Life in the Spirit

Pentecostals, Peacemaking, and Social Justice Series

PAUL ALEXANDER AND JAY BEAMAN, SERIES EDITORS

Volumes in the Series:

Pentecostal Pacifism: The Origin, Development, and Rejection of Pacific Belief among the Pentecostals by Jay Beaman

Forgiveness, Reconciliation, and Restoration: Mulitdisciplinary Studies from a Pentecostal Perspective edited by Martin W. Mittelstadt and Geoffrey W. Sutton

A Liberating Spirit: Pentecostals and Social Action in North America edited by Michael Wilkinson and Steven M. Studebaker

Christ at the Checkpoint: Theology in the Service of Justice and Peace edited by Paul Alexander

Pentecostals and Nonviolence: Reclaiming a Heritage edited by Paul Alexander

The Liberating Mission of Jesus: The Message of the Gospel of Luke by Dario Lopez Rodriguez

Pentecostal and Holiness Statements on War and Peace edited by Jay Beaman and Brian K. Pipkin

LIFE IN THE SPIRIT

*A Post-Constantinian and Trinitarian Account
of the Christian Life*

ANDRÉA D. SNAVELY

WITH A FOREWORD BY
JOEL P. OKAMOTO

PICKWICK *Publications* · Eugene, Oregon

LIFE IN THE SPIRIT
A Post-Constantinian and Trinitarian Account of the Christian Life

Pentecostals, Peacemaking, and Social Justice Series 9

Pickwick Publications
An Imprint of Wipf and Stock Publishers
199 W. 8th Ave., Suite 3
Eugene, OR 97401

www.wipfandstock.com

ISBN 13: 978–1-62032–513-5

Cataloging-in-Publication data:

Snavely, Andréa D.

Life in the spirit : a post-constantinian and trinitarian account of the christian life / Andréa D. Snavely.

xviii + 210 p. ; 23 cm. —Includes bibliographical references and indexes.

Pentecostals, Peacemaking, and Social Justice 9

ISBN 13: 978–1-62032–513-5

1. Holy Spirit. 2. Christianity and politics—United States. 3. Christian life. 4. Trinity. I. Okamoto, Joel P. II. Title. III. Series.

BT121.3 .S52 2015

Manufactured in the U.S.A.

In Memoriam

To my Father, Joe David Snavely (1930–2007)

and my three sisters, "Infant Daughter of Joe and Ann Snavely"

(b/d July 21, 1956), Sandra Jo (1960–1990),

and Casey Ann (1975–2000)

"And those who have died believing in Christ shall rise first."

—1 Thessalonians 4:1

Contents

Foreword

Christians are united when saying *that* the Christian life is a life in the Spirit. But the unity breaks down when explaining *how* the Christian life is a life in the Spirit. A stereotype of one extreme comes from my own Lutheran tradition. It can leave the impression that the Spirit's work in the Christian life consists entirely in bringing sinners to faith, doing nothing to transform believers and bring them to new life. This can happen when Lutherans explain good works by quoting Isaiah—"as filthy rags"—and when they regard the righteousness God conveys in justification as a fiction—"just as if I'd never sinned." A stereotype of another extreme comes from the Pentecostal tradition of author Andréa Snavely. It can leave the impression that life in the Spirit is all about special gifts like speaking in tongues and healing the sick.

These stereotypes may suggest that an appropriate explanation lies somewhere in the middle (unless, perhaps, you are a Lutheran or a Pentecostal). But this approach is reactive, not proactive. It assumes too much and questions too little.

For Snavely, this approach risks too much, even though he is a Pentecostal who appreciates the Lutheran tradition and who thinks the stereotypes are uncomfortably close to the truth. So the explanation he offers in this book is grounded in the life, death, and resurrection of Jesus Christ and in the ministry of the Apostles whom Christ sent into the world.

This explanation comes in four parts.

The first part considers the theology of the Christian life itself. Here Snavely follows the lead of John Howard Yoder. In *The Politics of Jesus*, Yoder showed how modern theology usually ignored or even denied Christ's life, death, and resurrection as the norm in its accounts of the

Christian life.[1] Some had historical reasons, others dogmatic, but all regarded Jesus as irrelevant for ethics and politics. Yoder outflanked all of them by pointing that they ignored or even denied the doctrine of the Incarnation. "What becomes of the meaning of the incarnation if Jesus is not normative man? If he is a man but not normative, is this not the ancient ebionite heresy? If he be somehow authoritative but not in his humanness, is this not a new gnosticism?"[2] Accordingly he proposed an account of the Christian life that presupposed the incarnation and therefore looked to the life, death, and resurrection of Jesus Christ as normative.

Snavely agrees with Yoder's post-Constantinian criticism and its dogmatic premise. He recognizes, however, that the two-natures Christology that Yoder's constructive proposal relied upon offers no help in giving an account of life in the Spirit. This takes us to the second part of his explanation: the pursuit of a different kind of Christology, namely, a Spirit Christology—an account of Jesus Christ and his life in which the Spirit's presence and power are essential.

Long neglected, the topic of Spirit Christology recently has drawn renewed attention. But not every proposal for a Spirit Christology is suitable. The requirements of an account of the Christian life as life in the Spirit comprise a strict and theologically valuable test. This account requires that a Spirit Christology make sense of Christ's life and mission, his crucifixion and his resurrection, and the mission he conferred upon the Church.

Snavely finds such a Spirit Christology in the proposal of Leo Sánchez.[3] This proposal is thoroughly Trinitarian. It takes seriously Karl Rahner's point that the Trinity "is a mystery of *salvation*" and follows his axiom that the economic Trinity is the immanent Trinity and vice versa.[4] The story of God's plan and work of salvation reveals not only that Jesus is the Incarnate Son of God and that the Spirit proceeds from the Father and the Son (*filioque*), but also that Jesus' person and life always were constituted by the presence and power of the Spirit. From his conception to his baptism, throughout his ministry all the way to his death, in his resurrection and exaltation, Jesus' identity and life were always from God "in the Spirit." Sánchez referred to this understanding of Christ as

1. Yoder, *The Politics of Jesus*, 1–21.
2. Ibid., 10.
3. Sánchez M., *Receiver, Bearer, and Giver of God's Spirit*.
4. Rahner, *More Recent Writings*. 87. Emphasis original.

an "*in Spiritu* model." This account of Christ is ideal for Snavely's purpose because it pays close attention both to the work of the Spirit and to the actual contours of his life leading to death and resurrection.

But any account of the Christian life also should explain how this life comes about. If the Christian life is life in the Spirit, then the life of Christ cannot be simply an example for Christians to follow. This life must come from the gift of the Spirit. How does this happen? Answering this is the third part of the explanation.

Snavely takes a typically Pentecostal approach by drawing an account from the book of Acts. But rather than focusing on what the new life consists of, he attends closely to the ministry of the Apostles by considering how their preaching and baptizing brought about new life in the Spirit. And to describe what he finds in the work of the Apostles, he draws on the typically Lutheran concepts of the "alien and proper works of God," or "killing and making alive."

The fourth part of the explanation draws out some contours of the life in the Spirit. You could say that Snavely returns here to post-Constantinian themes. Like Yoder, he portrays the Christian life as a cruciform life, which means non-violence, contentment, and harmony with all sisters and brothers in Christ. Borrowing from Yoder, we might say that what emerges here is "the politics of the Son of God" or "the politics of the Anointed One." Such labels highlight the Christian life grounded in the life, death, and resurrection of Jesus, not as the Incarnate One, but as the One Who Is the Son of God in the Spirit. But, as Snavely shows, it is equally true that these themes are genuinely Pentecostal. In fact, his choice of themes is decided even more by the life of Pentecostals than by the post-Constantinian theologians from whom he has learned.

If we want a label, however, that fits best not only with these choices but also for the entire book, then I would suggest that it is "catholic." This is the label that Yoder himself adopted for *The Politics of Jesus*: "[T]he view of Jesus claimed to be 'more radically Nicene and Chalcedonian than other views.' . . . the convictions argued here do not admit to being categorized as a sectarian oddity or a prophetic exception. Their appeal is to classical catholic Christian convictions properly understood."[5] Snavely also appealed to the classical catholic Christian convictions, and he justified his position by appealing to canonical Christian texts. There is noth-

5. Yoder, *The Priestly Kingdom*, 8, 9; quoting *The Politics of Jesus*, 102.

ing sectarian or denominational here. The Pentecostalism he portrays claims to be nothing less than a right way of being Christian.

This does not exempt his claims from argument or correction, addition or criticism. As one who subscribes wholeheartedly to the Lutheran Confessions, I have things to say about civil government and the use of force. And Snavely himself does not raise the Pentecostal position on spiritual gifts. These are important points to pursue. But they do not detract from or discredit what he has accomplished. Anyone who would assess, argue with, criticize, or even endorse his views must do so in this catholic way: grounded in the Gospel of Jesus Christ, drawn from the canonical New Testament, and consistent with the dogmas of the Christian Church.

Which also means that this is the "spirit" by which I encourage you to read and reflect upon this book.

Joel P. Okamoto
St. Louis, Missouri

Preface

To say this work is the culmination of a long and circuitous journey would be a great understatement. What ended as a PhD dissertation at Concordia Seminary began at a sale barn in Norwood, MO, when in 1960 my parents sold all their cattle, and later their farm, in order for my dad to spend all the money attending Central Bible College in Springfield, MO, beginning later that fall, to prepare for Christian ministry. A year later I would be born and a year after that my parents would begin pastoring small Assemblies of God churches, first in Kansas and then in Missouri, for the next twenty-five years. Having spent all their money and adding me, their fourth child, along the way, my parents were faced with obstacles far greater than poverty, such as standing up to racial discrimination from church deacons in 1963 for welcoming a black woman and her daughter into the church, social stigma for reaching out to the mentally handicapped and poor when it was not "the right thing to do," and for taking a stand against immorality within the church when it would have been much easier to "look the other way." Such events, and many others too numerous to recount, shaped my life at an early age in such a way that later ministry and education left me with a "hunch" that things within the church were just not right, even though I did not have all the theological ideas to understand why.

Fast forward to my first year of studies at Concordia Seminary where I met the likes of John Howard Yoder and Stanley Hauerwas through the classes taught by my dissertation advisor Joel Okamoto. Finally, I found the kind of theology my parents had been living and teaching me all my life, with the added dimension of the Lutheran faith that actually requires God to do something about the human predicament called sin. This might sound strange coming from a Pentecostal, but my upbringing was a throwback to an earlier time when Pentecostal preaching and living required the Holy Spirit to transform people into believers in order for them to understand what it means to be one of the saints of God. That is what made the testimony service so important, for it was mainly through the witness of God working Christ by the Spirit within a person that could explain the inexplicable. It was also a time when preaching was biblical, not the detailing of all the historical facts behind the text as a way of only explaining the text, but the preaching of the biblical story that places its hearers within God's story of his Son Jesus and requires repentance and faith *within* those who hear in order to believe it as one's own story.

Coming back full circle, it is my hope that, through the pages that follow, not only can Pentecostals be re-enlivened with the blessed hope in the resurrection that comes from the Spirit being "shed abroad in our hearts," but that Christians of all persuasions can appreciate the Holy Spirit's work in a greater dimension than what either a rational or an experiential description alone can provide. I must also sincerely thank Leopoldo Sánchez for not only helping guide my dissertation to its completion, but for providing the very theological framework upon which this work hopes to contribute in some way toward that greater dimension of the Spirit. May such a description of Jesus' life as lived in the Spirit contribute in some way to help others struggling to make sense out of their Christian faith when all other human explanations have failed, as they all must do at the foot of Jesus' cross and at the opening of his empty tomb.

Andréa D. Snavely
Springfield, MO
Three weeks before Resurrection Sunday, March, 2014

Acknowledgments

There are so many who have been instrumental in shaping my life and contributing in some way to see this project come to completion that I must limit my thanks to those whose contributions have been the most direct.

I want to first thank the teachers who have given so sacrificially to impart wisdom and knowledge into my life. High school teachers Karen Bullock and Louise Rhodes set me on a path of writing by sparking my interest in composition and research. College teachers Charles Harris, Opal Reddin, and Claude Black challenged me with deeper issues in church ministry, theology, and philosophy, respectively.

Many others have encouraged me in ways they might not have even realized. My late uncle John Snavely and my brother-in-law's late father, Bob Brand, encouraged me to continue my education even though they ministered for many years without the privilege of higher education themselves. Their words and smiles are etched in my memory forever and have been a constant encouragement during the long and difficult days of study. My "second family" of Pastor Royce and Elaine Beckett of Kansas City, MO and their children, Tammy, Sam, and Jonathon, encouraged me in my faith by their exemplary ministries of early-morning prayer and helping the elderly and socially marginalized. Written between the lines of these pages are the many expressions of compassion and social justice they have lived and taught to others.

Many have contributed directly to this dissertation simply through conversation. Former students Chris Lamberth, Don Yurmanovich, David Silverstein, Stephen Paddock, Kirk Sandstrom, and others helped me give clearer expression to difficult concepts by their probing questions. Pastor friend Harold Harrison provided great conversation and many helpful resources from his vast amount of reading. Central Bible College librarian Lynn Anderson and his assistant, Alice Harris, very generously secured sources for research. Krista Whittenburg provided expert editorial assistance. Thanks go to the many professors at The Assemblies of God Theological Seminary in Springfield, MO and Concordia Seminary in St. Louis who shaped my thinking and challenged me beyond what I thought was even possible.

This dissertation might not have ever been completed if not for the "Good Samaritans" of Global University of the Assemblies of God in Springfield, MO. Special thanks go to Undergraduate Dean Willard Teague, President Gary Seevers, and Provost Robert Love for taking the chance on "taking me in" and providing me the kind of environment necessary to finish this project. Any explanation this dissertation might offer for how people live sacrificial lives for the advancement of the gospel is only a reflection of how Willard and Jerlene Teague have served as faithful ministers of Jesus Christ for over fifty years, first in Ivory Coast, Africa, and now at Global University. Willard's phone call in July 2010 was a testimony to my family that God still works by his Spirit through "cross" and "resurrection," and that he does so most often through people who are still willing to believe in God against the odds.

The most thanks goes to my dissertation committee who graciously guided me and this project through the long journey! Committee readers Victor Raj and especially Leopoldo Sánchez offered many insights to help frame this discussion. My doctorfather Joel Okamoto has, of course, contributed the most to seeing this project through to completion. His patience, encouragement, unfailing tenacity, and theological concepts are woven throughout these pages.

Lastly, I wish to express my deep gratitude to my family. My late grandparents Joe Amos and Emily Snavely and Lon and Alice Bruffett set godly examples of selfless Christian service and moral character that continue to bear fruit. My in-laws Lindell and Hazel (Skaggs) Gowen have gone far beyond what earthly patience alone could provide with their support and encouragement while I moved their daughter and two grandchildren around for my education. A very special thank-you goes to Hazel for showing us all in very tangible ways what it means to live in the Spirit by trusting God with the outcomes of life. Her faith in me finishing this project was expressed in her many acts of selfless hospitality and kind spirit. My brothers Alex (and Karen) and Bruce (and Becky) have often encouraged me even in many small ways they might not have even realized. Offering spiritual encouragement at the most practical level has been my brother-in-law Ron Brand. Having gone through many trials of their own, both he and his wife Carla have walked side-by-side Darla and me through the many dark days of our lives as well, understanding how the Spirit works through Jesus' cross and resurrection in ways that go far beyond what many ever grasp in this life.

What would be adequate to express my deep gratitude to my parents, Joe David and Ann (Bruffett) Snavely, than to say that all I am is because of your lives of sacrifice and faith in God, even as you walked many times through the "valley of the shadow of death"? Your lives taught me early in life what it means to live in the Spirit in ways this dissertation only attempts to explain. May this be at least a partial return on your investment until the resurrection when all debts are "paid in full." Even though my dad did not live to see this work completed, his unwavering trust and faith in God through the deaths of three daughters has left a legacy of what faith really means in a time when so many twist it beyond recognition to satisfy their own fleshly desires. How many others would consider it an honor to be found worthy by God to suffer such tragedies? My hope is for this work to be a tribute to how you preached, lived, and taught us how to live in the Spirit as Jesus did. And to my dear mother who, with great faith in Christ, waits with the blessed hope in the resurrection; may the God of all comfort extend to you a double portion of his Spirit according to the great measure by which you have comforted us.

Finally, to my wife, Darla, and our two children, Titus and Tessa, who have made many sacrifices of their own by allowing me much time in solitary study. I trust that God will lead you, Titus and Tessa, in living lives in the Spirit that are worthy of your calling in Christ Jesus. And to Darla, my beloved gift from God, you have shown me and our children what it means to live in the Spirit in ways that are difficult to understand or express, even though you "got it honest" from your dear mother Hazel. It was your encouragement that sent me on this journey and your love and prodding that kept me on course. Your sacrifices can only be truly known by God, but may the completion of this work be a token of my appreciation for God *literally* bringing you into my life just when I needed you most! It is to you that I dedicate this work.

1

The Christian Life as Life in the Spirit

Introduction

This work will give an account of the Christian life as life in the Spirit. This should be obvious enough from the New Testament witness and especially Paul's description of the Christian life as the Spirit's work of making people into the image of Jesus Christ. However, we should not take it for granted that we have and in fact live by such an account for two reasons. The first reason is that the kind of life Jesus lived is not taken seriously for what it means for a Christian to live a life in the Spirit, or even for just living their life as a Christian. The second reason is that the Spirit's indwelling presence is not taken seriously as what led Jesus to live the kind of life he lived; which obviously fails to be the reason for his followers living the kind of life Jesus lived. Simply put, this account will show life in the Spirit as the basic way to describe a Christian's life, as a disciple of Jesus, and which, by the Spirit making people disciples of Jesus, also produces a life that looks like Jesus' life—a life lived in the Spirit.

The first reason recognizes how modern theology has distorted the nature of the Christian life by it not taking Jesus' life seriously. As John Howard Yoder pointed out in *The Politics of Jesus*, modern theology has in various ways denied or ignored the thesis that the life of Christ speaks to the shape and direction also of the life of the Christian.[1] Yoder ac-

---

1. Yoder, *The Politics of Jesus*, 4–8. Yoder originally gave six reasons for why Jesus is not seen as the norm for Christian ethics (adding five more in the second edition, cf. 15–18), the most notable for this account is his sixth one in which Jesus' death is a "dogmatic" assertion. "Jesus came, after all, to give his life for the sins of humankind. The work of atonement or the gift of justification, whereby God enables sinners to be

1

companied his "post-Constantinian" critique of modern theology with a "post-Constantinian" account of the life of the Christian that follows Jesus, and he justified it on christological grounds. As Yoder would put it, his account worked out the practical implications of a "more radical" Chalcedonian Christology.[2] What this working out consisted of was Jesus Christ's life *prescribing* the shape and direction of the Christian life. The way Jesus lived obediently unto God *prescribes* how Christians are also to live unto God.

The second reason is a characteristic of much of Western theology, that is, a distorted view of the Spirit in which a Christian remains in control of their own life rather than the biblical view which shows the Spirit as the indwelling presence that led Jesus to live the kind of life he lived that led to the kind of death he died—intrinsically—and which produces in his followers the same kind of life Jesus lived that might just lead to the kind of death he died. This biblical view sees the Spirit as what "kills" one's flesh so a person can be "raised" with Christ by the indwelling presence of the Spirit, making a Christ-centered life possible by the Spirit controlling one's life by producing Jesus Christ's life as one's way of life. While this characteristic of Western theology and its impact upon the Christian life is much more difficult to recognize or explain, it will nevertheless be more apparent once a proper account of the indwelling presence of the Spirit is understood as central to the life, death, and resurrection of Jesus Christ. Therefore, a more complete description of this theological misunderstanding, its manifestations, and corrections must come later. What must come first is an account of the Spirit's presence *within* the life of Jesus as the "constitutive ingredient" in how he lived the kind of life he did that led to the kind of death he died on a cross; not only that he lived in the Spirit but that he died in the Spirit. This account shows Jesus' life as *descriptive* of a life lived fully in the Spirit as the Son of God the Father.

---

restored to his fellowship, is a forensic act, a gracious gift . . . How the death of Jesus works our justification is a divine miracle and mystery; how he died, or the kind of life which led to the kind of death he died, is therefore ethically immaterial" (7–8).

2. Yoder, *The Politics of Jesus*, 102. "If we were to carry on that other, traditionally doctrinal kind of debate, I would seek simply to demonstrate that the view of Jesus being proposed here is more radically Nicene and Chalcedonian than other views. I do not here advocate an unheard-of modern understanding of Jesus. I ask rather that the implications of what the church has always said about Jesus as Word of the Father, as true God and true Man, be taken more seriously, as relevant to our social problems, than ever before."

As Jesus lived in the Spirit, his life not only *prescribes* his life as what it means to be a disciple, his life *describes* a life lived fully in the Spirit. His life in the Spirit is not simply a prescription (to take or not to take, in one's own ability) as in Yoder's account, but the actual description of what a life looks like that has the Spirit as the "constitutive ingredient" in their living as an adopted son of the Father. However, this account shows transformation by the Spirit, upon hearing the gospel, as the necessary condition for having and living in the Spirit, a transformation from being a son of "this age" in "this world" to being a son of God in his eternal kingdom to come. In this view, Jesus' followers do not just have "sonship," like an added quality or substance; they *are* adopted sons of the Father—by the *indwelling* Spirit of the Father that he gives through his only begotten Son Jesus Christ.

These two features of modern theology show that an account of the Christian life as life in the Spirit might still be an important task. Any tentativeness to such a pursuit is eliminated when we further consider that post-Constantinian accounts of the Christian life cannot actually yield a rich account of the Christian life as life in the Spirit precisely because its account of the person of Jesus Christ has no clear place for the Spirit's indwelling presence in his own life. Still yet, the move to relate the life of Christ and the life of the Christian in any account of the Christian life is correct and should be followed. What is therefore desirable for this kind of project—one that accounts for the Christian life as life in the Spirit—is an account of Christ in terms of the Spirit, that is, a Spirit-Christology of a certain sort.

This sort of Spirit-Christology is one that not only shows Jesus' life as what constitutes the Christian's life, as Yoder's account does, but shows, in a *descriptive* fashion, the kind of life Jesus lived as life lived in the Spirit— as an actual reality—in a way Yoder's account cannot. In doing so, I will follow a path laid out by Leopoldo Sánchez in his published dissertation, *Receiver, Bearer, and Giver of God's Spirit*.[3] Sánchez provides an account that establishes the life of Christ in the Spirit as *constitutive* for the proclamation of the gospel and for further reflection into the intra-divine life of the Trinity. Following Sánchez's account, I will further develop an account of Jesus Christ as he lived obediently unto the Father in the Spirit, showing his life to be life as the Son of God. As believers in Jesus as Lord, his followers *are made* fellow participants in Jesus' life as the Son, "caught

---

3. Sánchez M., *Receiver, Bearer, and Giver of God's Spirit*.

up" into the life of sonship as "other sons" of the Father by the same Spirit in which Jesus lived his life. This account follows a post-Constantinian account of the life of Jesus as what constitutes the Christian life, but, since the post-Constantinian accounts do not offer a clear place for the Spirit's indwelling presence that constitutes such a life, this Spirit-Christology will explain how the Christian life *is* life in the Spirit. My thesis then is this: as Jesus lived the kind of life he lived as the Son of the Father in the Spirit, the Spirit also *makes other sons* of the Father in the *image* of Jesus Christ who then, as a result of this *actual* transformation by the Spirit, gladly follow him in the kind of life he lived—in the Spirit.

As for methodology, this Spirit-Christology will proceed upon the basis of Pauline theology that sees the Spirit as making other sons of the Father. Whereas this might be obvious to most readers, the necessary corollary to understand Paul's dependence upon the work of the Spirit is the presupposition of the life Jesus lived in the Spirit and especially his death on a cross (Rom 6), which is never obvious to anyone (1 Cor 1:21; 2 Cor 4:4), that is, by identifying with a man who died on a cross one is actually given life. This way of making Jesus' life, death, and resurrection constitutive for the Christian life was the lasting contribution of John Howard Yoder. Following Yoder, my plan is to also provide an account of Jesus' life but one that sees the Spirit as the "constitutive ingredient" in Jesus living as the Son of God the Father. This account, in turn, will show how it is through the life, death, resurrection, and ascension of Jesus Christ that God pours out his Spirit of life (and thus, Jesus' kind of life) upon and through his church, making other sons of the Father who live like Jesus lived.

In order to accomplish this, I will first provide a certain reading of Jesus' life as he lived in the Spirit that opens up space for a more faithful reading of Luke's account in Acts of the Spirit's work of making and shap-ing people into the people of God, in the image of Jesus Christ, beginning at Pentecost and continuing until the end of this age. Chapter 1 will de-tail the post-Constantinian accounts of John Howard Yoder and Stanley Hauerwas, which show the significance of Jesus' life for the Christian life, but which are also limited by their neglect of the Spirit's presence both in Jesus' life and his followers to live such a life. Chapter 2 will navigate recent Spirit-Christologies and Pneumatologies that either do not take Jesus' life seriously as the Son of God or deny that his life demands trans-formation from the spirits of this age and the flesh in order to live life in the Spirit. This positioning within recent scholarship will yield a clearer place for seeing Jesus' life as what it means to have the Spirit and to live in the Spirit. Chapter 3 will then give such an account of Jesus' life in the Spirit as the Son of God that is constitutive for his followers' lives as adopted sons of God. This account of Jesus' life in the Spirit and his followers' lives in the Spirit, as described in Acts, will then yield a more faithful and coherent reading of Pauline theology of the Christian's life as life in the Spirit. Further implications of this more faithful reading of Scripture will provide a stronger critique of modern theology in chapter 4, along with some suggestions for theology's proper use and its implications for the proclamation of the gospel. Chapter 5 will outline some preliminary implications of this Spirit-Christology for the shape and direction of the lives of individual members of Christ's body. Chapter 6 will conclude this study with a summary of the question, the main points of the theological proposal, and some prospects for future theological reflection in related areas. To begin this journey, the first step in providing such an account of Spirit-Christology that takes Jesus' life in the Spirit seriously for the Christians' life in the Spirit must begin with John Howard Yoder's retrieval of the significance of Jesus' life for the Christian's life and its parallel theological diagnosis.

John Howard Yoder's Post-Constantinian Diagnosis: The Systematic Diminishing of Jesus' Life

To understand the significance of Yoder's larger contribution, one must first understand the significance of his post-Constantinianism in two related respects: in a diagnosis of Christian theology on the Christian life and in offering the kind of account that addresses this problem. As to the first, Yoder's diagnosis of Christian theology was very simple: Christian accounts of the Christian life did not take Jesus' own life into account. In *The Politics of Jesus*, the sixth reason he gives for this neglect of Jesus' life for the Christian life is that Jesus' death is seen only as the mechanism by which he gave his life as a ransom for sinners to provide forgiveness. This view of Jesus' death remains abstract, allowing sin to also remain abstract (if it exists at all). Yoder explains how the irrelevancy this view has for Jesus' life is the reason Jesus' life is regarded as insignificant for understanding the Christian's life.

> Just as guilt is not a matter of having committed particular sin-
> ful acts, so justification is not a matter of proper behavior. How
> the death of Jesus works our justification is a divine miracle and
> mystery; how he died, or the kind of life which led to the kind of
> death he died, is therefore ethically immaterial.[4]

This relationship between the life Jesus lived and the kind of death He
died is perhaps the single most instructive point to understanding Yoder's
correction to the wrong "content" of the Christian life; wrong "content"
being something other than Jesus' life. Not only does Yoder show the significance of Jesus' life for the Christian, he shows Jesus' life and death to
be all-encompassing of the Christian's life; political, economic, cultural,
and social. Yoder's significance is that, in his view, Jesus' life created a
completely new human existence.

For Yoder, Jesus' coming into the world was the creation of a new
human existence; the very re-creation of humanity. Caught in the web
of fallen human existence are the structures of the world; the political,
economic, and religious structures that God now uses against fallen
humanity for his own purposes, even for good.[5] God even used these
structures for the purpose of killing his only Son, thereby showing the
degree to which humans have "fallen" into violence. Could this view of
Jesus' death and his cross constitute the very essence of the Christian life?
If one answers "yes," this would be a new beginning for what it means to
be a follower of Jesus.

In form and content, *The Politics of Jesus* is a model for an account
of the Christian life. In form, by giving shape and purpose to life as a
Christian, it is perhaps unexceptional, but in content, *The Politics of Jesus*
is indeed exceptional. So exceptional, in fact, that Stanley Hauerwas says
it will never be a classic due to a classic being "the category of dominant
and dominating traditions."[6] Rather, it defies categorization into contemporary traditions by critiquing the usual approaches by re-establishing the
life of Jesus as the only paradigm for Christian existence.[7] In this sense,
it is Hauerwas's conviction that, in the future, Christians in America will
look back and see *The Politics of Jesus* as a "new beginning" for theology.[8]

4. Yoder, *The Politics of Jesus*, 8.

5. Ibid., 142.

6. Hauerwas, *A Better Hope*, 1.

7. Ibid., 131.

8. Hauerwas, "When the Politics of Jesus Makes a Difference," 982.

Yoder's Solution: Confession in Jesus as Lord Lets Go of the World

One of the most critical theological presuppositions to understanding Yoder's critique of modern theology's diminishing of Jesus' life for the Christian's life is his dependence upon Barth's "foundation" of belief to be the Trinity as opposed to a dependency upon natural theology as a foundation to Christian faith. Contrary to H. Richard Niebuhr, as Craig Carter points out, Yoder follows Karl Barth's rejection of theology's dependency upon natural theology as a foundation for understanding the Trinity because Barth "simply refuses to play by the rules by which Niebuhr assumes we have to play."[9] Yoder's *Politics of Jesus* shows how Niebuhr's liberal agenda no longer has any validity. Hauerwas explains this quite well.

> Yoder needs to be read in the tradition of liberal Protestantism not only because he helps us recognize the strengths of that tradition, but also because he helps us see why that tradition has come to an end (which accounts for why he remains something of an outcast in mainstream Protestant theology). Yoder cannot be made to fit into the presuppositions we have learned from the Niebuhrs and their successors. Such theologians keep saying, "We have seen this Christ-against-culture type before." In mainstream hands, such typologies become power plays to keep in their place those who might challenge the reigning explanatory categories.[10]

9. Carter, *The Politics of the Cross*, 125. Carter contrasts H. R. Niebuhr's "distributive Trinitarianism" seen earlier to Barth's christocentric Trinitarianism. "Barth's doctrine of the Trinity is christocentric, meaning that his doctrine of God the Father is developed not out of natural theology, but out of the biblical witness as it is interpreted christocentrically. Barth rejects the entire natural-theology project, including the analogy of being, apologetics, and reason and history as sources, independent of revelation, of the knowledge of God. For this reason, the doctrine of the Trinity is . . . the presupposition of all dogmatic theology. For Barth, the Christian God is the God of Abraham, Isaac, Jacob, and Jesus; the God of the Bible, not Aristotle's Unmoved Mover; the God of the philosophers. So we know the Christian God (as opposed to the God of the Deists, the Muslim God, and the God of idealistic metaphysics) through God's own self-revelation in Jesus Christ. Any other God is simply an idol for Barth."

10. Hauerwas, "When the Politics of Jesus Makes a Difference," 982–83; see also *A Better Hope*, 131.

Hauerwas says the reigning explanatory category of depoliticization (by both the right and left) of the gospel has "made Christianity a faithful servant of the status quo."[11]

By contrast, Yoder is calling the church to let go of its compromise with the world and return to living lives patterned after Jesus' life, which condemns the status quo as the servant to an unbelieving world. Compromise with the "world" necessarily means forsaking one's faithfulness to Jesus as Lord. On the other hand, declaring "Jesus is Lord" means forsaking one's compromise with "this world." Constantinianism is simply one's refusal to let go of the world and its structured unbelief. A follower of Jesus is able to let go of the world's unbelief and the structures that unbelief underwrites by their awareness of living within a whole new human existence made possible by Jesus' life, death, and resurrection.

Jesus' Life as a Whole New Human Existence

Yoder based the demands of Jesus' followers letting go of the world's structured unbelief solely upon the life, death, and resurrection of Jesus. Jesus' life as a new human existence of peace not only shows God's condemnation of human violence and the world's cultures that are established and survive by human violence but the calling of a people to a new community of human existence based on peace. Jesus' life cannot be made compatible to any form of human culture or religion since the very fabric of human existence is woven with threads of violence for its survival across time. Rather, Jesus' life, death, and resurrection denounce all others as false pretenders, allegiance to which is idolatry. Yoder not only refused, like Barth before him, to conform Jesus' life to the syncretism of a cultural religion that thrives by violence (and the artificial remedy for it seen in pluralism) he did so by retrieving and elevating Trinitarian theology to the pinnacle of what it means to know one's place in God's assembly of peace.[12]

Trinitarian theology becomes the starting point for knowing one's identity with God, something Yoder believed natural theology could nev-

---

11. Hauerwas, *A Better Hope*, 133.

12. Carter, *The Politics of the Cross*, 125. "Niebuhr's account of trinitarianism is inherently open to syncretism, to the blending of pagan and Christian notions into a culture religion. It was against trends perceived by Barth to hold the potential for this kind of deformation of the Christian faith, which Barth regarded as *more serious than anything faced by the church in many centuries*, that he uttered his famous 'Nein!'" (emphasis added).

er do. Whereas Yoder received criticism for not being Trinitarian enough, it was unfounded. Yoder's whole approach was even more Trinitarian, even though implicitly, than most other explicit attempts at Trinitarian theology due to his belief in the Trinity as the starting point and only foundation for all other Christian understanding. Carter refers to this method as "practical trinitarianism," by which Christian assertions "depend for their coherence on the truth of the doctrine of the Trinity."[13] This Trinitarian basis undergirds all of Yoder's critique against the status quo since Jesus' very life is both the full expression of God's divine nature, of God's critique upon humanity, and the re-constitution (re-creation) of human life.[14] As God's re-creation of human life, Jesus' life was the very condemnation of "this age" and the structures necessary to maintain its norms and status quo. Jesus inaugurated a "new age" of the Kingdom of God that broke in and declared "this age" fallen and awaiting God's final judgment. Yoder explained this breaking in of God's Kingdom by showing Jesus' life as the very center of God's life. For the follower of Jesus, there is no other social norm or social order for Christian life and ethics than Jesus himself. Therefore, "Yoder returns Jesus to the center of Christian ethics by freeing us from the political presuppositions sponsored by liberal social orders."[15]—and conservative ones too.

Yoder's Post-Constantinian Critique and Account of the Christian Life

Yoder's Critique of Theology that Ignores or Denies Jesus' Life

Yoder's account that takes the life of Jesus seriously for the Christian's own life has been his most significant contribution, which has done a great deal to help Christians return to *faithfulness* by making Jesus' life and his cross visible in ways many have never seen even for the first time. Yoder did so by linking the faithfulness of Christians to the faithfulness that Jesus lived before his Father even unto death on a cross.[16] Yoder's *The*

13. Ibid., 126.

14. "Full expression" here means the only legitimate one, an idea I will bring up later in comparing others who use other terms to describe Jesus as the "best" or "most complete" as a way to include other manifestations as also legitimate expressions of God's divine nature.

15. Hauerwas, *A Better Hope*, 133.

16. Yoder, *The Politics of Jesus*, 232. "The triumph of the right is assured not by the might that comes to the aid of the right, which is of course the justification of the use

Politics of Jesus made Jesus' life and death visible again simply by show-ing the political, economic, and cultural significance his life had in its historical context. Jesus did not live a life just so he would be able to offer a sacrifice for sin, although it was that. Yoder shows us that Jesus lived a certain kind of life that ended up getting him killed. He sees the cross that Jesus died on as the punishment of a criminal charged not for political insurrection (since He committed no such thing) but for social noncon-formity, which he did commit by offering the possibility of a radically new human existence.[17]

Yoder's Link between Jesus' Faithfulness and His Followers' Faithfulness

It was Yoder who explained persuasively how Christian answers about what constituted life, for Christians, went wrong: Christianity forfeited its identity of faithfulness to its Lord Jesus Christ in favor of a "wider wis-dom" compatible with nations and their cultures, which is more popular than carrying a cross and especially than dying on one. However, for Yoder, the faithfulness required for one to be a follower of Jesus means taking on Jesus' cross as one's own "way of life," paradoxically as that seems. Jesus did not see the cross he was about to die on "as a ritually prescribed instrument of propitiation but as the political alternative to both insurrection and quietism."[18]

This view of Jesus and his cross shows Jesus to be the inaugurator of a new human existence he called the Kingdom of God.

> Here at the cross is the man who loves his enemies, the man whose righteousness is greater than the Pharisees, who being rich became poor, who gives his robe to those who took his cloak, who prays for those who despitefully use him. The cross is not a detour or a hurdle on the way to the kingdom, nor is it even the way to the kingdom; *it is the kingdom come.*[19]

---

of violence and other kinds of power in every human conflict. The triumph of the right, although it is assured, is sure because of the power of the resurrection and not because of any calculation of causes and effects, nor because of the inherently greater strength of the good guys. The relationship between the obedience of God's people and the triumph of God's cause is not a relationship of cause and effect but one of cross and resurrection."

17. Ibid., 36–39, 51–53, 95–96, 129.

18. Ibid., 36.

19. Ibid., 51; emphasis added.

Jesus' kind of life led to the kind of death he died; death on "a cross identified as the punishment of a man who threatens society by creating a new
kind of community leading a radically new kind of life."[20] This new kind
of life that Jesus brought into existence by dying on a cross is exemplified
in Jesus' followers by their own "crosses" which are patterned after his,
but only in a certain way.

> The believer's cross is no longer any and every kind of suffer-
> ing, sickness, or tension, the bearing of which is demanded. The
> believer's cross must be like his Lord's, the price of his social
> nonconformity. It is not, like sickness or catastrophe, an inex-
> plicable, unpredictable suffering; it is the end of a path freely
> chosen after counting the cost . . . it is the social reality of repre-
> senting in an unwilling world the Order to come.[21]

The continuity between Yoder's description of the believer's cross and his
description of Jesus' cross can be clearly seen in the following.

> The cross of Christ was not an inexplicable or chance event,
> which happened to strike him, like illness or accident. To accept
> the cross as his destiny, to move toward it and even to provoke it,
> when he could have well done otherwise, was Jesus' constantly
> reiterated free choice. He warns his disciples lest their embark-
> ing on the same path be less conscious of its costs (Luke 14:25–
> 33). The cross of Calvary was not a difficult family situation, not
> a frustration of visions of personal fulfillment, a crushing debt,
> or a nagging in-law; it was the political, legally-to-be-expected
> result of a moral clash with the powers ruling his society.[22]

Yoder's understanding of Jesus' death on a cross and the requirement of
others to follow him in order to be his disciples (Matt 16:24–28; Mark
8:34–38; Luke 9:23–27) is the basis upon which he makes his case against
modern theology's abandonment of Jesus' cross in favor of a more "reasonable" or "effective" method that appeals to everyone, a method that
uses natural theology as the foundation for faith and abandons the biblical view of faith as the lens, or "foundation," through which one sees
natural theology.

20. Ibid., 53.
21. Ibid., 96.
22. Ibid., 129.

The Church's Unfaithfulness: Serving a "Wider Wisdom" of Natural Theology

Yoder's return of Jesus' life, death, and resurrection to their proper place is accompanied by a critique of modern theology that appeals to a "wider wisdom" that depends on natural theology for its supporting foundation. Properly understood, Jesus' life interprets, critiques, and supplies meaning to natural theology rather than natural theology serving as the filter through which to interpret and then diminish Jesus' life and death. Yoder's critique of the modern theological method that finds another "surer foundation" than the cross and resurrection of Jesus Christ is one piece with his account of Jesus and his cross explained above. In place of Jesus' cross and resurrection, modern theology has opted for a "wider wisdom" found in natural theology that appeals to human understanding of "'nature,' 'reason,' 'creation,' and 'reality,'" which are all "self-evident" and "ascribed a priori a higher or deeper authority than the 'particular' Jewish or Christian sources of moral vision, whether these be the Bible in general, or Jesus in particular."[23] These other "self-evident" foundations than Jesus and his cross served the church's unfaithfulness by supporting its Constantinian quest for control over history, to make history "come out right" for God and his church. Yoder calls this into question by suggesting Jesus' cross was the relinquishing, a "letting go," of any personal "responsibility" in favor of trusting his Father's control of history. Yoder explains this position of "letting go of history" in relation to Jesus' suffering.

> We have observed this biblical "philosophy of history" first of all in the worship life of the late New Testament church, since it is here that we find the most desperate encounter of the church's weakness (John was probably in exile, Paul in prison) with the power of the evil rulers of the present age. But this position is nothing more than a logical unfolding of the meaning of the work of Jesus Christ himself, whose choice of suffering servant-hood rather than violent lordship, of love to the point of death rather than righteousness backed by power, was itself the fundamental direction of his life. Jesus was so faithful to the enemy-love of God that it cost him all his effectiveness; *he gave up every handle on history.*[24]

---

23. Ibid., 19.

24. Ibid., 232–33; emphasis added.

In place of this early church's understanding of Jesus' cross and one's relinquishing control over history that follows Jesus' demands, much of the church since Constantine has opted out of this way of Jesus' cross by appealing to a use of natural theology that eclipses and, thereby, suppresses this view of Jesus and his cross as the way of life for his followers. Recent post-Constantinians, such as Yoder and Stanley Hauerwas, have identified and exposed this connection between the church's unfaithfulness and its use of natural theology. We will now examine their critiques of the church's unfaithfulness by which theology appeals to natural theology as a foundation for faith in Jesus Christ.

Yoder's Critique of H. Richard Niebuhr's Use of Natural Theology

John Howard Yoder and Stanley Hauerwas have mounted a two-fold critique against this liberal Protestant minimization of Jesus' life to the periphery of one's Christian life found in the theological method of H. Richard Niebuhr and his brother Reinhold Niebuhr, respectively, both of whom elevated natural theology to a higher authority than Jesus' life. First, John Yoder critiqued H. Richard Niebuhr's 1951 *Christ and Culture* in a 1958 article unpublished until 1996.[25] Yoder cites Niebuhr's methodology that allows culture a monolithic autonomy separate from the lordship of Jesus Christ. He explains Niebuhr's independent status given to culture that is contrary to the teachings of the New Testament.

> The church of the New Testament confessed that Jesus was Lord over the "principalities and powers." . . . The *autonomy* claimed by the powers of this world is not only independence of any higher will such as that of the Creator God, but also the claim to exercise dominion over men and women, who thereby become slaves of the law, of idols, or of other powers. The *unity* which these "powers" claim lies precisely in their pretention that independently of the will of the Creator God they are able to provide a person and to society a full, integrated, genuine existence. . . Now what the New Testament affirms in claiming that Christ is Lord is precisely that these structures of creaturely unity and meaningfulness have no such autonomy, but have rather been brought into subjection under the feet of our Lord. They have in their rebellion against him no unity, since rebellion is not a principle of unity. What for H. R. Niebuhr is the definition of

25. Stassen, Yeager, and Yoder, *Authentic Transformation*, 11.

> "culture" in its essence is for the New Testament the definition of perdition and demonic self-glorification, from which the "powers" need to be, and can be, saved in order to be brought under the Lordship of God in Christ.[26]

Yoder reveals Niebuhr's strategy of setting up five types of church stances toward culture as that which allows culture this monolithic autonomy. By using these five types, Niebuhr leads the reader along to eventually accept the fifth type, that of "transforming culture" as the best possible solution, showing this position to be the best by not listing any of its shortcomings but by using such words as "transform" and "convert" without any concrete or substantial clarity as to what either one would actually looks like if they happened.[27] Yoder calls this methodology into question since it serves as its own "grid" that eliminates any alternative and especially by how it criticizes others in the past, such as Tertullian, for not being consistent by ascribing exclusively to one particular type. Yoder shows Niebuhr's method indebted to Ernst Troeltsch by his categorization of history that uses "prior intellectual commitments and categories" to "determine what will be recognized as a 'motif'"[28] and then using that categorization motif as a way to show Jesus' life "pointing away from" the particularity of culture. Yoder shows how this "pointing away" from culture was, for Niebuhr, based on Jesus being a "moralist" and "radical monotheist."[29]

> [Jesus] does not condemn culture because it is particularly sinful, nor does he condemn aspects of culture because these portions of it are more sinful than others; in fact he does not condemn it at all. He simply "points away from" it towards something else incomparably more important.[30]

This something "more important" reflects a dualism that splits the spiritual from the material, leaving the earthly and worldly an independent autonomy of existence, allowing "nature," "reality," and even "creation" an independent status apart from Jesus Christ's lordship. As we will now see,

---

26. Yoder, "How H. Richard Niebuhr Reasoned," 69; emphasis original. Cf. 54–55.

27. Ibid., 40–42.

28. Iibd., 43.

29. Ibid., 59. Jesus as a "radical monotheist" is the fifth reason Yoder gives in *The Politics of Jesus* (7) for why Jesus is not seen as the norm for Christian ethics.

30. Yoder, "How H. Richard Niebuhr Reasoned," 59.

the independent status of creation and nature apart from Jesus Christ is due to Niebuhr's flawed view of the Trinity.

Ultimately, Yoder rightly suspects Niebuhr of making Christ into a "straw man" that points people away from the historical particularity of Jesus' life; the result of a Trinitarianism that is "modalistic" or "distributive," that is, seeing Father, Son, and Spirit as distinct and separate sources of revelation. In Niebuhr's Trinitarianism, the Father's creation of all things supports culture and necessarily uses other sources than Jesus Christ for moral judgment.[31]

> It is his rhetorically most powerful way of arguing that the teachings and example of Christ need to be "corrected" or brought into balance by appeal to nature or to history ([*Christ and Culture*] 81f, 114) . . . Nature and history are therefore channels of revelation from God the Father. What they have to say about "culture" is of course largely affirmative, and thereby stands in tension . . . with the authority of "Christ."[32]

Not only does the Father's creation as an affirmation of culture serve as an alternative source of revelation apart from Christ, but Niebuhr's view of the Sprit does as well. "Thus the term 'Spirit' can serve as a general code label for not further specified sources of valid moral insights, which can be complimentary to (or prima facie contradictory to) the revelation received in the teaching and example of Christ."[33] Yoder asks whether this sharp distinction between the Father, Son, and Spirit's work, especially for differing sets of moral obligation for the Christian, can hold up under the scrutiny of Scripture. "Can we thus distinguish between the teaching and example of the Son and the will of the Father? Can we distinguish between creation, as the work of the Father on the one hand, and radical discipleship or redemption on the other, as the work of the Son?"[34] Yoder shows how this cannot be the case and that, in the history of church doctrine, the concept of "Trinity" was later developed to combat this tendency exhibited by Niebuhr in order to safeguard against any modalistic tendency that would make unwarranted distinction between Father, Son, and Spirit.

31. Ibid., 62–63.
32. Ibid., 61.
33. Ibid.
34. Ibid.

The entire point of the debate around the nature of the Trinity was the concern of the church to say just the opposite, namely that in the Incarnation and in the continuing life of the church under the Spirit there is but one God. The point of the doctrine of the Trinity is not to affirm distinctions or even complementary differentiations between Father, Son, and Spirit, but rather to safeguard the unity of these three ways in which we know of God. It was not to relativize Jesus or to cut the later church loose from his normativeness.[35]

In *The Politics of Jesus*, Yoder gives reasons why Jesus is not seen as the norm for Christian ethics, such as a later systematic theological filter that serves as an epistemological grid through which Jesus' life must be translated. Yoder uses H. Richard Niebuhr's "distributive epistemological understanding of the Trinity" as an example of this theological grid through which Jesus' life is "filtered," a position Niebuhr articulated in an article prior to *Christ and Culture*.[36] Yoder explains how Niebuhr's grid of "distributive Trinitarianism," that allows for other sources of authority than Jesus Christ, diminishes the life Jesus lived for constituting Christian ethics.

One should not make Jesus too important for ethics . . . since God the Father would call for a different (perhaps more institutionally conservative) social ethic, based on an understanding of creation or providence whose content is derived otherwise than from Jesus. God the Spirit might guide us toward another, also different ethic, based on the further revelations received since Pentecost, during the history of the church.[37]

Niebuhr's "distributive Trinitarianism" is instructive for understanding Yoder's critique of its diminishing of Jesus' life to the periphery of the Christian's life. Niebuhr's Trinitarianism did not allow Jesus' life to be the sole expression of what it means for humans to know God

---

35. Ibid., 62.

36. Niebuhr, "The Doctrine of the Trinity," 371–84.

37. Yoder, *The Politics of Jesus*, 17n33. By the "guidance of the Spirit" H. R. Niebuhr did not mean the Spirit's application of Jesus' life into believers' lives through the church. He meant the church's "progress" by its adaptation into its present culture. Thereby, Niebuhr validated American Constantinianism by allowing the church to learn from the "'lessons of history,' the adjustments made by the churches over the centuries to the intractable constancies of the fallen world, i.e., structures like ethnicity, the state, or the economy, which one can appeal to the guidance of the Holy Spirit to validate."

and live in his new creation of human existence, since Jesus' life did not "translate" very well into 20th century politics, economics, and culture. This "epistemological grid" softened Jesus' life to merely a *moral example* in favor of a Trinitarianism more compatible with an American form of Constantinianism in which Christianity becomes pluralistic and eclectic to agree with those same qualities found in American culture. Niebuhr's distributive Trinitarianism, which combines all three Unitarianisms of Father, Son, and Spirit, is an adaptation of the classical Christian doctrine to an increasing American emphasis on pluralism that accepts all voices as legitimate ways to know the truth. Niebuhr's Trinitarianism accepts even heretical theologies into a "synthesized formula in which all the partial insights and convictions are combined."[38] In this method, the doctrine of the Trinity serves as "an ecumenical doctrine providing not for the exclusion of heretics but for their inclusion in the body on which they are actually dependent."[39]

For Niebuhr, the particularities of Jesus' life, and especially his death, could not be made to fit into or to be made compatible with an American culture that was becoming increasing monolithic in its acceptance of pluralism and in its prescribing that acceptance as the equal right of everyone to achieve the "American Dream" following World War II. In such a time, the particularities of Jesus' life, death, and resurrection had to take a back seat to the more formidable cultural pressure of acceptance and unity. As a result, Jesus' death became obscured and spiritualized in mainstream American Christianity as a way to hide the true significance of his life and death.

Niebuhr's Trinitarianism, in Yoder's view, "seems therefore rather to be a slogan, symbolizing in a superficial way our author's urbane, pluralistic concern for a balance between Christ and other moral authorities."[40] These other moral authorities for Niebuhr exist because the "world," in its autonomous and independent status, exists in and of itself. This is the power Niebuhr's *Christ and Culture* exhibited upon its readers, who, largely responded by assuming "a 'rational' or 'natural' epistemology, according to which the moral content of 'culture' is simply given, already 'out

---

38. Niebuhr, "The Doctrine of the Trinity," 383. Niebuhr's Trinitarianism was simply the combination of all three Unitarianisms, a pluralism by which "the three Unitarianisms are interdependent."

39. Ibid., 384.

40. Yoder, "How H. Richard Niebuhr Reasoned," 63.

there,' defined by the way things are."[41] Yoder rightly exposes this faulty epistemology: "The Gospel alternative we have gradually been watching unfold will rather deny that there is any such thing as an already given 'nature' of things, 'out there' or 'as such,' ..."[42] For Yoder, the Christian life is a call to be a disciple of Jesus as Lord, who, as Lord over the universe, has already subjected the rebellious "principalities and powers" under his lordship as they await their final judgment. The monolithic pretention of culture's power to dominate has been broken by Jesus so that his disciples, rather than being responsible for culture's ongoing "progress," are freed from its domination in order to be witnesses of Jesus' victory over all of it. In the end, Niebuhr's call for "transforming culture" parallels his inability to call cultures fallen and standing in judgment, a vision that "correlates with a low estimate of the power of evil."[43]

STANLEY HAUERWAS'S CRITIQUE OF REINHOLD NIEBUHR'S USE OF NATURAL THEOLOGY

Yoder's critique of liberal Protestant theology's filtering of Jesus' life through the lens of natural theology is complemented by Stanley Hauerwas's explanation of how powerful Reinhold Niebuhr (H. Richard's brother) used natural theology as a "supporting foundation" for Christian faith. For Reinhold Niebuhr, Christ was the culmination of the "best" of what humanity lacked; a method that minimized Christ to merely the remedy for the inner longing "for more." Hauerwas, following Yoder's post-Constantinian critique, explains Reinhold Niebuhr's methodology of correlation with this natural characteristic of human longing.

> Yet exactly because he was such a vital Christian believer, Niebuhr felt free to provide an account of our knowledge of God that seems little more than a pale theism. In short, Niebuhr's practice, his use of Christian speech, prevented him, as well as those influenced by him, from seeing that metaphysically his "god" was nothing other than a [William] Jamesian sense that "there must be more." ... As it turns out, the revelation that is required for us to know Niebuhr's god is but a reflection of ourselves.[44]

41. Ibid., 88–89.
42. Ibid., 89.
43. Ibid.
44. Hauerwas, *With the Grain of the Universe*, 122.

In good liberal Protestant fashion, Reinhold Niebuhr sees Jesus' death on a cross as the triumph of God's love over his wrath, making salvation one of personal forgiveness of sin and the healing of a troubled conscience; all by which even the particularities of special revelation can be validated by human experience.[45] This use of natural theology uses human experience and understanding as the basic foundation to make faith in Christ "reasonable," even "desirable," to an unbeliever. In providing an account of Christian ethics that works for anyone,[46] it is understandable that Niebuhr made little room for the church in his ethics, seeing it as a "sociological necessity for Christianity to exist across time."[47] Without the necessity of Spirit transformation to make one a member of Christ's body, Niebuhr's Christianity is reduced to a moral perfecting of the world without any salvation from it.[48]

As revealing as Yoder's and Hauerwas's critiques of the Niebuhr brothers' failed use of natural theology and flawed use of Trinitarian theology are, a basic element to their critique of modern theology is their view that Constantinianism, at its most fundamental level, is simply the church's unfaithfulness to Jesus as Lord. We now turn to this element of their critiques.

The Constantinian Confusion of Church and World: Unfaithfulness to Jesus as Lord

Yoder gave this systematic and intentional failure of the church to live as though Jesus is Lord the name "Constantinianism" and defined it as the unfortunate confusion between the church and the world; identified in five stages in Western church history.[49] Others have explained it in less

45. Ibid., 125.

46. Ibid., 133.

47. Ibid., 137.

48. Ibid., 138. "Niebuhr's god is not a god capable of offering salvation in any material sense. Changed self-understanding or attitude is no substitute for the existence of a church capable of offering an alternative to the world. Of course, Niebuhr did not seek to offer an alternative, which is why he could not help but become a theologian of a domesticated god capable of doing no more than providing comfort to the anxious conscience of bourgeoisie."

49. Yoder, *The Royal Priesthood*, 195–97. The church's current state of compromise with America's Post-Christian culture is seen in the "transposition of the gospel into terms of nonreligious language [that] has been proposed as the price for bringing the message of the church to the new 'world.' . . . This preoccupation of the church to be allied even with post-religious secularism, as long as this is *effective and popular*, could

nuanced ways or have studied particular aspects of its development,[50] but Yoder described it best in relationship to Jesus' lordship and the church's unfaithfulness to that lordship. At the present stage of Constantinianism, much of the church is even resistant to its own self-critique due to the depth of cultural compromise and unfaithfulness into which it has fallen. It has its own built-in self-defense mechanism of the human proclivity to power and domination that various forms of Constantinianism afford it. Most ironically, it is this proclivity to power and dominion which still holds captive the Western church in the clutches of Constantinianism. Those most afflicted with this proclivity to power are the very ones most adept at "grabbing" and "holding on" to the power structures that enable their own domination to continue, even if now those structures within America's most Constantinian segments of the church are maintained by those most qualified to appease a following that is bent on the renunciation of all authority and their interdictory commands that demand faith to follow.[51] This domination is held through the complete inversion of a hierarchical system where those in "authority" only hold onto it by appeasing the whims of those at the grass roots in order to maintain their own popularity and control over those whose only authority is their own "fictive selves," Philip Rieff's definition of the false prophets in Jeremiah who serve their own selves and "speak visions of their own minds."[52] This parallels Yoder's description of the future stage of Constantinianism (which is actually already here) in which the church will align itself with whatever is *en vogue* within the wider culture out of a desire to be "on the right side" of the "winning cause" of history, even if that cause has not yet appeared.

> Convinced that the future belongs to some particular cause, that history is assured a move according to the insights of some particular system, it is possible already in the present to take sides with this cause so that we will not be discredited when the old

---

perhaps be called 'neo-neo-neo-Constantinianism'" (197; emphasis added).

50. Bercot, *The Kingdom that Turned the World Upside Down*; Boyd, *The Myth of a Christian Nation*.

51. Elshtain, *Sovereignty: God, State, and Self*. Elshtain elaborates a fascinating narrative of the chronological progression that has resulted in the Western monistic sovereignty of God, then the state, and now the self that finds its greatest expression in modern existentialism of Jean-Paul Sartre and Albert Camus. See also Rieff, *The Feeling Intellect*.

52. Rieff, *Charisma*, 43.

order collapses and the new is victorious. Something of this seems to have taken place in North America with the predictions of how the church will be radically transformed in the age of urbanization . . . Such advance approval of an order that does not yet exist, tending to be linked with approval of any means to which people resort that hope to achieve it, we would call "neo-neo-neo-neo-Constantinianism."[53]

In its fullest extent, Constantinianism is the church's denial that Jesus is Lord in favor of a quest for power through "elitism" or "dominionism" over the world's structures (or structures of its own making) that is self-perpetuating. Yoder's post-Constantinianism calls for the church to let go of this quest for power in order to declare Jesus as Lord, not as the goal of faith but as the very essence of faith. However, overcoming Western Constantinianism is a daunting task, one that requires critique of some firmly-held, yet "invisible," theological assumptions. Ultimately, it is only the church's awareness of its own essence and mission that will free it from its self-delusion that its mission to the world is advanced by worldly power, prestige, and popularity.

The Post-Constantinians' Lack of an Explicit Account of the Spirit's Necessity

While Yoder's account represents a "new beginning" for the content of the Christian life, it is noticeably lacking in an explicit account of the Holy Spirit's role in establishing and living out the Christian life. Yoder's and Hauerwas's post-Constantinian accounts have no prominent place for the Holy Spirit's necessary presence to live out such a life. No doubt they believe in the Spirit's necessary presence in forming people to the life of Jesus, they just fail to make such a presence explicit.

Yoder's account does acknowledge the role of the Spirit, but how the Spirit works remains implicit and presupposed. His understanding of Spirit is based in large part on his historical studies of the various versions of sixteenth century "radical" reformations and their claims as to the purpose and role of the Spirit.[54] Of the five types he identifies within the sixteenth century radical reformation, Yoder commends two that place

---

53. Yoder, *The Royal Priesthood*, 197.

54. Yoder, "'Spirit' and the Varieties of Reformation Radicalism."

the Spirit's work in the believing community as a whole.[55] Yoder places
the Spirit's work within the community of believers as distinguished
from "other spirits, subjectivity, unaccountability, and the Spirit [sic] of
this world."[56] By working within the community, the Spirit leads people
to "simple obedience to biblical commands."[57] This rightly elevates the
Spirit's work in the church, but the Spirit's role in shaping such a community and how one obeys with "simple obedience" is neglected. It is hard to
believe that "simple obedience" to Yoder's kind of Christian life is a simple
thing, even if one's life is constituted by a certain kind of community that
shapes one's life. Thus, his view of the Spirit's role in the community is
shaped by his ecclesiology; how one is transformed into a disciple in the
community is subsumed within his ecclesiology. Yoder's view of the Spirit
neglects the need for personal transformation necessary to live out the
kind of new human existence that Jesus lived in his own life.

In being greatly influenced by Yoder and applying his methodology
to ethics, Stanley Hauerwas follows in the same path of obscuring the
necessary transformation of the Spirit in making disciples who take Jesus'
life seriously as their own way of life. Hauerwas's assessment identifies the
loss of not only our ability to locate the church but, by implication, the
Spirit's work in the church. Hauerwas cites an article by Michael Hollerich
in which he identifies Dietrich Bonhoeffer's assessment of "locating the
Church" at the end of Constantinianism.[58] Hauerwas relates this problem of locating the Spirit's work within such a misplaced church after
Constantinianism by asking, "What does the Spirit's work look like and
how is it to be identified?"[59] But as much as he identifies the problem of

55. Ibid., 303–4. (1) Unity is in "the Spirit of Christ" by the congregation's account-
ability to "Scripture as exposited by the Spirit in the assembled community" and (2) in
the "power of obedience whereby the individual makes his own what is already known
as God's will."

56. Ibid.

57. Ibid., 304. See also Yoder, The Priestly Kingdom, 33–35.

58. Hollerich, "Retrieving a Neglected Critique of Church," 305. Quoting
Bonhoeffer: "The question is whether, after the separation from papal and from secular
authority in the church, an ecclesiastical authority can be established which is grounded
solely in Scripture and confession. If no such authority is possible, then the last possibility of an Evangelical Church is dead; then there is only return to Rome or under the
state church, or the path of individualization, of the 'protest' of Protestantism against
false authorities." See also Hauerwas, In Good Company, 21.

59. Hauerwas, In Good Company, 21–22. "The problem is, quite simply, that we can
talk all we want about the church as the body of Christ, but in fact such talk is more

locating the Spirit's work in the church, he succumbs to his own critique of theology mainly talking about other theologians and their theologies rather than actually writing theology that explains the Spirit's work.[60] With all due fairness, Hauerwas views all human existence as theological and, above all, the activities of the church: so too, the Spirit's work of making disciples of Jesus encompasses all of life.

Hauerwas also identifies this all-encompassing aspect to theology in the work of James Wm. McClendon. For McClendon, theology in this post-Constantinian era can no longer be only a specialization or "systematic theology" for the professional clergy trained in the seminary. That method served well in a past Constantinian era as a service to the state to keep theology in its place, obscured, private, and mute. Hauerwas shows how McClendon's theology is problematic for Christian institutions still subservient to the state or especially to those who would challenge that subservience by making theology an all-encompassing reality for Christian identity.[61]

James McClendon does come closer to articulating the role of the Spirit as the "constitutive ingredient" for the Christian life, in "which Christians experience the moral world itself . . . as the new world in formation, revised and under revision by the Spirit and the power of the risen Christ."[62] Later, in volume 2, McClendon suggests the Spirit's inner working in Stephen's martyrdom in Acts 7, *"for the Spirit, intimate enabler, was within him,* allowing Stephen to see the vision of Jesus in his place and die a faithful death."[63]

Like Yoder and Hauerwas, McClendon does well at explaining *that* the Christian life is a life lived in the Spirit and *that* it requires an inward work of the Spirit for inner transformation. He even criticizes H. Richard Niebuhr's "rejection of the efficacy of the Holy Spirit to make Christians Christ-like, his downplay of the new birth as a real transformation of human life, and his neglect of the resurrection in favor of an exclusive

---

than likely to be just that–i.e., talk. We have no means of knowing if the Holy Spirit has abandoned the church because we have no means of knowing what it would mean for the *spirit to matter as matter.* In short, we have few ways to resist what seems unavoidable everywhere but in Sneem [Ireland]; namely, the 'spiritualization' of the church" (emphasis added).

60. Hauerwas, *Wilderness Wanderings,* 176.

61. Ibid., 175–76.

62. McClendon, *Ethics,* 66–67.

63. McClendon, *Doctrine,* 291; emphasis original. Cf. ibid., 240.

emphasis on the cross."[64] In speaking of the end or goal of the Holy Spirit's mission in creation and humanity, McClendon uses marriage as an example in which "sacrifice is altogether appropriate, every social organism must be for its members an 'other' and an 'all' that as Christians know, can be supported only by sacrifice, by taking up a cross."[65] Here the shape and direction of the Christian life is made explicit as the same shape and direction of Jesus' life; that of taking up a cross. But *how* is the cross defined and *how* does one come to make Jesus' life one's life as a Christian? McClendon acknowledges that "for this ideal unity to be realized, it must enter and rule 'the kingdom of matter and death' by rising *within* each individual human being."[66] In the end however, McClendon also falls short by not fully explaining *how* this transformation by the Spirit takes place in the Christian's life. Even McClendon's advancement of the Spirit's role still falls short of explaining how the kind of life Jesus lived in the Spirit becomes the inward presence for the believer to live the same kind of life. As much as he says at times *that* the Spirit's work is an inward work, his overall methodology conveys the same tendencies as Yoder and Hauerwas; a deficiency in articulating *how* the Spirit becomes the "energy" for one's very existence as a Christian.

Are Yoder's, Hauerwas's, and McClendon's lack of an explicit account of the Spirit's role in conforming one's life to the life of Christ only a lack? Or, is there a more fundamental reason? I propose the post-Constantinians lack an explicit role of the Spirit due to the Spirit not adequately supplanting human "freedom of the will." Yoder's *Politics of Jesus* begs the question, "How does one *freely choose this kind* of Jesus whose very mission it was to condemn human freedom by allowing humans to use their freedom to kill him?" Yoder's account of the Spirit is too weak to overcome human's inability to pick up a cross and follow Jesus on his road to a tragic end. Humans cannot and do not freely choose to pick up a cross and submit to their own "public executions" or even to live a life of social nonconformity that led Jesus to die the way he did. Yoder's presupposing of human freedom as sufficient enough to do God's will is one

---

64. McClendon, *Ethics*, 320.

65. McClendon, *Doctrine*, 449. McClendon suggests Russian philosopher Vladimir Sergeyevick Solovyov's imperfect, but helpful, analogy of marriage between a man and woman as an example of ultimate intimacy and ecstasy where one finds in the "other," the "all."

66. Ibid; emphasis original.

reason for the Spirit's neglect in his account of Christian identity. While the presence and power of the Holy Spirit frees one from bondage to sin, his presence certainly does not free one from God and his will. Rather, the Spirit's presence ties one to God's will: a freedom that frees one to obey God's will and from bondage to doing one's own "free will." This dilemma puts the status of the question back into its most simplest and basic form: Did Jesus come to enhance human freedom or did he come to condemn human freedom as sin and replace it with his obedience to the Father in the presence and power of the Spirit? Or, asked a different way, is the human condition of sin only partial or are humans entirely sinful, including their will? How this basic question is answered determines not only how one does all subsequent theology but the entire essence and mission of the church and the shape and direction of the Christian life as life in the Spirit as a member of Christ's body of the church.

Excursus: A "Test Case" of Non-violence for the Spirit's Necessary Transformation

The relevance of this issue comes up when dealing with a crucial test case of the Christian life: non-violence, especially since it is the stance held by these post-Constantinians. That the Christian's life should be non-violent is clear: you shall not murder, you are to love your enemies, turn the other cheek, love your neighbor as yourself, etc. *How* anyone can be non-violent is not so clear. Maybe more than any other, this test case shows clearly the distinction and reciprocal relationship between material content and motivational energy; that is, the content of "what to do" and the energy of "how is it possible to do it." How does one "freely will" to not use one's naturally violent will as the "energy" to be non-violent? This becomes especially evident by how *violently* even Christians *reject* the notion of non-violence as a constitutive element of the Christian life, defending their rights to violently defend themselves against their non-violent enemies. But what if Jesus' non-violence was due to the Spirit's presence?

A good example of this test case of non-violence is the Pentecostals of the early 20th century, who lived lives "fully in the Spirit" even better than they knew or were able to theologically explain. Their lack of an explicit theology to explain the otherworldly aspects of their lives (such as sharing material goods, racial unity, proclamation of the Scripture for transformation, pacifism, etc.) caused their lifestyles among Pentecostals to largely lose out to the greater force of gaining the "American Dream" following World War II. They simply took these social and community elements of their lives for granted; thinking anyone who lived "fully in the Spirit" would live as they did. They lived lives that resembled post-Constantinianism before it was ever a theological construct and movement. Some historians, such as Grant Wacker, think these early elements lost out due to their minority status, but his theory bears the burden of proof since pacifism was an official stance of the major Pentecostal movements up until or after World War II and their other worldly lifestyles were the very marks of their Christian Pentecostal identities.[67] Their lifestyles of contrast to, even condemnation of, worldly cultural norms proportionately lost out over time due to the greater pressure to conform to the larger American monolithic culture. In short, early Pentecostalism's cultural critique caved in to the greater pressure of the American form of Constantinianism. In order to better explain this Constantinian compromise of Pentecostalism to the larger American culture, this work will propose a *theological* account to affirm these early Pentecostals' otherworldly lifestyles as what it means to live lives fully in the Spirit. The theological reasons for the early Pentecostals' lifestyles and why they lost out to American Constantinianism is brought into clearer focus by the impressive nature of Yoder's work. His work helps us make better sense of their lives. However, for both early Pentecostals and present-day post-Constantinians, the content is there but they both lack, possibly for different reasons, an explicit account of the Spirit's work to live out such a culturally-contrasting content. The former lived lives fully in the Spirit without an explicit theology able to explain their lives as living in the Spirit while the latter have an explicit account of the Christian community as a contrast society without an explicit account of the Christian life as life in the Spirit. The reason for this separation in both accounts is the nature of the Spirit; seen as an "added extra" rather than as the very "constitutive ingredient" or the very principle of life itself for the Christian life.

The contribution this work intends to offer is an account of the Christian life as life in the Spirit that makes sense out of such transformed and radically otherworldly lives of the early twentieth-century Pentecostals and the recent post-Constantinians; both *transformation* by the Spirit and the *relinquishing* of one's own will (even life itself) by the indwelling presence of the Spirit. Such an account is able to be seen only

---

67. Wacker, *Heaven Below.*

when Jesus' life is first seen as a life lived fully in the Spirit; from conception by the Spirit to surrendering his spirit for the will of the Father. As Jesus lived his life as the Son of God the Father in the presence of the Spirit, so too do Christians live their lives as adopted sons of God the Father in the Spirit with Jesus as their older brother.

2

A Spirit-Christology That Works for the Christian Life

Introduction

In this chapter I intend to lay the theological groundwork for an account of Spirit-Christology to be given in the following chapters that explains the Christian life as life in the Spirit based on the constitutive events in Jesus' life and death, showing that the Christian life is not only life in the Spirit but that such life in the Spirit is also a cruciform life. To do so, I will examine other Spirit-Christologies and Pneumatologies to see whether they contribute to the kind of Spirit-Christology given here that begins with Jesus' life and death as the basis for showing what it means to live in the Spirit. By engaging these other accounts the case will be made for a certain kind of Spirit-Christology that serves as the foundation for constructing a post-Constantinian and Trinitarian account of the Christian life. The end result will demonstrate the need for a Spirit-Christology that begins with the life Jesus lived in the Spirit as the *actual* life that constitutes the Christian life, that is, life lived as an adopted son of God on account of the life, death, and resurrection of Jesus.

This chapter will establish the theological basis for such a Spirit-Christology by evaluating the field of scholarship to find a framework that truly serves as a complementary account to the prevailing framework of Logos-Christology. Such a framework will need to postpone the need to establish the ontology of Jesus' divine person as God-man in order to first examine his life and death the way the synoptic gospels portray it—as he lived. This will serve our purposes three ways. First, it will be compatible with the post-Constantinian focus on the way Jesus lived his life as constitutive for the Christian life. Second, it will explain Jesus' life as a Trinitarian life by reflecting on his identity in the gospels as the Son of God in the Spirit. Third, it will show the Christian life to be the kind of life in the Spirit God brings about by doing Jesus' cruciform life in others through Spirit transformation. Such a cruciform life in the Spirit may be described as participation by the Spirit in Christ's death and resurrection.

Summarizing to this point, the post-Constantinians have explained Jesus' life and death in such a way that one cannot "add Jesus on" to any foundation or wider wisdom that uses natural theology as a support mechanism to make Jesus' life more reasonable for anyone to believe. Yoder and Hauerwas corrected this wrong use of natural theology by showing how it distorts Jesus' life. Yoder gave the best correction of all to this faulty reliance on human reason simply by describing the life Jesus lived and what it meant for his follower. However, this led us to realize the post-Constantinians lack an explicit account of the Spirit's presence in Jesus' life due to their indebtedness to Logos-Christology, which takes *how* Jesus lived largely for granted due to their focus on *what* constitutes Jesus' ontological identity. This hinders theology's ability to describe *how* one becomes a follower of Jesus. Providing a more adequate answer to this question has now led us to the task in this chapter of finding a Spirit-Christology that explains how Jesus lived by the Spirit's presence.

Now I will examine other Spirit-Christologies and Pneumatologies that do not explain the Spirit presence *beginning* with Jesus' life. While these do offer contributions that advance Spirit-Christology in various ways, we will see how they eclipse giving an answer to *how* one becomes a follower of Jesus by their equating the Spirit with the general religious experience in all people in their quest to find and know God or by relying mostly on an Incarnational framework to explain Jesus' life and death. Since they do not begin with Jesus' life and death for what it meant for Jesus to live in the Spirit, they eclipse Jesus' life and death as the basis for showing what it means for his disciples to also live in the Spirit. Laying this groundwork will establish the basis upon which I will give an account of Jesus' life and death for ascertaining what it means to live in the Spirit. Beginning with the narrative description of how Jesus lived and died in the Spirit will yield a view of the Christian life as life in the Spirit that is none other than Jesus' way of life that led to the kind of death he died on a cross—a cruciform life God brings about through Spirit transformation.

Other Accounts That Eclipse Jesus' Life as Constitutive for Life in the Spirit

To this end, a selection of other Spirit-Christologies and Pneumatologies will now be explained as helpful in delineating the criteria for constructing a Spirit-Christology solely from Jesus' life but which are also inadequate, to various degrees, for the task of describing the Christian life as life in the Spirit. Therefore, this survey is more representative than it is exhaustive. These other representative accounts of the Spirit fall short in accomplishing the task called for here for two reasons. First, they do not take the Spirit's presence seriously for what it meant for Jesus to live and die as the obedient Son of God as attested in the passion narratives and, as a result, are not able to take Jesus' life seriously as the basis for describing what it means for a Christian to live as one of God's adopted sons in the Spirit. This neglect calls for a fully developed Trinitarian view of Jesus' life as the obedient Son of God in the Spirit. Secondly, they do not take the life of Jesus seriously for what it means for a Christian to live a transformed life of death to one's own life in this world and life in Jesus' resurrection. This neglect calls for a fully developed post-Constantinian view of Jesus' life. However, a discussion of their contributions and methodologies will open up a clearing in which to demonstrate the need for a Spirit-Christology that is both post-Constantinian and Trinitarian.

Pneumatologies of Religious Experience That eclipse Jesus' Life and Death

We begin our examination of Pneumatologies by returning to our test case of Pentecostalism in order to show its increasing emphasis upon developing a Pentecostal theology of the Spirit as the completion of the general religious experience that desires to know God. Rather than beginning with the life Jesus lived, and the historical context in which he lived and died in order to describe the Spirit in relation to Jesus' mission, many Pentecostal Pneumatologies work from the other direction, by starting with one's own culture, experience, or theological persuasion to explain the Spirit, a common trend in modern theology. With humans and their experience as the "subject," these view God as the "object" of humanity's quest, longing, or desire, which leads to an understanding of the Christian life that keeps one in control and their Pentecostal experience as the litmus test of spiritual success or control over one's own life but with little or no connection to the life Jesus lived. While this is a sweeping generalization of the Pentecostal movement in America, it is obvious that such a methodology has led many to view their Pentecostal experience as the renewal of God's order of dominion over the earth by which one has the God-given right to achieve possessions or prestige formerly prohibited. I will discuss this specifically in chapter 5, but I mention it here to highlight a presuppostional methodology that elevates an experience in the Spirit in order to circumvent the particularity of Jesus' death and resurrection for defining what life in the Spirit entails. With Jesus' death and resurrection marginalized or, at the very least, generalized to accommodate religious experience in all people as legitimate expressions of the Spirit, Jesus' life is relegated to the "best" moral example.

This methodology, as we will see in more detail, is an attempt to establish a Third Article theology from the perspective of the Pentecostal tradition's emphasis on the manifestations of the Spirit as operational in the church today. Ironically, the more the Pentecostal experience or Pneumatology in general remains the starting point through which one views Jesus and his relationship to the Spirit, the less significant the experience becomes by it losing its biblical meaning altogether and, more particularly, the Spirit's presence in Jesus' life. Without Jesus' life and his death on a cross as the starting point for understanding the Spirit's presence in his life, the Spirit's presence in the Christian's life has the potential to mean just about anything a Christian desires it to mean. If Jesus death on a cross and his resurrection from the dead are not the starting point for understanding the Spirit's activity in the church, the lack of desire to get back to Jesus' cross always persists since Jesus' cross is antithetical to one's human desires.

There has been an increase in Pentecostal Pneumatologies that derive their impetus from not only the Pentecostal movement itself, but from Pentecostal spiritualities that desire to engage the wider theological spectrum regarding Trinitarian theology in general and Spirit-Christology in particular. However, Pentecostal theologians are susceptible to basing theological truth first on the immediate context of their Pentecostal spirituality or cultural context and then, secondarily, by reading their own contexts back into the biblical narrative for it to come out right. An emphasis on developing a Third Article theology based on the Spirit as known through Pentecostal experience tends to bypass the life of Jesus as the *person* who received and bore the Spirit from his Father and, on account of his resurrection and exaltation to the Father's "right hand," what it means for him to be the sender of his Spirit upon the church. Due to this eclipse of the life of Jesus as defining for what it means to live a life in the Spirit, they are susceptible to falling into a pantheistic Pneumatology of "ultimate concern" to meet one's needs or to complete the desire for God that people generally experience.

Within Pentecostal theologies of the Spirit, Veli-Matti Kärkkäinen and Amos Yong represent the most prolific Pneumatologies based on general religious experience or, at best, on one's own Christian experience. Kärkkäinen believes that one's personal experience of the Spirit is primary to theological reflection since the biblical record clearly shows that a powerful experience came first and "only afterward, and in a slow tempo, came theological reflection."[1] A primacy of experience leads Kärkkäinen to emphasize context over content and to construct Pneumatology in a way that fits into the common religious experience of all people by way of a distributive Trinitarianism.[2] Such an emphasis on the Spirit seeks a way around the church's traditional emphasis on the particularity of Christ's salvific work in order to take into account the "potential salvific value"[3] of other religions.

Fellow Pentecostal Amos Yong sees Kärkkäinen representing a pneumatological theology of the Third Article that seeks a new starting point.[4] However, this new starting point equates personal religious experiences with the Spirit, lending credence to an ecumenical approach that seeks unity through experience formerly unattainable through doctrine. "This pneumatological reframing of older theological subjects has shed light on the issues of our time. . . . This is especially the case given the increasingly ecumenical direction of theology."[5] In Yong's own admission, Kärkkäinen's perspective seeks a vantage point on the Spirit within the traditional sequencing of theological studies of "patrology (God the Father), christology (God the Son) and pneumatology (God the Spirit)" that "appeals to educators looking for Pentecostal and ecumenical perspectives on the last named topic."[6] By beginning with common

---

1. Kärkkäinen, *Pneumatology*, 15.

2. Kärkkäinen, *Toward a Pneumatological Theology*, 235.

3. Ibid., 238.

4. Yong, Introduction to *Toward a Pneumatological Theology*, xvii.

5. Ibid., xvi–xvii.

6. Ibid., xviii.

religious experience as a way to break down doctrinal barriers, Yong says Kärkkäinen "traverses grounds heretofore considered to be in opposition . . . This is a testimony to Kärkkäinen's capacity to cross over, return, and therefore bridge multiple worlds."[7]

This pneumatological perspective, that equates experience with the Spirit, is necessary, according to Yong, since pluralism calls for the adoption of another starting point than the one Christian theology has traditionally maintained—the life of Jesus Christ. In order to accept other Christian traditions as valid and even certain aspects of other religions, the starting point of Jesus is replaced with a starting point of the Spirit. For Yong, Kärkkäinen's "is truly a theology that emerges from living on the boundaries and walking along the margins, especially since, in our time, *the center which once held no longer holds*."[8] What no longer holds for Yong is the Christian life that takes Jesus' life and death as its starting point and center.

Amos Yong's own Pneumatology represents an explicit articulation of a Hegelian and Niebuhrian philosophical Trinitarianism by relativizing Jesus' life as defining what it means to live in the Spirit. He does so by elevating the preexistent Logos to a higher level of divine existence than the particularity of the incarnate Logos in the gospel accounts, stating, "God is *fully* revealed in Jesus Christ, the *supreme incarnation* of the Word by the power of the Spirit."[9] He identifies the Logos's work through the Spirit in creation in order to posit other partial incarnations of the Logos in other religions and in creation in general.[10] Yong's premise of the Spirit as "the life breath of the *imago Dei* in every human being"[11] agrees with Paul Tillich's view of religion as humanity's "ultimate concern"[12] by which he elevates human experience of God (or a god) to a place of authority about God.

This elevated view of humanity and creation is but another example of what Yoder critiques as a wider wisdom normative for the Christian's life over that of Jesus' life, thus relegating Jesus' life to that of best example. "Every determination of being exhibits the presence and activity

7. Ibid., xviii.

8. Ibid.

9. Yong, *Discerning the Spirit(s)*, 118; emphasis added.

10. Ibid., 120–22.

11. Yong, *Beyond the Impasse*, 45. See also Habets, *The Anointed Son*, 237.

12. Yong, *Beyond the Impasse*, 15–17.

of the divine being: Father creating something through the Logos by the Spirit. The person of Jesus is simply the *most complete* instance of this."[13] The basis for Yong's foundational Pneumatology is the quest for wholeness in a fragmented and pluralistic religious world. As is already evident, Yong works from within a certain appropriation of pre-Nicene Logos-Christology that takes for granted Jesus' identification as the Logos, even if Jesus is only the Logos' *most complete* manifestation. The problem Yong seeks to overcome is the particularity of Jesus' life, death, and resurrection as the *only starting point* for knowing God, calling this traditional approach from Christology an "impasse" and "dilemma."[14] To do so he attempts to develop a Pneumatology able to circumvent the life of Jesus as the *only* incarnation of the Logos. While presupposing a certain form of early Logos-Christology, he identifies Logos with seeds of reason within creation in general, providing a framework in which the Spirit can be seen as the force by which the Logos is incarnated in various forms in other religions.

As a way around this christological impasse, that is, the Christian tradition's exclusivist view of salvation being only through Jesus Christ, Yong develops the idea of a "trinitarian metaphysics of creation and a theology of symbolism"[15] so as to appropriate a Pneumatology that recognizes the Spirit's work in other religions that is not accomplished with Christology. The most foundational premise that serves as the basis of Yong's proposal is his Pentecostal experience of the Spirit: personal experience being for Yong the avenue through which we experience the Logos. He follows the foundational Pneumatology of his Doctorfather Robert C. Neville,[16] the pragmatism of Charles S. Peirce, and the empirical theology of Donald Gelpi. His anti-Cartesian claim is but a foil for replacing

---

13. Yong, *Discerning the Spirit(s)*, 120; emphasis added.

14. Ibid., 33–58.

15. Ibid., 62. "The economy of the Spirit is such a conception would then be considered to be 'larger' or 'broader' than the economy of the Word . . . More appropriate would be to begin by recognizing the economies of the Word and Spirit as overlapping dimensionally." Yong follows Paul Tillich's use of dimensions to refer to the economies of Word and Spirit rather than spatially "because the notion of dimension does not spatialize or hierarchicalize reality but rather *recognizes its unity above the conflicts*" (emphasis added).

16. Yong's foundational Pneumatology of religions has drawn much from Neville's Hegelian-based speculative metaphysics in *God the Creator*.

René Descartes' foundation of cognition with a foundation of experience (which he then equates with Pneumatology), seen in the following.

> My own foundational pneumatology follows Gelpi in eschewing the strong Cartesian foundationalism that bases all beliefs ultimately on self-evident intuitions. It proceeds instead from what Peirce called a "contrite fallibilism" wherein all knowledge is provisional, relative to the questions posed by the community of inquirers, and subject to the ongoing process of conversation and discovery.[17]

In other words, by his own admission, Yong does not believe that the revelation of God through Jesus Christ is final, or even normative or constitutive, only that God's "wisdom is *most fully manifest* in the cross."[18] By elevating Logos to a higher level than the life of Jesus, Yong is able to marginalize Jesus' death on a cross and, in its place, regard personal spiritual experiences through the Spirit just as legitimate for determining manifestations of the Logos in history as Jesus' own life and death.[19]

As we have now seen in Kärkkäinen and Yong, a pneumatological "method of correlation" only serves to minimize the particularity of Jesus' cross; choosing rather an accommodation of other spirits in other religions as legitimate manifestations of the Logos and as activities of the Holy Spirit. For our purposes here, of articulating a biblically based Spirit-Christology to explain the Christian life, these Pneumatologies based on "creation" or "reality" or, now, "religious experience" are inadequate to the task of demonstrating Jesus' life and death as the foundation for ascertaining what it means to live in the Spirit. Without Jesus' life being God's re-creation of the human condition and without the Spirit's indwelling presence as the very "constitutive ingredient" in Jesus' living

17. Yong, *Discerning the Spirit(s)*, 100.

18. Yong, *Spirit-Word-Community*, 39; emphasis added.

19. Yong, *Discerning the Spirit(s)*, 117. In line with H. Richard Niebuhr's "distributive trinitarianism" Yong hopes to "help fill out, and thereby strengthen, the pneumatological component of Neville's abstract trinitarian theology of creation" (111). Yong elevates personal experience up to a level through which the Logos communicates God directly to humanity through "religious experience," Logos being the "mind of God" revealed to humanity by the Spirit, not *only* through Jesus, but through "creation" and "reality." In this reductionist Trinitarian theology, Yong's starting point is the human spirit's engagement with the divine through "pneumatological imagination." His Hegelian dialectical framework values tension for continual investigation but without a final synthesis or resolution, upholding a tension between unity and plurality. See also Yong, *Spirit-Word-Community*, 101–9.

his life as the Son of God, Jesus' life and death lose their biblical sense of condemning humanity's most incipient sin of all, the "religious desire" to be like God or be God.

Such a priority of Pneumatology over Christology is parasitic upon salvation as defined by being a disciple of Jesus because it replaces knowledge of what Jesus Christ *has done* with a subjective spiritual experience one *has had*, regardless of what kind of experience. This equates the Spirit's work with one's inner quest for self-righteousness and is the reason much of recent Christianity in general, and Pentecostalism in particular, has slid down the slippery slope toward viewing the Christian life as the fulfillment of one's inner spiritual desire through personal experience rather than basing one's Christian life in Christ's own life, the narrative of Scripture that defines Christ's life, and the ecclesial use of Scripture and theology for shaping the body of Christ. Especially diminished in this approach is the proclamation of the gospel as necessary for transformation. As seen earlier in the Niebuhr brothers' distributive Trinitarianism, these other Pneumatologies closely resemble G. W. F. Hegel's philosophical Trinitarianism that equates the persons of the Trinity with the goodness of the world; in effect, negating the curse of estrangement and rebellion God placed upon humanity and within creation at the fall.

Spirit-Christologies of Divine Presence That Deny Jesus' Life as Transformative

These Pneumatologies, which view the Spirit as continuous with the general human spirit, are not the only accounts that discount the life and death of Jesus as constitutive for the Spirit's presence. There are also Spirit-Christologies that do the same. They claim to offer an account of the Spirit based on Jesus' life but do not see Jesus' life as transformative, a result of their minimizing his death on a cross and resurrection from the dead as constitutive for what it meant for him to live in the Spirit as the Son of God. As a result, they offer little if any discontinuity between Jesus' life and humanity's. Any discontinuity there might be is only by degree but not in kind. Without a discontinuity between Jesus' life and ours, Jesus' life becomes, at best, a moral example of what people are able to do in their own strength and the Spirit becomes synonymous with the striving of the human spirit in all people to be like God. In these accounts, the Spirit only comes to help a person be a "better person." These views of the Christian life are based on an account of the Spirit in Jesus' life as

God's presence that comes down to help him live a more divine life but is in no way constitutive for his identity as the Son of God.

As the post-Constantinian accounts of Jesus presuppose belief in the doctrine of the Two-Natures founded upon Logos-Christology, the Spirit-Christologies of Geoffrey W. H. Lampe[20] and James D. G. Dunn[21] are examples that go too far in this opposite direction by denying Jesus' divine nature altogether in favor of a mere functionality of the Spirit as an outside aid. As their own writings show, they work from within a false dichotomy between what Jesus is and how he lived rather than one between God's Spirit in Jesus and the generalized human spirit in all people. Their basic frameworks are similar to what we have already seen in Yong and Kärkkäinen of a generalized religious anthropological experience of "Spirit" in all people that is read back into the life of Jesus to affirm continuity between God and humanity. However, their lack of discontinuity between Jesus' life and the rest of humanity discounts the Spirit's work of making disciples of Jesus Christ who live lives in continuity with the way he lived. It especially minimizes Jesus' death and resurrection as the ground for both Jesus' discontinuity with humanity and for the Spirit's work of making Jesus' cross and resurrection the defining work in a Christian's life.

Geoffrey Lampe emphasizes the functional aspect of Jesus' life in relationship to God over against an ontological relationship by positing a Spirit-Christology as a replacement to Logos-Christology. Believing Logos-Christology to be the problem, Lampe sees its development as a departure from what he thinks could have been a better way of seeing Jesus as the point of reference between God and humanity, as God's greatest example of a Spirit-inspired human. He does this in an effort to show how Jesus Christ is present to believers in a way Logos-Christology has always had difficulty doing. He says the Logos was "well suited to express Christ's relationship to God . . . It was less fitted to express Christ's im-

---

20. Lampe, *God as Spirit*. Lampe works from the standpoint of humanity's spirit as God's continual activity of creation that leads to the perfecting of humanity. Thus, Lampe replaces the ontological claim of Jesus' Trinitarian existence with a relational one rather than showing how the relational aspect of Jesus' Trinitarian life *is* his ontological Trinitarian existence.

21. Dunn, *Christology*, 47.

manence in his people."[22] "Logos," which "lent itself least readily to this double reference,"[23] was later adapted to bridge this gap.

> Only when the idea of "Logos" had acquired a new and dominant role in Hellenistic philosophical theology could it be applied both to the "putting forth" or "generation" of God's immanent Reason for the "economy" of creation and redemption, and also to the rationality which unites the rational creation, by an innate kinship, to the Reason or Logos of God; men are *logikoi* because they participate in the Logos.[24]

While Logos adequately expressed Christ coming from God, Lampe believes a "different image was required for the corresponding interpretation of the relation between Christ and believers, the immanent presence of Christ as the source of their new life."[25] Rather than the Logos as the image of God coming down from God, Lampe proposes the Spirit as its alternative. "It might be expected that the most appropriate concept for the expression of this image would be Spirit-possession. God's Spirit is his own active presence: God himself reaching out to his creation."[26]

As much as Lampe's account might seem attractive as this point, filling a gap that Logos has always struggled to fill, his replacement model ever so subtly uses Jesus' life of Spirit-possession to confirm, by completion, humanity's experiencing of God's presence in all people.

> It also stands for the immanence of the presence of God within men's souls. The Spirit may possess a man and in some measure unite his personality to God. Yet this is without any diminution of his humanity; rather, it means the *raising of his humanity to its full potentiality, the completion of the human creation* by the re-creating influence of the creator-Spirit. Through Spirit-possession a man may be divinely motivated and act divinely— he may be at one with God—and become at the same time, and because of this, fully and completely human.[27]

---

22. Lampe, "The Holy Spirit and the Person of Christ," 114.

23. Ibid.

24. Ibid.

25. Ibid., 115.

26. Ibid., 117.

27. Ibid.; emphasis added.

While denying his account is adoptionist, by his own admission he places the uniqueness of Jesus as God's agent upon the *degree* of his Spirit-possession and thus Jesus is not distinct from the saints in kind but only by degree. At this point one is able to perceive Lampe's methodology as one that begins with the human condition of experiencing the divine, for which the Spirit in Jesus serves as the greatest example, as one's union with God, an account that ends up being modalistic[28] and involving "a considerable re-structuring of the trinitarian dogmatic formulations."[29]

Lampe's re-structuring is one in which Jesus' life is reduced to the greatest example of God's continual creativity within humanity. His desire is to see how the Spirit's active presence in Jesus can be related to God's presence in others.[30] As he sees it, the basic problem of the particularity of Jesus' life is solved in much the same way as we have already seen in Amos Yong. By defining the Spirit in Jesus as God's general presence in all creation, Lampe ascribes to Jesus the Spirit as God's perfecting of humanity's relationality begun at creation, but in no way sees the Spirit's presence in Jesus as discontinuous in some significant way with the Spirit's presence in humanity.

> If, then, we ask again, "What has God in Jesus done for man that man himself could not do?," our answer can be: "Created him"; or, rather, "Brought the *process of creation to the point where*

---

28. Ibid., 129. "The threefold distinction may be retained, God in his transcendence (or the being of God) being distinguished from God 'reaching out towards' and addressing (or God's Word) and from God operating immanently and influencing, inspiring and possessing (or God's Spirit). Or, on the other hand, it may be thought sufficient to distinguish between God as transcendent Spirit and God as immanent Spirit. In either case the concept of the pre-existent personal Son, or pre-existent Christ, would have to be re-expressed in terms of the eternal Spirit who was manifested at a particular point in history operating humanly in the person of Jesus Christ."

29. Ibid.

30. Lampe, *God as Spirit*, 13. At the most basic level, Lampe is operating from within the dominant framework of Logos-Christology, but, in denying it, is offering a non-Trinitarian functional view of Jesus to overcome the dilemma posed by not believing it; either God not being fully present in Jesus or, what he thinks is worse, "that God whom we acknowledge in Jesus was united in him with something less than a fully human personality. The history of the ancient controversy shows that the one defect can be remedied only at the cost of making the other worse; that the Nicene denial that God the Son is other than God the Father, except in a sense which it was ultimately found impossible to determine, prevented a fully personal meaning being given to the assumption of human nature by God the Son."

perfect man appears for the first time." "Perfect," in this context, means "perfect in respect of his relationship to God."

Creation is a continuing process, and for God's continuous creation of man in *ever deeper and richer* communion with himself the model of God as Spirit is very apt; for the term "Spirit" properly refers, not to God's essence but to his activity, that is to say, his creativity. Salvation, in one meaning of the term, denotes "making whole." Salvation is that part, or aspect, of the divine creative activity by which man comes to be informed by God's presence, made in his image and likeness, and led to respond with trust and willing obedience to the love and graciousness of his Creator. This is not to say that man is already and has always been a participant in the divine nature, needing only, as Gnosticism supposed, to have his eyes opened to his authentic nature. On the contrary, the Spirit transforms man into that which he was not; yet this *transformation is continuous with creation*; it is *the completion of creation.*[31]

God's Spirit (read God's *presence*) is equated with all of God's dealings with humanity in general, but with only a heightened presence in Jesus from what is generally experienced in all humanity. This provides a leveling effect by which Jesus' life is unique but only by degree. In Jesus, the Spirit's indwelling is reduced to God's presence,[32] which Lampe proposes to be the best way of explaining how Christians understand that "Jesus is alive today."

For this purpose, so we shall find, "the Spirit of God" is to be understood, not as referring to a divine hypostasis distinct from God the Father and God the Son or Word, but as indicating God himself as active towards and in his human creation. We are speaking of God disclosed and experienced as Spirit: that is, in his personal outreach. The use of this concept enables us to say that God indwelt and motivated the human spirit of Jesus in such a way that in him, uniquely, the relationship for which man is intended by his Creator was *fully realized*; that through Jesus God acted decisively to cause men to share in his relationship to God, and that the same God, the Spirit who was in Jesus, brings believers into that relationship of 'sonship' towards himself and forms them into a human community in which, albeit partially

31. Ibid., 17–18; emphasis added.
32. Webster, "The Identity of the Holy Spirit," 4–7.

> and imperfectly, the Christlike character which is the fruit of
> that relationship is re-presented.[33]

This explains Lampe's view of Jesus' sonship to God as a perfecting of
what was begun at creation, yet it is sonship as an abstraction of relationality that can be seen apart from the concrete existence of Jesus' life,
death, and resurrection. The Spirit of God is seen by Lampe as the source
of the human spirit and continuous with it, the conflation of which he
attributes to the wide spectrum of *ruach* and *pneuma* inclusive of both
God's Spirit and the human spirit in Scripture.[34] In Jesus, the Spirit as
God's divine presence in all people and the human spirit's desire for God
come together in a way continuous with both. Jesus is the fullest expression of this general incarnation but only by degree. It is this continuity
that provides the ground of communication between God and humans,
but which ends up being just another way of domesticating God's transcendence in favor of an immanence of God's Spirit in the spirit of all
people, even creation itself. Such a view turns Jesus' life into a metaphor
for the cooperation between the divine presence and the created (human)
spirit.[35] With the Spirit in Jesus equated with the presence of God in all
created reality, the extent to which the events of Jesus' life are constitutive
for the Christian life as life in the Spirit are necessarily diminished and
vague. They in no way define Jesus' life in a way that is discontinuous with
the rest of humanity and, as such, cannot save humanity out of its plight.

James Dunn likewise sees the Spirit's presence in Jesus metaphori-
cally, much as he does later church doctrine. By presupposing later
Trinitarian doctrine as the church's development, Dunn prefers a metaphorical view of Christ's preexistence, but in a way that is ideal rather than
real.[36] He believes John's gospel to be the beginning of a later theological
redefinition of Jewish monotheism by describing Jesus' life in Trinitarian
terms; seeing in John "the strains which caused rabbinic Judaism to reject
such redefinition as in effect an abandonment of the unity of God."[37] To

---

33. Lampe, *God as Spirit*, 11; emphasis added.

34. Ibid., 44. See also Lampe, "The Holy Spirit and the Person of Christ," 116.

35. Lampe, *God as Spirit*, 45. "Indeed; it points us further, to the truth that all personal communion between transcendent God and man involves God's immanence
within man—nothing less, in fact, than an incarnation of God as Spirit in every man
as a human spirit."

36. Habets, *The Anointed Son*, 99.

37. Dunn, *Christology*, 25.

avoid what he thinks is an inevitable polytheism, he favors a Wisdom/ Word Christology that claims "Jesus is the person/individual whom God's Word *became*."[38] In this sense, Jesus was a man who the Spirit of God adopted by anointing him with an ever-increasing consciousness of God's presence, "a consciousness of Spirit without real parallel at the time."[39] Dunn views Jesus as bringing about the kingdom of God only because of his unique possession of the eschatological Spirit.[40] Attributing to the resurrection and exaltation the point at which Christ and the Spirit are linked together by the disciples, Dunn believes notions of Jesus as the incarnated Logos of God stem from the later reflection of the disciples back upon Jesus' life, just as we have already seen in Lampe's account.[41] At least Dunn is consistent by applying his own anachronistic hermeneutics, of reading his own experience back into Scripture, to how the later New Testament writers read their understanding of the post-resurrection exalted Christ back into the life Jesus lived.

Dunn's methodology works upon the assumption that much of the New Testament writings, especially John and Paul, are later christological developments which are better interpreted as the church's later establishment of Trinitarian theology, which therefore should not be read back into Jesus' life if we are to get at the real historical Jesus.[42] The question is "How much post-resurrection Christology should one read back into the evangelists' accounts of Jesus' life?" Or, is this even a fair reading of the gospels, since the synoptic gospels put a greater stress on the narrative of Jesus' life in the face of even the disciples' unbelief? Could it be the synoptic writers wrote in an effort to portray Jesus' life *as he was living it*, that is, as a *narrative* in order to give the reader an awareness of not only what

38. Ibid., 47; emphasis original. "The incarnation doctrine which comes to expression in the New Testament is properly understood only if it is understood as the incarnation of God's self-revelation, in the sense as that incarnation of God himself. The issue which caused the breach with Jewish thought and with Judaism is the charge against the Johannine Jesus that 'you being a man, make yourself God' (John 10:33)."

39. Dunn, *Jesus and the Spirit*, 53. See also Habets, *The Anointed Son*, 154.

40. Dunn, *Jesus and the Spirit*, 46–49. See also Habets, *The Anointed Son*, 153.

41. Habets, *The Anointed Son*, 178.

42. Dunn, *Christology*, 30. Referring to Jesus' "incarnation" in terms of the Logos and Nicene description of "truly God and truly man," Dunn says, "this certainly reflects what has been the dominant meaning of the term itself in Christian thought. But it is doubtful whether the concept in such a developed sense can be found anywhere in the Bible, since clearly presupposed therein is the full-blown trinitarian doctrine as that came to expression in the fourth and fifth centuries of the Christian era."

Jesus was but in how he lived as the Son of God? If so, this would show the synoptic gospels to be complementary to John's view of the incarnation not its antithesis. This would show the dichotomy between Logos-Christology and Spirit-Christology to be that of *what* he was versus *how* he lived rather than, as Dunn believes, between Jesus being divine and merely a Spirit-inspired human adopted by God.

Both Lampe and Dunn, while attempting to show the significance of the Spirit's work in Jesus' life, forfeit the possibility of a relational ontology of Jesus' identity with the Father in the Spirit due to their constraints of seeing ontology only in terms of a thing's "substance." This in itself is a methodology constrained by the limits of Logos-Christology that attempts to dichotomize between a thing's substance and its relationality or functionality. Their denial of Jesus' divine nature in favor of a functionality of Spirit (understood broadly as human experience of the divine) prohibits their ability to provide an account of Jesus' relational Trinitarian existence as a complement to Two-Natures Christology. By interpreting any divine element of Jesus' life as a later post-Pentecost theological development, they believe they have discovered the real Jesus to be a man in whom there was Spirit, like any other man, except to the degree for which he was anointed. As much as they attempt to overcome the constraints of Logos-Christology, they still work upon the basis of its presuppostional methodology; that is, they still attempt to explain Jesus by *what* he was, or in their case *what he was not*, rather than strictly by *how* he lived. By not seeing Jesus' life in the Spirit as the presupposition and complementary framework to Logos-Christology, they bypass the very reason upon which their view of christological development is based; that Jesus was seen later by the evangelists as both Lord and Christ, true Son of God, *because* he was crucified, raised on the third day, and ascended.

This move towards seeing Jesus as a man in whom there is a greater degree of Spirit, demonstrates the basic inadequacy of Lampe and Dunn for explaining the Christian life. By not showing *true* continuity from Jesus' life to the lives of his followers, based *first* on his discontinuity with humanity, they have no means of describing the Spirit's transformational change to the human condition based on how Jesus lived his life in the Spirit. But what constitutes *true* continuity from Jesus' life to his followers? Why would anyone risk their life by becoming a follower of Jesus if the continuity was not real and true, that is, if it is not, in itself, an *actual* work of the Spirit? Their reading back into Jesus' life later theological developments eclipses their ability to see the Spirit's presence in Jesus' life running forward, as God's narrative of salvation, into the lives of his disciples following Pentecost. What is needed is an account of the Spirit's presence in Jesus' life and death that serves as the basis for how his life and death *become* the life and death of his disciples, both in Acts and to-day. For such a task we need a Spirit-Christology that explains the Spirit's presence defined by the life Jesus lived; one that describes Jesus' identity as a complement to the incarnate Logos' identity with the Father in the Spirit by *how* he lived and died in the Spirit.

Spirit-Christologies That Eclipse Jesus' Life and Death as Defining for Life in the Spirit

The previous section outlined accounts that begin with either general religious experience or with particular Christian experience, both of which were shown to be inadequate to serve as a model upon which to construct an account of Jesus' life as constitutive for the Christian life. This section will now outline Spirit-Christologies that do begin with the Trinity as a way to explain the Christian life but do so within a Logos-Christology framework that takes Jesus' divine nature as a given. This leads theologians to read their traditions back into Jesus' life and death; Sammy Alfaro starts from his context of Pentecostal experience based on Hispanic liberation theology, David Coffey and Ralph Del Colle from their scholastic Trinitarianism, which begins with Christ's intra-divine life within the immanent Trinity, and Myk Habets from a Protestant context, which also uses immanent Trinitarianism as a framework to describe Jesus' death. As a result, these accounts will also be shown to be inadequate to explain the Christian life as life in the Spirit due to their eclipsing of *how* Jesus lived his life as constitutive for defining the Spirit's presence in the body of Christ.

Pentecostal scholars, especially Hispanic ones, have begun to weigh in on the subject of Spirit-Christology and Spirit-empowered praxis in general from their own cultural contexts of liberation, social ethics, and even orthopathos within the Christian community.[43] Hispanic Pentecostal Sammy Alfaro has advanced the discussion of Spirit-Christology from within this tradition with the publication of his disser-tation *Divino Compañero: Toward a Hispanic Pentecostal Christology.*[44]

43. Villafañe, *The Liberating Spirit*; Solivan, *The Spirit, Pathos and Liberation*.

44. Alfaro, *Divino Compañero*.

Alfaro admits his goal is to "construct a Hispanic Pentecostal Christology that is rooted in the experience of the Hispanic community and developed with an interest toward a liberative praxis."[45] Realizing the dearth of Christologies from a Pentecostal perspective as a "significant thematic gap," especially since the "main task of the Spirit is to glorify Christ," Alfaro says, "a main task for Pentecostal theology today should also be to work out a Christology that focuses *concretely* on Jesus' person, life, and work from its unique Pentecostal standpoint."[46] Alfaro rightly sees a major impediment to the development of a Christology from a Pentecostal standpoint to be its indebtedness to the long-standing dominance of Logos-Christology in mainstream protestant theology upon which Pentecostal Christologies have been dependent.[47] Alfaro contends that "by adopting a two-natures Chalcedonian model, the development of a distinctive Pentecostal Christology was hindered in early Pentecostal writings, as in later systematic theologies and even in more recent attempts."[48]

Ironically however, the strength of Alfaro's account is also a weakness. Both are shown in how he uses his Hispanic Pentecostal context as a "lens" through which to view the liberative aspects of Jesus' life and death. The strength of his account is his ability to see the liberative aspects of Jesus' life and death on account of his context. In relying heavily on Jon Sobrino,[49] Alfaro distinguishes the Latin American liberative approach to Jesus' life from the European approach that takes from Jesus' life whatever "fits into" the life of a modern European.

> European Christologies embarked on the quest with the aim of discovering the reasonableness and meaning of the Christian faith for individuals. The quest from a Latin American perspective, however, attempts to rediscover Jesus' call to the church to do as he did—to discipleship.[50]

Alfaro is right to distinguish a Spirit-Christology of discipleship within Christ's community of the church from that of the predominantly indi-

---

45. Ibid., 5.

46. Ibid., 7; emphasis added.

47. Ibid., 5–15, 52–57.

48. Ibid., 6.

49. Sobrino, *Jesus the Liberator*.

50. Alfaro, *Divino Compañero*, 100.

vidualistic Christologies which are generally dependent upon a Logos-Christology framework that focus on Christ's *individual* constitution as fully God and fully man. Alfaro's strength is his offering a Spirit-Christology from his Hispanic Pentecostal context of social and economic oppression that opens up a view of Jesus' life in its more dynamic historical enactment of liberation; a view one is not likely to see from within a European vantage point of political, social, and cultural freedom based on individual "rights." As seen earlier in Yoder's view of Jesus' life, Alfaro's liberationist view allows Jesus' life, which led to his crucifixion, to not be seen simply as atonement for sins but as the result of a political clash between the dominant and the oppressed.

> The depiction of the Jesus of history provided by the Gospel narratives reveals the destiny of those who counteract the religious, social, and political forces that foster an environment of oppression: death. Thus liberation theologians develop the argument that Jesus did not die; *his enemies killed him.* What led Jesus to the cross was his life of solidarity with the poor, which drove him to disturb the structures that oppressed them.[51]

While Alfaro's account shows a Hispanic Pentecostal view of Jesus' liberating life and death from a liberationist position, it is deficient for the same reason. It does not go far enough into what liberation in Christ truly means because it does not begin with the life, death, and resurrection of Jesus for what it means to live a life fully in the Spirit as a contrast to human sinfulness, which is the root cause of structures of oppression in this world. Making a distinction between European or Latin American oppression misses the mark since the kind of liberation Jesus enacted was not limited to only replacing the structure of this world with a better one. Jesus liberated people *from* this world by releasing them from their sins.

As much as Alfaro recognizes the need for a Spirit-Christology to serve as a complement to Logos-Christology, his Hispanic Pentecostal context is also a hindrance by it serving as a grid of interpretation from the context of liberation. Liberation accounts are inadequate to construct a proper Spirit-Christology because they base their views of Jesus' life on their context first and then read their context back into Jesus' life and death. This places Jesus' life and death only within the context of religious, social, and political dominance and oppression in this world but

---

51. Ibid., 104; emphasis original.

not as transformation to a life of freedom *from it* and within the church as a contrast community *to it*. As such, their Constantinian framework still confuses the world and the church.

As we will see, a Spirit-Christology that begins with Jesus' life yields a *different* liberation from the kind Alfaro attempts to construct based on socioeconomic liberation, even though he does draw some helpful implications for social justice from his Hispanic Pentecostal context. Another Hispanic Pentecostal, Samuel Solivan, has critiqued the North American theological emphasis on orthodoxy from his Hispanic Pentecostal liberation theological context, calling for an *orthopathos* based on the holistic work of the Spirit's transformation that is both personal and social.[52] Solivan suggests that liberation within a Christian perspective must first deal with human sin for there to be any real freedom.[53] Otherwise, any promise of freedom will only mask the Spirit's work in Jesus' life and death that must bring death to human sin for resurrection to life in Christ's freedom. If not, what looks like liberation is still only bound to political, economic, and cultural expressions according to this world.

Also working from within their own context to offer a Spirit-Christology are Catholic theologians David Coffey and Ralph Del Colle, both of whom attempt to advance beyond the constraints of scholastic and Neo-Scholastic methodologies based on an immanent Trinitarian model. However, both remain firmly in a tradition very much indebted to Augustine's psychological model of the Trinity. David Coffey moves beyond scholasticism's emphasis on the Spirit as the mutual love between the Father and the Son by developing a *bestowal* model or, what he later calls, a *return* model of the Trinity.[54] Coffey's return model attempts to reinvigorate incarnational Christology by emphasizing the Father's bestowal of the Spirit upon Jesus from his conception but with the added reciprocal return of the Spirit back to the Father from the Son at his death on the cross. This bestowal of the Spirit upon Christ and return from Christ is predicated on Karl Rahner's transcendental Christology which sees the hypostatic union of the divine and human in Jesus as "the unique,

---

52. Solivan, *The Spirit, Pathos and Liberation*, 39–46.

53. Ibid., 104–5.

54. Coffey, *Deus Trinitas*, 5. Coffey says a return model gives greater contrast from the traditional procession model (Johannine) and "also encompasses the entire process by which Jesus, having been sent forth from the Father, returns to him through his life and death in the power of the Holy Spirit."

supreme, case of the total actualization of human reality, which consists of the fact that man *is* in so far as he gives up himself."[55] Coffey says "this means Rahner understands the human being as obediential potency for hypostatic union with the Son of God, and Jesus Christ as the only man in whom this fullness of being human has been actualized."[56] With the help of Rahner's elaboration of the *enhypostasia* of Christ's divine nature in relation to his human nature, Coffey says he was able "to understand the divinization of the humanity of Christ . . . as the work of the Holy Spirit."[57] This gives a basis for Coffey to propose an alternative model of return, latent within Augustine and St. Thomas, of the Holy Spirit as the mutual love of the Son for the Father.

> Its substance can be stated quite simply: the Holy Spirit is the mutual love of the Father and the Son. Notice that is not said that the Holy Spirit is the result or term of this mutual love; His is the love itself. In St. Thomas' words, he is an *operatio subsistens*, a subsistent operation, and in this respect is to be contrasted with the Son, who is the subsistent *term* of an immanent operation in the Trinity.[58]

Here Coffey shows how his methodology continues to work from the immanent Trinity into the economic, saying the Holy Spirit, as the Father's love, when "directed beyond the Godhead into the world . . . will exhibit . . . the following two characteristics of personal love. It will be *creative* and it will be *unitive*, with the former characteristic subordinated to the latter, as is the case in all love."[59] Coffey goes even further, explaining the economy of the "incarnation" of the Holy Spirit in Jesus with the use of immanent Trinitarian language.

> In its unitiveness it draws the humanity of Christ into the unsurpassable union of love with the Father which belongs only to the Son in the immanent Trinity, and here the radicalness is seen in the fact that the result is not a mere union of persons but *unity of person* with the Son. And as an act of assimilation, i.e., ultimately

---

55. Rahner, *More Recent Writings*, 110; emphasis original. See also Coffey, "The 'Incarnation' of the Holy Spirit in Christ," 467.

56. Coffey, "The 'Incarnation' of the Holy Spirit in Christ," 467.

57. Ibid., 469.

58. Ibid., 471; emphasis original.

59. Ibid., 472.

an inner-Trinitarian act, it is the work of the Holy Spirit alone, or better, of the Father acting *by* the Spirit.[60]

The Spirit's unitive presence in Jesus serves as the love the Son has for the Father whereby he gives himself up for the Father, his human nature becoming more consciously aware of his divine Sonship through "a direct communication of being, of subsistence, from the Father to the humanity of Christ constituting him Son of God in humanity."[61] This "psychological relationship of unity with the Father" by the Spirit provides Jesus with not only sole orientation to the Father as constituting his ultimate being but with the Father as the object of his love; so that "dedication and obedience to God's will marked his life . . . and that love of God was the whole motive force of his life and the inspiration of his ministry."[62]

For Coffey, the unitive bond of the Spirit between the Father and the Son serves as the "progressive actualization of the Holy Spirit in Jesus' transcendental love of the Father. . . . and this process continued throughout his life, coming to its completion in his death."[63] In his death, Jesus attained the limit possible in this life of his transcendental love of the Father.

> Here, then, we have the perfect "incarnation" of the Holy Spirit in Christ. It is the incarnation of divine love in human love. And the "scandal" of the Incarnation is complete; for the Son of God stands fully incarnate in Christ, i.e., has penetrated his humanity totally, i.e., in the very perfection of its act. That is to say, the Son of God has penetrated the human being of Christ not just as it was at the first moment of its existence, but in the highest activity, which orders and subsumes all other activities, viz., his love of God, and this in its consummation.[64]

In Coffey's account, Jesus' death on a cross is the highest activity of the Spirit's presence of mutual love for the Father. While this might be an accurate description of Jesus' death and the Spirit's presence in his death within the inner-Trinitarian life of God (but then, who would presume to know?) it certainly eclipses seeing Jesus' life as he lived in the Spirit

60. Ibid; emphasis original.

61. Ibid., 474.

62. Ibid.

63. Ibid., 477.

64. Ibid., 478.

from below due to its attempt to secure humanity's relationship with God on the basis of a Rahnerian interpretation of the hypostatic union as the highest instance of divine self-communication to a human creature and the human creature's self-transcendence to accept such divine communication (grace). As such, it is insufficient to use as a model for explaining the Christian life as a life in the Spirit as it does not first deal with the main obstacle to the Spirit working "actualization" within people as he did in Jesus, that of human rebellion and sin that was responsible for putting Jesus on a cross in the first place. Without this element, Jesus' death remains something he did only for his Father in the Spirit but in no way can his life or death be *for us*. Hence, Jesus' death is not salvific for us in Coffey's account but works more within the context of Rahner's assumptions about the hypostatic union as the highest example of the cooperation of God's grace and the human (graced) will.

Another notable Catholic who takes as a starting point Jesus' life from an immanent Trinitarian framework rather than from an economic one is Ralph Del Colle,[65] He is indebted to David Coffey's earlier attempt to transcend the limits of scholasticism's mutual love model of the Trinity and the Neo-Scholastic processions model with his bestowal/return model.[66] However, like Coffey, Del Colle is unable to fully transcend Neo-Scholasticism due to his own account being largely constrained by questions tied to the scholastic tradition which gives preeminence to the immanent Trinity and the theology of infused grace for understanding the missions of the Son and the Spirit in the economy of salvation. This constraint to answering Neo-Scholastic questions concerning God's intra-Trinitarian relations is seen in Del Colle's reliance on Orthodox

---

65. Del Colle, *Christ and the Spirit*, 4–5. Del Colle develops a Spirit-Christology that "attempts to inform christology with an equally important and central pneumatology, while at the same time preserving the integrity of the doctrine of the trinity" and also "quite profoundly enriches trinitarian faith and thus our understanding of the Christian knowledge of God." He first establishes his position of Spirit-Christology (14) as following Karl Rahner (as opposed to Thomism) in being "explicitly Trinitarian" by seeing the "Father as communicating the divine being in the missions of the Son and the Holy Spirit, so that the latter two persons are not self-communications of divinity in addition to the Father, but the two modalities of the one divine self-communication of the Father."

66. Ibid., 114. Del Colle believes Coffey takes a "step beyond the limitations of scholastic trinitarian theology" inherited from Augustine and Aquinas, but "he nevertheless does not envisage his project as a restoration of early pre-conciliar Spirit-christology" (121).

theologian Vladimir Lossky, who maintained separate missions of the Son and the Spirit beginning first with their intra-Trinitarian distinctions and only secondarily in the economy.[67] Del Colle proposes a similar methodology that begins with the immanent Trinity as a way of understanding the divine economy and the inhabitation of the Holy Spirit in the Christian.[68]

Following in the same line as David Coffey's Spirit-Christology, Del Colle proposes that Trinitarian theology takes into greater consideration the Spirit's role in mediating the divine persons to the graced individual, especially the Spirit's mission of mediating Jesus' sonship.[69] According to Del Colle, "a Roman Catholic Spirit-Christology would need to negotiate the general framework of trinitarian theology. . . . [and that] the relation of the graced soul to the individual persons of the trinity and the relation of the trinitarian persons to one another cannot be separated."[70] By this he means Spirit-Christology offers a framework in which the Christian life can be seen as conjoined with the intra-divine relations between the Father, Son, and Spirit, which a bestowal model of the Trinity provides since "the Christian encounters first the Holy Spirit, then the Son, and finally the Father."[71] Recognizing the Christian life as life in the Spirit is an important feature of Del Colle's account,[72] but it is a life conjoined with the persons of the immanent Trinity and not the singular life of Jesus Christ. Rejecting fellow Catholic Piet Schoonenberg's insistence that one begins with the economic Trinity,[73] Del Colle follows Coffey in retaining traditional scholastic methodology of reading the economy through immanent Trinitarian lenses so that what comes through the economy are the intra-divine relations.

This role of the Spirit in mediating the divine persons to the graced individual is the very basis for Del Colle's insistence that the

---

67. Ibid., 27.

68. Ibid., 27–28.

69. Ibid., 118.

70. Ibid., 78.

71. Ibid., 124.

72. Ibid., 78. "In other words, if the pneumatological dimension of Christian salvation is to be fully articulated—e.g., that the Christian life is life in the Spirit— then it is necessary to explicate how the being and event of incarnation/redemption is pneumatological."

73. Ibid., 148–57.

intra-Trinitarian opposition of relations serves as the basis for a proper Spirit-Christology. Del Colle agrees with Coffey in upholding the Neo-Scholastic tradition that begins with the immanent Trinity to understand the economy.

> Coffey's assertion that a doctrine of the economic trinity is the product of a reconception of the immanent trinity on the basis of the biblical testimony . . . [is] consistent with the scholastic tradition's emphasis that only the opposition of relation can distinguish the persons. In fact, it has been the argument thus far that from within the perspective of the traditional Latin paradigm, it is necessary that a properly pneumatological mission be developed that is consistent with a coherent doctrine of intra-trinitarian distinctions in order for Spirit-Christology to be a viable theological construct.[74]

He extends the intra-Trinitarian relations even further, describing Jesus' life and death as first of all events within the Son's intra-divine life with the Father in the Spirit.

> Through the Spirit of sonship, the humanity of Christ is assumed by the divine Son. Through the power of the Spirit, Jesus ministered and entered into his passion. By the same Spirit he was raised up, and now as the risen one he communicates divine life by the Spirit. All of this follows because in its hypostatic being the Spirit is not only gift and sanctifying power (as Schoonenberg argues) but also the communion of love of the divine persons for one another (Coffey's point). In other words, the distinctiveness of the Spirit's economy is predicated on the distinctiveness of the Spirit's hypostatic relation to the other persons in the Trinity.[75]

This methodology shows both Coffey's and Del Colle's accounts to be Trinitarian yet constrained by questions based upon and asked within the scholastic tradition. As much as they strive to propose ascending Spirit-Christologies, their accounts are not truly from below due to a reliance on Incarnational Christology that presupposes a certain Rahnerian understanding of the hypostatic union for understanding the economy of salvation. In the end, Del Colle's Spirit-Christology is inadequate for explaining the Christian life as life in the Spirit *for us* because his Trinitarian approach does not begin with an account of the Spirit in Jesus that lays

74. Ibid., 152–53.
75. Ibid., 155–56.

bare human complicity in the death of the Son and thus our human inability to choose to live in the Spirit of Christ.

The more recent work of Myk Habets goes further towards developing a Spirit-Christology from the perspective of the economic Trinity, a theology from below, even though he still relies, even if subtly, on the thought structure and language of Logos-Christology.[76] Habets rightly says a Spirit-Christology from below takes a prior faith commitment in that it necessitates a belief in the resurrection, which, in turn, informs one's belief in the identity of Jesus.[77] As such, Habets's approach is an attempt to bridge the two approaches, even though he insists on the proper movement as beginning from below and moving to the above.[78] However, in attempting to bridge the two approaches, he dichotomizes, in good Western fashion, "from below" as epistemological (*how* we come to know

76. Habets, *The Anointed Son*, 38. "According to a Christology from above the Trinity is a concrete idea that is reflected onto Christology. Jesus must be *this* sort of person and act in *this* sort of way to be consistent with our trinitarianism. But the reverse is actually the case. A Christology from below presents us with the New Testament revelation of the person of Christ and says that God must be like this, and do this sort of activity, because that is what Christ did and who Christ was and is. Jesus is God's revelation, and that revelation is a Trinitarian event. The real issue therefore is the movement from the economic to the immanent Trinity" (emphasis original).

77. Ibid., 47. Habets rests the believer's conviction of Jesus Christ's divinity and Lordship upon his exaltation and outpouring of the Spirit at Pentecost. "It was not until the Pentecostal outpouring that the disciples really understood, and believed. Pentecost formed the foundation for the early Christian understanding of the identity of Jesus; an identity informed by the Holy Spirit. The New Testament indicates that the early believers viewed Pentecost as God's confirmation and vindication of Jesus's claims about himself and his mission. Through this act of exaltation/coronation, God himself confirmed Jesus's claim concerning his own uniqueness." Habets recognizes an approach from below is epistemological or gnoseological in nature, not beginning from an ontological priority that assumes Jesus' divinity or that his divinity can be readily perceived or understood by those without a prior faith commitment (51). However, he then proceeds on the comfortable and well-trodden path of Logos-Christology by appealing to Calvin's use of the *unio mystica* as the benefit of Christ's atonement for the believer. Habets credits Calvin of overcoming extrinsicism, saying he "cuts out any extrensecist notion of justification by positing justification as a benefit of union with Christ" (245–46). For Calvin however, the believer's union with Christ is based on Augustine's Trinitarian axiom in which the Spirit is the unitive bond of love between the Father and the Son which is appropriated to the believer as well. "Calvin appropriates the Augustinian notion of the Spirit as the 'bond of love' (*vinculum caritatis*) between the Father and the Son *and equally applies it* to the bond of union between Christ and the believer" (246; emphasis added).

78. Ibid., 50–51.

Christ) and "from above" as ontological (knowing *what* Jesus is as divine). One can see how he subtly divulges his underlying framework as still operating upon the assumption of incarnational Logos-Christology, seen in the following.

> We only come to know Jesus and what he did, from below. Thus, Christology from below is not concerned with ontology as if Jesus *became* divine from below, that is, that the man Jesus became increasingly divine as he grew in knowledge and intimacy with God. Ontologically, we affirm that the Incarnation is always from above as an orthodox Logos Christology maintains. Only because the Word became flesh from above can we come to know the Son of God from below.
>
> When we start from below we are confronted with Jesus Christ, the God-man. We allow him to speak and act and "reveal" his essential being to us. As the New Testament will witness, Jesus is none other than God himself; God in the flesh and that will be the doxological culmination of any orthodox Christology.
>
> In the awkward language of theological precision the model of Spirit Christology presented here in an inspirational-incarnational Christology, a Christology that proceeds *from below to above* . . . I propose a Christological methodology that seeks to bridge the gulf between Jesus's humanity and divinity (the two nature Achilles heel of classical Christology) by means of the Holy Spirit. This movement lays equal stress on faith and understanding, on Spirit and reason, and on transcendence and immanence. Spirit Christology is a method that holds out the great promise of returning Christian discipleship to its roots; the simple faith and practice of seeking to be like Jesus.[79]

This reveals Habets's difficulty in fully distinguishing a methodology of Spirit-Christology that is from below from one that presupposes a Logos-Christology that begins from above. If his desire is to begin Christology from below, he makes plenty of references throughout his account that work against such a construction. By relying on knowledge of Jesus' divine nature supplied by a *post-Pentecost* theological understanding, his account eclipses Jesus' death on a cross, the result of the kind of life he lived as the Son of God, for what it meant for Jesus to live in the Spirit.[80]

79. Habets, *The Anointed Son*, 51–52; emphasis original.

80. Ibid., 21, 29, 59.

Habets makes this more explicit in describing his methodology from below as resting upon the foundation of Jesus' exaltation. While crediting Wolfhart Pannenberg and his follower, Stanley Grenz, with providing the "most comprehensive example of a Christology from below"[81] and as "the most consistent Evangelical representative of a Christology from below," respectively,[82] Habets also believes "they have formed a premature conclusion in perceiving the resurrection event as the foundation of a Christology from below."[83] Rather than locating knowledge of Jesus' divine nature in the reality of his resurrection, Habets locates it in Jesus' exaltation and sending of his Spirit at Pentecost, the confirmation of his exaltation.

> It was not until the Pentecost outpouring that the disciples really understood, and believed. Pentecost formed the foundation for the early Christian understanding of the identity of Jesus; an identity *informed by* the Holy Spirit. The New Testament indicates that the early believers viewed Pentecost as God's confirmation and vindication of Jesus's claims about himself and his mission.
>
> . . . Pentecost confirmed his exaltation historically, and today it still remains, that each coming of the Spirit upon believers confirms that historical event—the exaltation/ coronation of the Son of God to the right hand of the Father. In these pentecostal outpourings the link is made between the cosmic Christ and the personal Lord. They are one and the same person.
>
> . . . We have already considered how this unity is to be understood—not just functionally (although that is the start of it)—but also ontologically. Jesus is God because he does what God can do and was confirmed as God's only Son; our knowledge of this today is based on the receiving of his Holy Spirit which authenticates Jesus's proclamation and witnesses to his exaltation.[84]

It is apparent here that Habets is reading a post-Pentecost epistemology of Christ's divine nature back into a pre-resurrection ontology of Jesus' two-natures, an approach that is still indebted to Incarnational

---

81. Ibid., 43. See also Pannenberg, *Jesus—God and Man.*

82. Habets, *The Anointed Son*, 46. See also Grenz, *The Social God and the Relational Self.*

83. Habets, *The Anointed Son*, 47.

84. Ibid., 47–48; emphasis added.

Christology that takes Jesus' divine nature as the starting point for not only Jesus' life but also for the Christian's life. This theological reading of a post-Pentecost understanding to Jesus' life is such a common assumption in Western Christology that even Myk Habets identifies this element of interpretation as somewhat positive even for Spirit-Christology, believing it lays greater emphasis on the "proleptic element" and "retroactive reading" of Jesus' life by the evangelists.[85] However, it also short-circuits a view of Jesus' life as he lived in the Spirit which, as a result, obscures the cross Jesus died on as the result of *how he lived* in the Spirit.

I propose that such a move is not an authentic complementary Spirit-Christology because it does not begin fully from below according to how Jesus lived and died. Habets's account of Jesus' dependency on the Spirit's presence, even in death, still uses language borrowed from a later knowledge of the Spirit's relationship to the Son within the intra-divine life of the Trinity, and that through the letter to the Hebrews.[86] This theological "jumping ahead" to pick up and depend on later Incarnational and immanent Trinitarian language actually eclipses the Spirit's presence for explaining what Jesus' life, death, resurrection, and exaltation mean for the Spirit's later outpouring upon Jesus' followers at Pentecost. In short, by always reading back into Jesus' life, even subtly, a later theological understanding, the full import of Jesus' life and death is eclipsed for what it means for the Christian life to be life in the Spirit, an understanding that can only be fully realized by "reading it forward." Only a Spirit-Christology that sees Jesus' life *as he lived it* is truly from below, a certain reading of Jesus' life in view of the coming cross by which the synoptic writers most certainly intended their narratives to be read. By not providing this kind of cruciform reading, Habets's Spirit-Christology does not truly begin with Jesus' life[87] and, as a result, does not describe Jesus' death as the result of the kind of life he lived unto the Father. Likewise, Jesus' death on a cross is eclipsed as defining for Jesus' followers as well, which hinders one's ability to see the Spirit's work as necessary to transform sin-

---

85. Ibid., 160; cf. 94–100.

86. Ibid., 165–66.

87. Ibid., 252. "A Soteriology that starts with the Spirit has as its concern from the very beginning the transformation of the material, the embodied, and the social. Believers are raised to new life and baptized in the Spirit through the risen Christ and as such their new lives are to imitate that of Christ. As Jesus was obedient not to the spirit of the age but to the Father through the Holy Spirit, so we too are obedient to Christ in the self-same Spirit."

ners into believers in Jesus as the risen and exalted Son of God and in living a life of sonship to the Father as Jesus lived.[88]

Even so, Habets's Spirit-Christology is helpful for appropriating the Spirit's necessary presence in declaring Jesus as Lord by showing us the need for a Spirit-Christology consistent in its approach from below in every respect. A consistent complementary Spirit-Christology would carry through with the implications of Trinitarian theology derived solely from an economic Trinitarian reading that moves us towards the cross, that is, strictly from the chronological sequencing of Jesus' birth, life, death, and resurrection *as his life was being lived in the Spirit.* If one must begin, especially epistemologically, from below to arrive at a theology from above, as Habets suggests, why not begin with Jesus' life as he was living it without importing a prior epistemological understanding of his divine nature from a post-Pentecost theological foundation back into his life and death? Would this not show Jesus' life and death more for what it actually was than does a view that reads later theology back into it? Would this not also require the full necessity of the Spirit's presence in Jesus' life, as the Son of God, to live and die the way he did? I suggest it does and, furthermore, I also suggest that a more robust account of Jesus' life as he lived in the Spirit not only requires the Spirit's necessity to believe it, even from a post-Pentecost perspective, as Habets rightly says it does, but also adds the necessary component of the Spirit's presence in the church to live and die trusting God, possibly even as Jesus did, as one of Jesus' disciples.

For this reason, Habets's Spirit-Christology does not identify Jesus' sonship to the Father in the Spirit by the constitutive events in Jesus' life and, as such, is too weak to call sinners to repentance through the proclamation of Jesus' life, death, and resurrection. Habets's most telling weakness resides in his account not allowing for Jesus' life and death to first *bring death* to the sinner and *resurrection* in the Spirit within one's own

---

88. Ibid., 250. Even though Habets remains committed to the particularity of Jesus' death on a cross as constituting atonement for humanity by his perfect obedience, his account of Jesus' obedience unto death remains a "God-event" by which the Spirit's work is an intra-divine work. As such, this account of Spirit-Christology is only able to account for how Jesus was able to live such a life. It does not adequately provide an account for how humanity is able to live such a life, that is, other than the *unio mystica* by which Christ's obedience can only be transferred in the spiritual realm to the believer by way of an exchange that "is experienced and further developed through the sacraments and the life of piety lived out in the Spirit's power."

life *solely* on account of Jesus' life and death. Although Habets does touch on the epistemological dimension of the Spirit's work in the believer's knowledge of Christ, he does not incorporate it as an underlying principle of God adopting "other sons" through the Spirit's work of "death" and "resurrection" in those who hear the gospel proclaimed. Through what he describes as an "epistemology of critical realism," Habets says "the role of the Spirit is constitutive for the apprehension of truth."[89] For Habets, Jesus' death and resurrection is mediated to us by the Spirit as *knowledge about* Jesus Christ but Jesus' death and resurrection are not the work by which the Father also does sonship in others, thereby making them his adopted sons. It still only remains *what* we know but it never quite gets back to *how* we know. This is the classic mistake of reading one's priority of the Western emphasis of ontology back into one's diminished view of faith and then forgetting (or never fully developing) one's account of *how* one believed in the first place.

Now we are beginning to see not only the need for an account of the Christian life as life in the Spirit that is based *first* on how Jesus lived and died but, more specifically, we see the difficulty in navigating our way through the maze to find a proper framework upon which to base such an account. With an appreciation for certain aspects of Habets's and Alfaro's Spirit-Christologies, the account I wish to develop here is based on a reading of Jesus' life, death, and resurrection as descriptive for what it means to live a life fully in the Spirit, both for Jesus and his followers. This will provide an explicit account of Jesus' life and his followers' lives that gives a more adequate biblical foundation and explanation for not only Alfaro's Pentecostal account but for others attempting to give a reason for their Christian faith and the kind of lives their faith informs, Pentecostal or otherwise.

For such an account we need to see Jesus' life as constituting an *actual change* in the human condition, which requires transformation by the Spirit to believe and to live. In order to yield such an account for the Christian life, Jesus' life must be seen first in the framework of its biblical narrative account that, only secondarily, informs the Christian life. I argue that such a Spirit-Christology provides just this kind of necessary framework and trajectory, which not only resists reading back into Jesus' life one's own cultural context,[90] but will be better able to "read forward"

89. Ibid., 239.

90. Even in this approach it is recognized that one can never or should never com-

Jesus' life in the Spirit as constitutive for the Christian's life in the Spirit. In due course, we will also look at the implications for the Christian church from Jesus' identity as the faithful Son of God in the Spirit, a Trinitarian view of relationality with the Father made possible by the Spirit's presence in Jesus and through him in his church. In truly complementary fashion, a Spirit-Christology from below must not begin with either common human experience or even one's Christian context, whether theological, cultural, or otherwise. Rather, it must *first* look at how Jesus lived and died as defining for his life as the Son of the Father in the Spirit and *only then* let his life in the Spirit define what it means for others to live in the Spirit as God's adopted sons.

A Post-Constantinian and Trinitarian Spirit-Christology

Now that Christians in the west live in post-Constantinian cultures, this investigation is crucial for at least two reasons; first, it can no longer be assumed people are *able* to believe Jesus is divine and, second, even if they do, it can no longer be assumed Christians have an adequate understanding of *how* they are Christians or what shape their lives are to take once they become Christians. Offering a Spirit-Christology based on how Jesus lived and died in the Spirit will offer an answer to both of these dilemmas: *how* one believes in Jesus as the Christ and *how* one lives their life *as a life in the Spirit* once they do believe. To this end, we need a framework for understanding Jesus' identity as the Son of God derived strictly from the Spirit's presence in his life and in his death, from his conception in the Spirit to his death and resurrection in the Spirit.

In contrast to these other Spirit-Christologies that, in various degrees, depend on a Logos-Christology framework, the Spirit-Christology proposed here locates Jesus' identity within a Trinitarian understanding based solely on the life Jesus lived and the death he died as Son of the Father in the Spirit. In the Western Trinitarian tradition, the former has been historically conducive to a focus on Jesus Christ's *intra-Divine relations* that, following Augustine, tends to locate personhood first within one's own individual substance with relationality of "three-ness" within

---

pletely divest themselves of their theological persuasions, especially their faith, even if it is their theological persuasion (like it is mine) that one should try to divest all of their other persuasions, besides their faith in Christ, so as to allow their faith to be the very power by which they live so as not to be ashamed of it, as Paul describes faith in Romans 1:16–17.

the inner self as its product.[91] The latter, developed here, by focusing on Jesus' life and death as the *relational* Son of the Father in the Spirit, posits personhood as one's relationality first with individuality a concomitant feature of one's relationality.[92] The relational focus in contemporary Trinitarian theology has an affinity with the economic trajectory of a Spirit-Christology. Such Christology speaks of Jesus not in terms of his ontological or substantial make-up as God-man (as in a two-natures Logos-Christology) but in terms of his identity as Son of God the Father in the Spirit. In a complementary approach, such Spirit-Christology will not deny a two-natures Christology but rather infuse it with a much needed pneumatological element and trajectory that can link the life of the Son in the Spirit to the life of God's adopted sons in whom the Spirit dwells.

With the demise of Constantinianism, a Trinitarian Spirit-Christology of this kind is critical for not only the church's evangelism in fulfilling the Great Commission but for the church's understanding of its very own essence and mission in and to the world as witness to the lordship of Jesus Christ as King over his Father's Kingdom. As we have seen so far, Yoder and Hauerwas have opened up for us an understanding of Jesus' life and death that denies human nature the ability to believe or live out the Christian faith in Jesus as Lord. In the process of describing Jesus' life truthfully, however, they have also opened up our ability to see their own lack of an explicit account of the necessity of the Spirit for others to believe in and live out the kind of life Jesus lived. For this task, we need a framework by which we can describe Jesus' life and death as a result of the Spirit's presence, as receiver and bearer of the Spirit, and one by which we can describe Jesus, as a result of his exaltation, also as sender of the Spirit into others' lives. We need a Spirit-Christology that, in contrast to ones we have examined, "runs forward" through Jesus' life into the lives of his followers in order to properly account for Jesus' life constituting a *funda-*

---

91. Boersma, *Violence, Hospitality, and the Cross*, 126–27. This development of the person by Augustine as an inner realm parallels his psychological analogy of the Trinity. This "substance" of the inner person, known as "self" has three parts that parallel the threeness of God's inward nature as Trinity. As the Trinity has one substance (*ousia*) with three persons (Father, Son, and Spirit), so does the individual have three "parts" (one of mind, knowledge, and love or one of memory, intelligence, and will). See also Cary, *Augustine's Invention of the Inner Self*; Boff, *Trinity and Society*, 56.

92. Macmurray, *The Self as Agent*, and *The Form of the Personal*; Zizioulas, *Being As Communion*, and *Communion and Otherness*.

mental change to humanity that requires transformation by the Spirit to believe and live. Since these other accounts explored thus far do not begin with Jesus' life, which led to the kind of death he died, as the basis for describing what it means to live in the Spirit, their ability to see Jesus' life as constituting actual change to the human situation is also profoundly limited. As a result, the Christian life is subtly reduced to one's ability to *work* for one's own change, usually by "moral improvement" with Jesus as the forgiver of sins for those who cooperate with him and the Spirit as a mere aid to "meet my needs."

This view of Jesus' life, at best, leaves Jesus "outside" the human condition, "added on" to one's sinful life without the need of first killing our sinful flesh. Moreover, such a view of Jesus' life does not deal with the problem of the sinful will, bound to sin, because it promotes the common assumption that one's will is "free" to do as it pleases, giving one warrant for keeping their will of the flesh alive and well. This is hardly in line with Paul's description of the Christian as one who has died with Christ and has shared in his death in their baptism (Rom 6:4). What I am proposing is a Spirit-Christology that accounts for Jesus' life and death as God's Son in the Spirit and, by accounting for Jesus' life in this way, is also able to fully account for Jesus' death and resurrection as what God does in others by his Spirit to make them his adopted sons. For this task, we need a framework that fully accounts for the Spirit's presence in Jesus' life, death, and resurrection and, by doing so, shows Jesus' life to be God's fundamental change to the human condition for others to be made God's other sons in the image of his Son Jesus.

Leopoldo Sánchez Provides the Conceptual Framework of Jesus' Life in the Spirit

Our search leads us to Leopoldo Sánchez, whose Spirit-Christology offers an account of the life of Jesus as the receiver, bearer, and giver of the Spirit as defining for Jesus' identity as the Son of God. Sánchez provides us with the necessary conceptual framework to describe Jesus' relational Trinitarian identity by mining the fuller pneumatological dimension of his life and begins to suggest how such christological ground has implications for the Christian life and begins to explore the usefulness of a Spirit-Christology for the task of proclamation.[93] I will use Sánchez's framework

93. Sánchez M., *Receiver, Bearer, and Giver of God's Spirit*. Sánchez's Spirit-Christology seeks to develop the pneumatic dimensions of Jesus' identity within the

to explain the Christian life as life in the Spirit because he explains Jesus' identity as constituted by the Spirit's presence in him throughout the concrete "constitutive" events in Jesus' life, death, and resurrection. As my discussion moves forward, Sánchez's framework will be helpful for understanding Jesus' identity on the basis of the biblical narrative as it moves forward towards the cross. This cruciform trajectory and approach, unlike many others we have seen, gives clarity to Jesus' identity by beginning with God's revelation of himself in the gospels rather than how people might already perceive God prior to or apart from his revelation through Jesus' death and resurrection. Contrary to other approaches "from above," Sánchez develops a more consistent approach to Jesus' sonship "from below" as the basis for knowing who he is "from above." As a result, Jesus' life as Son in the Spirit is shown to have not only ontological importance but more significance for church proclamation and thus for shaping the believer's identity as a son of God. By offering a pneumatological trajectory to the mystery of Christ that moves towards and is centered in the death and resurrection of Jesus, Sánchez provides a systematic framework that is helpful to my own account for three reasons.

First, Sánchez develops a view of Jesus' identity as receiver, bearer, and giver of the Spirit from the constitutive events of Jesus' life. As we have already seen in this chapter, many other accounts of the Spirit do not begin with the constitutive events in Jesus' life to define his sonship. Even when they do account for the events of Jesus' life they do so within a Logos-Christology framework that already presupposes Jesus' divine status *from birth*. They presuppose the incarnation of the Logos into human flesh. While there is a place for describing Jesus' sonship in terms of his pre-existence as the Logos who at birth becomes flesh, the Spirit-Christology developed here relies heavily on Sánchez's framework because it shows Jesus' identity not from his pre-existent divine status but from the concrete historical narrative of how he lived his life in the Spirit as the obedient son of the Father; that is, it describes sonship from an economic Trinitarian perspective.[94] In other words, my account begins

context of God's acts in history (the economic Trinity) for their greater significance for salvation and the Trinitarian relations before creation (the immanent Trinity).

94. Sánchez, "Praying to God the Father in the Spirit," 292. See also Sánchez, *Receiver, Bearer, and Giver of God's Spirit*, 122. Sánchez elevates the economic Trinity for a greater understanding of the immanent Trinity. He clarifies his approach by affirming John Zizioulas: that of the Cappadocians' insistence on the priority of Trinitarian relationality as a way to safeguard against the Greek culture's ontological monism that

with Jesus' life as constituted by the Spirit of sonship (or as Sánchez puts it, as life "in the Spirit" or *in spiritu*). As such, it works upon the premise that Jesus' life, death and resurrection are constitutive for his identity as the Son of God.[95] By using Sánchez's framework of Spirit-Christology, I will also show that Jesus' identity as the Son of God is constituted by his death on a cross and his resurrection from the dead, for it is Jesus' death and resurrection that is defining for faith by the very requirement of faith necessary to believe Jesus is the Son of God. Sánchez's account of Jesus' life in the Spirit is also helpful because its cruciform trajectory promotes seeing Jesus' sonship in terms of his cross and its implications for the proclamation of the gospel and of our participation in his death and resurrection.[96] Since one's faith in Jesus as the Son of God begins at the cross and resurrection; the cross and resurrection of Jesus are constitutive both for Jesus' identity as the Son of God and for the Christian life as an adopted son of God. By further extension, how one becomes a Christian and how one lives a Christian life will also be shown to be constituted by the death and resurrection of Jesus' life in the Spirit.

Second, Sánchez's account will provide the framework from which to gain a greater understanding of Trinitarian relationality as the basis for the Christian life. Whereas my account will not discuss the implications of a Spirit-Christology for discussing models of the inner life of the Trinity (including the place of Jesus' life *in spiritu* for the immanent Trinity), Sánchez provides a much-needed contribution to our un-

---

has heavily influenced the Western Trinitarian emphasis on substantialist language. "After the Cappadocians, person (*prosōpon*) is no longer secondary to being (*ousia*) but its hypostasis; therefore, hypostasis (being) is essentially relational (being-in-relation). Since the real existence of substance (*ousia*) is to be found in person (=hypostasis), then the cause cause (Gk. *aitia*) of the divine existence must also be found in a particular person (not in the common divine essence)."

95. Sánchez, M., *Receiver, Bearer, and Giver of God's Spirit*, x; see also 30–85 for its full development, especially 45 and 52. Sánchez sees the identification of Jesus' life not only within the static or individual existence of incarnation derived from Logos-Christology, but as an *incarnating* throughout Jesus' life and mission in all of its dynamic and relational aspects so that one is better able to "speak of Jesus' identity in 'dynamic' and 'relational' (social or ecstatic) terms—namely, according to his 'being-in-act' and 'being-in-relation' or 'being-in/through/with/for-another')."

96. Ibid. For the importance of this cruciform approach to the Spirit in Jesus' life for gospel proclamation, see Chapter 7, "Preaching Jesus in the Spirit." This chapter was also published as Sánchez, "God against Us and for Us," 134–45. For an earlier account of what Sánchez calls constitutive and paschal accounts of Jesus' anointing with the Holy Spirit, see his article "A Missionary Theology of the Holy Spirit," 28–40.

derstanding of the relational aspects of the Christian life based on the Trinitarian relationality[97] of Jesus' life as the Son of God in the Spirit (the economic Trinity). This kind of approach gives us a Trinitarian framework to develop the relational aspects of Jesus' life in an ecclesial direction or trajectory, highlighting how the Spirit, whom the Son bears in his life and mission, shapes the lives of adopted sons today. Therefore, the ecclesial trajectory of Sanchez's Spirit-Christology will help us draw out further implications of Jesus' Trinitarian life in the Spirit for the shape and direction of the Christian life in chapter 5. As we have seen with some other Spirit-Christologies, many Trinitarian discussions eclipse the full import of Jesus' sonship in the Spirit for himself (Jesus) and for us (his disciples). This diminishing of the pneumatic movement and cruciform trajectory of the mystery of Christ in the economy of salvation diminishes and distorts our understanding of the gospel. Sánchez's proposal provides us the right framework for proclaiming the story of Jesus in such a way that sinners are "killed" and "made alive" in the Spirit, which will be our discussion in chapter 4.

Third, Sánchez's emphasis on the economic Trinity has major methodological implications not only for declaring that Jesus is Lord but, more basically, reflecting on how Jesus is declared Lord.[98] Sánchez' Spirit-Christology is based on the eschatological and pneumatological reality of Jesus' resurrection and exaltation. For Sánchez, our resurrection and exaltation in the Spirit of Jesus is the very "ground" of the believer's faith in declaring Jesus as Lord and God. He explains this *a posteriori* epistemology in Jesus' resurrection and exaltation.

> In the order of knowledge (*ordo cognoscendi*), Jesus is a man who is fully recognized and confessed as Lord, Son of God in power, and finally God only upon the completion of his life and mission in the Spirit at the moment of his exaltation. In the light

---

97. Sánchez, M., *Receiver, Bearer, and Giver of God's Spirit*, 55–60, 99–106, 109, 120–23, 214–15. In this chapter we will be helped by Sánchez's approach to Trinitarian relationality as described by the Cappadocians who emphasized being-in-relation over subsisting in their common divine essence. Rather than seeing the persons of the Trinity subsisting in their common divine substance, the prevalent tendency in Western Trinitarianism, Sánchez sees their divine hypostases subsisting *as* their divine relationality. Following the Cappadocians in this manner, Sánchez's approach clearly articulates a Trinitarian relationality that subsumes a substantialist approach *within the relational*, thus giving priority to the economy of salvation for proclamation.

98. Ibid., 46–49.

of the resurrection, the presence of the Spirit in Jesus—his identity as receiver, bearer, and giver of the same—point us to his
divinity, to the fact that Jesus is none other than the Logos upon
whom the Spirit remains. We can speak of a Logos Christology
operating *within* a Spirit-oriented Christology.[99]

This methodological approach is my basis for drawing further
implications from a Spirit-Christology for Christian identity in a post-
Constantinian era. Sánchez's methodology helps us to speak of Jesus
pneumatic identity as Lord in the terms of its implications for his lordship by the Spirit in our lives over against idolatrous attempts to conform
the church to other lords. As Sánchez says, "reading the story of 'Jesus in
the Spirit' facilitates 'preaching in the Spirit' that aims at our being crucified and raised with Christ."[100] Sánchez's account will help us understand
both Jesus' life and the Christian life as a sacrificial giving to the other; the
other of the Father and the other of humanity.

Expanding upon his dissertation, Sánchez draws out implications
of his Spirit-Christology for the Christian life in the areas of preaching,
prayer, and sanctification rooted in a sacramental pneumatology.[101] In
this same vein, I will draw out further implications of my own in order to
expand on Sánchez's account for what it would mean today for Christians
to see their lives as lived in the Spirit. This is not to imply Sánchez's adoption of these implications as his own; it is strictly my own attempt to further his work in Spirit-Christology in a way that promotes a certain kind
of life in the Spirit today in line with the post-Constantinian critique of
the church. I want to further his work by describing some of the ecclesial
and ethical implications of Jesus' suffering and death as a result of his
obedient trust and submission to the Father by the indwelling presence
of the Spirit. This hopes to explain Jesus' life, death, and resurrection as
Trinitarian events. The end result should be a clearer understanding of
how Jesus' life, death, and resurrection are not only *what* his followers
believe but are also *how* they believe—a life in the Spirit (or as Sánchez
would say, a life of sonship *in spiritu*).

99. Ibid., 160; emphasis original. See also 157–164.

100. Ibid., 183.

101. Ibid., 181–240

A Spirit-Christology That Begins with Jesus' Life and Death as the Son of God

The theological method that serves as the basis for this account is one that *begins* with Jesus' narrative identity described by the New Testament gospel writers, but especially by Luke's account. Beginning with Jesus' narrative identity will allow us to trace that identity into the identities of his followers, showing the continuity in Scripture from the Spirit's presence in Jesus to the Spirit's presence in his followers. Especially helpful for this account are Luke's writings of Luke-Acts and Paul's epistles, which will be used to show the theological continuity from Jesus' life to his followers of actual change in the sinful human condition. This continuity will be traced from the constitutive events in Jesus' life (which Luke attributes to the Spirit) to the actual change made by the Spirit in the lives of Jesus' followers in Acts (which Luke portrays as living the same kinds of lives as Jesus' life). Other accounts neglect this theological continuity of the Spirit from Jesus' life to his followers in three ways. First, they eclipse the life of Jesus by neglecting the historical narrative of Jesus' life, as we have seen in recent Pentecostal Pneumatologies. Second, they do not see the Spirit's presence in Jesus' life as constituting his Trinitarian existence as the Son of God, as we have seen in recent non-Trinitarian Spirit-Christologies. Third, they do not fully engage Jesus' life or his death on a cross as the foundational starting point and center in their Spirit-Christologies, as we have seen in recent Trinitarian Spirit-Christologies. With these other approaches, the life of Jesus is stripped of its power for describing and effecting what it means to live a Christian life or for what it means to live a Christian life in the Spirit because they do not see Jesus' life constituting any *actual change* in the sinful human condition, a change which necessitates transformation of a person's life by the Spirit to live in the Spirit.

Without any actual internal change to the human condition by Jesus' life, death, and resurrection, the Spirit is likewise left "outside" and becomes a mere aid to "help" people live better lives or to simply cope with their struggles of life. This reduces the church's preaching to being *about* Christ and the way Christians understand their faith in Christ from this kind of preaching as a form of therapy. This is why much preaching today serves mainly as a "coping mechanism" to help Christians manage their own lives the best way possible as their own lords over their own kingdoms. This is also the reason why much Christian worship is only people getting together to worship their own imaginations, offering incantations to help appease their inner "existentially experienced absence"[102] of God, like a hamster running faster on a wheel to make up for the feeling of not going anywhere. Such worship offers no real hope due to the neglect of real transformation of the Spirit that "ends" one's life on account of the life, death, and resurrection of Jesus. Without the Spirit in whom Jesus lived and died, all one can hope for is to try to makes sense out of one's own life or to "find a purpose" for it in an otherwise meaningless existence. Obviously, these approaches are only an attempt by the old Adam to affect one's own salvation. However, as I will demonstrate, with the Spirit's transformation of the person, by "killing" the flesh of human sin and "making alive" in Christ's resurrected life, the need for therapy dies in repentance and baptism. In repentance and baptism one's own fleshly desires "die" and the new believer "rises" in Christ's resurrected life by the Spirit's presence; a whole new creation spoken out of the chaos of one's inner darkness. On the other hand, without the Spirit "killing" human flesh, by the fashion in which Jesus lived and died, there is no reciprocal "being raised" by the Spirit to live in the new life of Christ's resurrected life. Faith in Christ then is matter of death and life; and *only* in that order.

Without the Spirit's "killing" and "making alive" to live in Jesus' life, Jesus' obedience to the Father's will remains dependent on his divine nature as explained in Chalcedonian Christology, as we have seen in Yoder's account. By extension, this places the burden of responsibility to live like Jesus solely on the backs of his followers. However, reliance on human ability to choose to live the way Jesus lived begs the obvious question, "How can anyone live *that kind* of life, especially if it would entail *willingly* going to one's own death on a cross for doing God's will?" How can anyone willingly suffer such an unjust death for living such a just life and, all the while, claiming to be doing God's will in the process of being condemned? But such a life, and its result in death, was that of Jesus' life and death, an account that owes much to Yoder's post-Constantinian account that explains the real reasons why Jesus died on a cross.

On this basis, Yoder's account of the Christian life as the life Jesus lived is not only an accurate biblical way of seeing Jesus rightly (simply because it starts with Jesus and takes his life seriously) but is also a helpful starting point for constructing a methodology that sees Jesus as the *only foundation* for describing such an account. The account of Jesus' identity as the Son of God in the Spirit given here will proceed upon the basis of

102. Thielicke, *Prologomena*, 227.

Yoder's account of Jesus but will clarify both Jesus' life and death as results of the Spirit's indwelling presence by using Sanchez's Spirit-Christology as its framework. This will allow us to do what other accounts do not, providing a biblical account of Jesus' life as the Son of God in the Spirit that fundamentally changes the sinful human condition by the Spirit's presence.

Only through the Narrative of Jesus' Life Does God Transform Others by the Spirit

A common characteristic of these other approaches is their methodological inadequacies that do not see Jesus' identity strictly from within the biblical narrative itself. Other extra-biblical criteria, whether philosophical or theological, are allowed to marginalize the life of Jesus as depicted by his narrative identity. Without the narrative as the sole descriptor of Jesus' identity, not only is Jesus' life marginalized but the Spirit's work and presence in Jesus' life is distorted or marginalized as well. When the biblical descriptors of Jesus and the Spirit are marginalized or skewed, other criteria take over as the controlling criteria for the Christian life and the continuity from Jesus' life to the lives of his followers is severed as a result. The proceeding account that describes the theological continuity from Jesus' life to his followers depends upon the scriptural narrative's historical development in a way that causes the reader or hearer to be confronted with the very life Jesus lived *in the same way* he confronted people during his earthly life, death, and resurrection. The biblical description of Jesus and the Spirit, as portrayed by their narrative identities, reveals their relation to the Father and to each other, revealing God as a Trinity of Father, Son, and Spirit. Since the biblical narrative description of Jesus' life is the only window through which we can see and know God as Trinity in the first place, the life, death, and resurrection of Jesus is revealed to be the only view of God. This means Jesus' cross and resurrection is not merely the way to the kingdom, as if God's kingdom were an "idea" or "thing" apart from Jesus' life, death, and resurrection, but the biblical narrative shows the cross and resurrection of Jesus to *be* the kingdom of God.[103]

A major premise of this approach to Spirit-Christology is that the biblical narrative not only carries the content of Jesus' identity, but the

---

103. Yoder, *The Politics of Jesus*, 51.

narrative description itself *performs* the Spirit's transformational act in the reader's or hearer's life in order to know Jesus' identity. The narrative not only points to Jesus' identity it *demonstrates* Jesus' identity, in a way that propositional statements cannot, since it was the narrative life that Jesus lived and the death he died that *enacted* God's reconciliation of rebellious humanity back to himself and to each other. Along with Hans Frei, others have realized the biblical narrative not only points to theological truth, but that God chose to reveal himself to humanity in and through the historical narrative of the person of Jesus in the time and place of first-century Palestine.[104] Only through the priority of the biblical narrative do we know who Jesus is and knowing Jesus' identity is equated with salvation itself and having his presence. It was Frei who reminded us of the proper relationship between Jesus' identity and his presence to believers. In relating Jesus' presence to the Christian, Frei insisted on the identity and presence of Jesus Christ being "so completely one that they are given to us together."[105] Contrary to what one might think, this requires the priority of Jesus' identity over questions of his presence, which get us nowhere. Frei reversed the order.

> We cannot know *who* he is without having him present. But I also want to suggest that if we begin with the often nagging and worrisome question of *how* Christ is present to us and *how* we can believe in his presence, we shall get nowhere at all. It is far more important and fruitful to ask first, "*Who is* Jesus Christ?"[106]

As we will see later, Frei's description of Jesus' identity is first and foremost established by his own intention, from inside the story itself, to be obedient to his Father's will.[107] The identity of Jesus then is not what he was but what he did. Frei asks, "Who then was Jesus? He was what he did, the man completely obedient to God in enacting the good of men on their behalf."[108] Seeing Jesus as the one perfectly obedient to the Father in the Spirit puts the emphasis on the Father enacting his will through Jesus' life, Jesus being obedient to that will, and enactment of the Spirit's pres-

---

104. Frei, *The Identity of Jesus Christ*. See also Frei, *The Eclipse of the Biblical Narrative*.

105. Frei, *The Identity of Jesus Christ*, 67

106. Ibid; emphasis original.

107. Ibid., 151.

108. Ibid., 152.

ence in power bringing about the Father's will. This lets Scripture be seen not merely as God's narrative by which he reveals knowledge *about* him but as the God who actively reconciles humanity back to himself through the faithful obedience of his Son Jesus by the Spirit.

Conclusion

We are now at a place to begin to explain Jesus' life as the one who, as receiver and bearer of the Spirit, lived out his intention to accomplish the Father's mission as his obedient Son; the mission for which the Spirit anointed him at his conception and baptism to fulfill. With our two theological constructs in hand, the post-Constantinian account of Jesus' life and the Trinitarian Spirit-Christology account of the Spirit's presence as necessary for Jesus to live the kind of life he lived, we are now able to integrate these two into one account of Jesus' life in chapter 3. This will serve as the basis for describing how the Christian life begins as life in the Spirit, in chapter 4, and what shape the Christian life takes as life in the Spirit, in chapter 5. We must now turn our attention to the task of describing Jesus' life as receiver and bearer of the Spirit.

3

A Trinitarian Spirit-Christology
Jesus, Son of God in the Spirit

Introduction

The criteria previously discussed will now be used to establish Jesus' life, death, and resurrection as constitutive for not only what it meant for him to live in the Spirit as the unique Son of God but what his life in the Spirit means for Christians to live in the Spirit as adopted sons of God. These criteria will be used here in the following progression to arrive at a Trinitarian Spirit-Christology: first, it must derive strictly from the narrative of Jesus' life described in the gospel accounts; second, it must locate constitutive events in the narrative that speak directly to Jesus' identity as receiver, bearer, and giver of the Spirit; third, it must show how Jesus' followers receive the Spirit's presence in their own lives; and fourth, it must show direct continuity from Jesus' life to his followers' lives, both in Acts and today as described in the New Testament epistles, especially the Pauline epistles that speak directly to the Christian's life as life in the Spirit. This chapter will follow this progression to arrive as a Spirit-Christology for the Christian life as life in the Spirit.

To achieve this purpose, I will depend on Luke's account of Jesus' life for three reasons. First, Yoder applied his post-Constantinian account to Jesus' life from Luke's gospel in his *Politics of Jesus*; second, many other Spirit-Christologies and Pneumatologies also depend heavily on Luke's gospel and Acts for their accounts, and third, and most obvious, Luke's account of Jesus' life and the fellowship of his followers in Acts flow together in a continuous narrative that demonstrates the Spirit's presence as constitutive for both.

The Importance of Narrative for Understanding Jesus' Life, Death, and Resurrection

Arriving at a Spirit-Christology strictly from the narrative of Jesus' life is our first task. Based on what we discovered in chapter 1 concerning the historical nature of Jesus' life and what we found in chapter 2 concerning the life Jesus lived as constitutive for describing the Holy Spirit, by way of an adequate Spirit-Christology, it is now necessary to examine Luke's narrative to understand what it meant for Jesus to live in the Spirit's presence. For such a task, following the contours of Jesus' life in Luke's narrative is particularly crucial. For, as we have learned from Sánchez, we only realize the identity of Jesus as the Son of God who bears the Spirit through the constitutive events in how Jesus lived and died.

Others have also been helpful in appreciating the development of Jesus' identity strictly from the unfolding of his life's narrative. Hans Frei, for instance, has helped us see how the gospel writers posit Jesus' identity solely from *within* the narrative itself, not through an idea brought to the narrative from outside or by some theological "grid" laid over the text. Frei saw the narrative description of Jesus entailed *within* the story, yielding an identity of Jesus from the reciprocal relationship between his intentions and the occurrences which happen to him.[1] Frei explains how Jesus' identity is not found in any description of his inner personality, but in the story of his life; by the relationship between his intentions and the enactment of his intentions that come together in the last few days of his life.

> Jesus' very identity involves the will and purpose of the Father who sent him. He becomes who he is in the story by consenting to God's intention and by enacting that intention *in the midst of the circumstances that devolve around him* as the fulfillment of God's purpose. The characterizing intention of Jesus that be-

---

1. Frei, *The Identity of Jesus Christ*, 138. "The identity of Jesus in that story is not given simply in his inner intention, in a kind of story behind the story. It is given, rather, in the enactment of his intentions. But even to say that much is not enough. Rather, his identity is given in the mysterious coincidence of his intentional action with circumstances partly initiated by him, partly devolving upon him. The latter kind of occurrence also, in part, shapes his identity within the story."

comes enacted—his obedience—is not seen "deep down" in him, furnishing a kind of central clue to the quality of his personality. Rather, it is shown in the story with just enough strength to indicate it characterized him by making the purpose of God who sent him the very aim of his being.[2]

Jesus' identity is not outside the story of his life, it is his life. Frei sees the identity description of Jesus as the events of his life through which he does his Father's will as *the aim of his very being*. This type of narrative description of Jesus' identity is formative for a Trinitarian Spirit-Christology. It will show how Jesus lived in the Spirit's presence to fulfill the purpose of God as a reciprocal relationship between Jesus' intentions and the result of those intentions that *devolve around him*. Only by showing this reciprocal relationship will we be able to adequately account for both what Jesus does and the events that happen to him as results of the Spirit's presence in defining his life as the Son of God, an identity that is only realized as he lives his life intending his Father's purpose.

As was discussed in chapter 2, accounts of Jesus Christ that do not begin with how he lived in the Spirit nor that he died by crucifixion as a result of how he lived are not adequate to explain the Christian life as a transformed life. Without the Christian life being transformed by the Spirit into Jesus' life of sonship, they must necessarily take on mistaken anthropologies in which human experience serves as the hermeneutical basis upon which Jesus' life is made to "fit into" the modern empirical or existential understanding of human possibility. Hans Frei explained this modern problem as the reversal from an earlier view of Scripture as sacred text, through which one sees the world, to the more recent view of human existence in the world as the "lens" through which one interprets Scripture, which is a distortion of the church's entire theological enterprise.

> I am saying that we have lived for almost three hundred years in an era in which an anthropologically oriented theological apologetic has tried to demonstrate that the notion of a unique divine revelation in Jesus Christ is one whose meaning and possibility are reflected in general human experience . . . Hence, I should want to draw a sharp distinction between the logical structure as well as the content of Christian belief, which is the business of theologians to describe but not to explain or argue, and the to-

2. Ibid., 149; emphasis added.

tally different logic of *how one comes* to believe, or the possibility of believing immanent in human existence, on which the theologian has relatively little to say and on which in any case cannot base the structure of his theology. Yet doing so has been the preoccupation of theologians for nearly three hundred years.[3]

With all due respect to Frei, this dichotomy between theological content and how one comes to believe is a notion I want to show in this chapter as false; at least in regards to the narrative description of Jesus' life, death, and resurrection as the Son of God and how one comes to believe in Jesus as the Christ by way of that same narrative description of Jesus' life. Besides, how can there be such a sharp distinction between what one believes and how one believes if Christ is what one believes and the Spirit is how and why one believes? If one can show the gospel of Jesus Christ to be not only the content of belief but how one comes to believe in the content as *inherent within the message itself*, then it follows that the content not only brings about repentance and baptism, faith and faithfulness, it must be the object of one's faith and faithfulness to Christ as well. It is the story of God within which one lives by faith, both objectively and subjectively. As God's story, there is no independent theory, reality, history, or even theology or hermeneutics that can interpret Jesus' death on a cross and his resurrection in a way that affirms some independent human existence apart from it. As Frei helped us see, Jesus' crucifixion and resurrection have become the paradigm through which all other reality, human existence included, finds it true meaning. "They [the gospels] have become the paradigm for the construal not only of what is inside that system but for all that is outside. They provide the interpretive pattern in terms of which *all* of reality is experienced and read in this religion."[4]

---

3. Frei, *Theology and Narrative*, 29–30; emphasis original.

4. Ibid., 148; emphasis original. It was Frei (142–43) who demonstrated most convincingly that any hermeneutical theory, even "realistic narrative" itself, only serves to overpower the narrative description of Jesus' life. "To take [a theory] as a general category of which the synoptic Gospel narratives . . . are a dependent instance is first to put the cart before the horse and then cut the lines and claim that the vehicle is self-propelled." This view of hermeneutics (139) that uses Jesus' life and teaching to disclose some higher order of possible human experience, the "truth and reality of a secondary and transcendent world," transforms the narrative description of Jesus' life into a metaphor. "Hence their preference in the synoptic Gospels for the metaphorical and disclosive character of the parables over the realistic, literally descriptive character of the passion and resurrection narratives."

Now we are beginning to see how that much modern church life is simply a reflection of this mistaken priority of human experience over the life of Jesus Christ himself and that, as a result, the church's understanding of the Christian life as life in the Spirit is distorted as well. Without the narrative description of Jesus' life in the Spirit as solely determinative for Jesus' identity as the Son of God, it is certainly doubtful his life is able to be seen as determinative for the Christian's for what it means to live in the Spirit or that the Christian life is fundamentally and inherently a life in the Spirit in the first place. It is becoming clearer how the Spirit is many times seen as an extrinsic "extra," added on to how one gets along in the world, even as a Christian. The Spirit might well work faith or give gifts, as if to fill up what one lacks or make up for what people are unable to do in their own ability, but still not be seen as the very "constitutive ingredient" in either what one believes or how one lives.

C. Kavin Rowe also helps us see the importance of the narrative for understanding Jesus' identity. Rowe builds on the work of Frei and others, such as Paul Ricoeur and Hannah Arendt, to rightly suggest Jesus' identity in Luke to be relational and dynamic instead of static and ontic,[5] a distinctive feature seen earlier in Sánchez's account. In agreement with Hans Frei and Kavin Rowe, a post-Constantinian and Trinitarian Spirit-Christology sees a reciprocal relationship between the Spirit's presence in Jesus' life, formative for his identity and ministry, and also for the reaction it causes in people opposed to his ministry. In other words, it is a holistic view of Jesus' life that sees the Spirit's presence responsible for not only the healings, exorcisms, releasing from sins, and ministering to society's outcasts and despised, but also accounts for the rejection he receives from those most threatened by his life lived in the Spirit.

Accounting for this rejection is most important for distinguishing this Spirit-Christology from the many others which marginalize or ignore Jesus' sufferings. As we have already seen, other accounts do not view Jesus' life as fully Trinitarian by how he lived and died on a cross; they do not show the significance of the Spirit's presence in Jesus carrying out the Father's purpose that causes people to reject him and his mes-

---

5. Rowe, *Early Narrative Christology*, 18–19. Rowe says a static approach, which predicates identity on some other notion than from within the narrative itself, commits "an epistemological error that involves a false notion of identity in which the identity of a character is somehow 'out there,' outside of the narrative and accessible by other means of reflection."

sage. Without this element of the Spirit's presence causing people to reject Jesus, Jesus' cross becomes an embarrassment or an "impasse" that must be circumvented to avoid the shame and scorn that one might receive from believing it in rightly. However, using these narrative approaches to view Jesus' life in the Spirit, this account will describe Jesus' life in the Spirit as causing his rejection, suffering, and death. By accessing the Spirit's presence through the narrative of his life and death, we will come to an understanding that Luke truly meant; by Jesus living in the Spirit he did his Father's will that brought about his suffering, scorn, shame, and death. This will be a reading of Jesus' life that not only accounts for his rejection, suffering, and death, but one that shows a proper reading of Jesus' life to be accessed only *through* his suffering and death. This will show life in the Spirit, both for Jesus and for his followers, to begin with and defined by his suffering and death, not something added on later.

This account of Jesus' life in the Spirit also depends on a narrative identity of Jesus as the Son of God that culminates in his death and resurrection, not an identity previously defined by a divine status that marginalizes the constitutive events of his life. Describing Jesus' identity as the Son of God through his life's narrative in first century Palestine has been the contribution of N. T. Wright. Wright's description of Jesus' identity as "son of God" requires the narrative to set its own agenda.[6] By allowing the narrative to describe Jesus' identity, Wright shows Jesus' messianic self-understanding as "son of God" to be within Jesus' own context, not ours.[7] Wright believes "son of God" in Jesus' context means Israel's Davidic messiah and not a divine status, especially since "in the first century the regular Jewish meaning of the title had nothing to do with an incipient trinitarianism; it referred to the king as *Israel's representative*. Israel was the son of YHWH: the king who would come to take her des-

---

6. Wright, *Jesus and the Victory of God*, 121. Wright says that "if we play the game properly—if, that is, we leave the meaning of 'divine' and 'human' as unknowns until we have looked at the material—then there can be no advance prediction of what the result may look like." This historical context to Jesus' life is the reason Wright puts "son" in lower case, putting off Jesus' divine status as "Son" for later theological reflection.

7. Wright's approach can be described as being closer to a theology from below that looks at the life of Jesus from the human perspective that appreciates all the "unbelievability" of Jesus' life as the representative of YHWH, *how Jesus lived out his life* as the messianic "son of God." This approach is in contrast to a theology from above that immediately posits Jesus' title, "Son of God" in a divinely Trinitarian understanding (thus eclipsing the role Jesus first lived out relationally and historically as the "son of God").

tiny on himself would share this title."[8] As God's son, Jesus' messianic claims "cannot be a matter of fitting Jesus neatly into a carefully designed and pre-packaged framework of 'what Jews believed about the Messiah.' No such thing exists."[9]

If no such air-tight framework exist by which Jesus' life as the Son of God can be rightly ascertained, where does one begin in order to investigate what it meant for Jesus to be the Son of God, Israel's messiah king? To begin the task, two items of caution are in order. First, one should avoid reading one's theological beliefs back into Jesus' life by an anachronistic method that eclipses seeing Jesus' life *as he lived it*. This helps one stay open to all the ambiguity and uncertainty in which the gospel writers tell the story of Jesus' life in the concrete and historical context of first-century Palestine. Wright helps us appreciate the ambiguity of Jesus' messiahship in contrast to the "certainty" of many accounts that eclipse the events of his life as constitutive for Jesus' life as the Son of God. Could realizing this uncertainty about Jesus' messiahship help us be more honest about Jesus' life? After all, is not Jesus' messiahship open to even more uncertainty, even denial, in our own post-Constantinian context than when he lived? Wright suggests this uncertainty of Jesus' identity insures our main task to be one of honest inquiry. "Because Messiahship is itself in question *throughout the gospel story*, . . . the task . . . is to see things as far as possible *through the eyes of the people of the time*."[10] This perspective of Jesus' identity, seen through his life's narrative, will help us understand his life as the Son of God as defined by the constitutive events in which he receives, bears, and gives the Spirit.

Second, one should appreciate how the gospel writers describe Jesus' life and death even though they wrote from a post-resurrection perspective. We will see how Luke weaves together the various aspects of Jesus' life from a kind of eye-witness account in order for the reader to be *encountered by* Jesus' life, death, and resurrection. By appreciating Wright's contribution that gives us a more honest depiction of Jesus' life, one can better see how the gospel writers connect "anointed son" (Messiah) to the *way he lived* relationally rather than a static view that depicts "Jesus the Messiah" like a title, especially since Messiah was not a

---

8. Ibid., 485–86; emphasis original.

9. Ibid.; cf. 489.

10. Wright, *The New Testament and the People of God*, xiv; emphasis added.

title until much later anyway.[11] In keeping with Wright's approach, this Spirit-Christology begins with how Jesus lived and died as the Son of God in the Spirit relationally and not merely as a divine status. This will serve the purpose of showing how he lived in the Spirit to not only perform God's kingdom but in being rejected and yet still accepting the suffering and death for doing so.

This will then allow for the appropriation of Jesus' rejection, suffering, and death as paradigmatic for what it meant for Jesus to live his life as the Son of God in the Spirit's presence. As a result, we will also be able to say his life, death, and resurrection are paradigmatic of the Spirit's presence in bringing others into a participatory life through the very proclamation of Jesus' life and death. As the Spirit was the presence in Jesus' sonship with the Father that brought his death and resurrection, the Spirit works "death" and "resurrection" through gospel proclamation that "kills" the hearer in their estrangement from God but "makes alive" in Christ's life; bringing the hearer to faith in Christ in repentance and baptism. In keeping with Sánchez's account, reading Jesus' life in the Spirit facilitates proclaiming his death and resurrection in the Spirit that "kills" and "makes alive." Reading Jesus' life through the constitutive events of his life, death, and resurrection, both the events that he performed and that happened to him, brings out a view of his identity as Son of God that is dynamic and relational. Jesus' identity, seen through the constitutive events of his life's narrative, will also be shown to be defining for both *how* people are adopted as "other sons" of God through the proclamation of Jesus' life, death, and resurrection and for the shape and direction the Christian life takes when Jesus' life is seen in this fashion.

Luke's Constitutive Events That Identity Jesus as Son of God in the Spirit

By following Luke's narrative in the manner just described, there are constitutive events in Jesus' life that we should pay particular attention to in order to understand his life as constituted by the Spirit's presence. I will use this narrative method to show how Luke describes Jesus' life, the kingly Son of God, as receiver, bearer, and giver of the Spirit.

---

11. Ibid., 84.

Jesus Received the Spirit at His Conception to Live Faithfully as the Son of God

From his conception, Jesus Christ's life and mission were tied to the presence and power of the Holy Spirit. In the language of Sánchez, the Spirit's presence and power are "constitutive" for the Christ from his very conception. Before Mary conceives, Gabriel announces to her that she will conceive when the "Holy Spirit will come upon" her and the "power of the Most High will overshadow" her (Luke 1:35), tying all that Jesus will be and do to the Spirit's presence and God's power, referred to by Rowe as a "doubleness" in the narrative.[12] Jesus' identity from birth is one constituted by the Holy Spirit as the constitutive ingredient in his life to fulfill God's mission as his Son, his king. However, Luke does not portray Jesus' identity in the sense of a preexistent divine status, as John does, a distinction that is crucial for this account of Jesus' life as life in the Spirit.

Sánchez helps us make this distinction between these two perspectives, a divine mission versus a divine status, in relation to Jesus' conception and birth.[13] He points out that Luke's designation of Jesus as "'Son of God' does not refer to the child's preexistence in the Father's eternal bosom (cf. John 1:1–2, 18), but to his conception by the Spirit as the Davidic Messiah-king (cf. Luke 1:32–33). The Spirit is God's dynamic power in history bringing forth God's kingdom in the Son."[14] Robert C.

12. Rowe, *Early Narrative Christology*, 48. "Such dynamism within the life of God is played out in the movement of the narrative, as God's Spirit is indeed God himself but in repetition or doubleness in the conception of Jesus: God remains God 'above' the world and at the same time in the Holy Spirit 'comes upon' and 'overshadows' the earthly woman Mary. The silence regarding Mary's pregnancy is broken with the introduction of Jesus in the narrative, and the life-giving activity within the gap is the presence of the Holy Spirit."

13. Sánchez, *Receiver, Bearer, and Giver of God's Spirit*, 35. Early on in post-apostolic formulations, the Spirit's overshadowing of Mary so that she would conceive a Son of God gave rise to an emphasis upon Jesus' identity that focused on his "inner-constitution as human and divine [that] led early patristic exegetes to relativize the pneumatological dimensions of the incarnation . . . [and] fostered what later came to be known as 'two-natures' christology."

14. Ibid., 34–35. "The Holy Spirit, 'the power of the Most High,' comes upon and overshadows the virgin; '*therefore* (Gk. *dio*), the child to be born will be holy; he will be called Son of God' (Luke 1:35, emphasis original). Luke's identification of the Holy Spirit with "the power of the Most High," as the mediator of the Father-Son relation in the economy of salvation, preserves God as the Father, but the Spirit's identity and role is also preserved as distinct from both Father and Son. Sánchez explains further, "Consequently, the Holy Spirit (and not the preexistent Son) effects the conception and

Tannehill also makes this distinction by connecting the nature of Jesus' conception by the Spirit to his life as Israel's anointed messiah.[15] This emphasis shows the kingly nature of Jesus' birth in Luke as God's divine call and mission.

> Jesus as Davidic messiah and fulfiller of Israel's hope for a king has greater continuing importance in Luke-Acts than the virgin birth does. For the author, the virgin birth is an indication of God's purpose and power at the very beginning of Jesus' life, and this wondrous beginning does not compete with the view that he is Son of God as Davidic king but attributes his kingship to prevenient divine action.[16]

Gabriel's announcement of Jesus' birth identifies him as "Son of the Most High" who will inherit "the throne of his father David" to "reign over the house of Jacob forever" as the fulfillment of Nathan's prophecy to David in 2 Sam 7:12–16 (Luke 1:32–33). However, Jesus' kingly birth also "goes beyond the Old Testament idea of the king as God's son."[17] Identifying Jesus as Son of God with the Davidic kingly line immediately connects his life with Israel's messianic hopes of an "anointed one" to come but one who would carry out God's justice and righteousness, a feature already seen in Mary's song of praise (1:46–55). Seeing Jesus' birth

---

sanctification of the Christ child in the new times of salvation, constituting or making him messianic 'Son of God' (Luke 1:35), 'Emmanuel' (= 'God with us,' Matt 1:23, quoting Isa 7:14), and the *enfleshed* Word (John 1:14). We may say that the Word alone *assumes* and *becomes* flesh, but he does so *in the Spirit*, namely, in a manner that the preexistent Son receives from his Father in the economy of salvation, and therefore for us, the Holy Spirit who creates and perfects in holiness what the Son at once assumes" (39; emphasis original). This pneumatological emphasis and distinction allows the Holy Spirit to function, from the very beginning of Jesus' life, as the one who "is a personal agent of acts in and through the man Jesus, who is none other than the incarnate Logos" (39).

15. Tannehill, *The Gospel according to Luke*, 25–26, 37–38.

16. Ibid., 25. Sánchez M., *Receiver, Bearer, and Giver of God's Spirit*, 35. See also Neufeld, *Recovering Jesus*, 106–7. Neufeld points out that Matthew takes the liberty of quoting the Septuagint reading of Isaiah 7:14 which uses the Greek word *parthenos* (virgin) for the Hebrew word *almah* (young woman), yet Luke retains the idea without the Isaiah quote. Whereas much emphasis has been placed in Western theology on the virgin birth, which conveniently lends support to the divine nature doctrine, "The quotation from Isaiah 7 adds, or at least supports, yet another element in the narrative, namely, the name *Emmanuel*, which means 'God is with us.' Allusions to the hopes and dreams of Israel continue to pile up."

17. Tannehill, *The Gospel according to Luke*, 25.

as *both* the work of the Spirit's presence *and* embodying Israel's expectations as the long-anticipated heir of the Davidic kingdom, two themes are already running together that might, at first glance, seem incongruous.[18] That Jesus is called from birth to fulfill this kind of mission and that God chose the humble and despised through which to do it is no marginal issue. Just how this mission will be fulfilled, given Jesus' lowly birth, Luke alludes to but only in clues that anticipate the narrative's further development.

Luke does give some clues as to just what sort of mission Jesus is called by his Father to fulfill as the receiver of the Spirit. Even before Mary conceives by the Spirit, God is bringing about deliverance for Israel by the most unconventional means. Mary and Joseph are lowly peasants but their son Jesus will take the throne of David and rule over the people of Jacob forever (Luke 1:32–33). Seemingly set at odds with one another are these two themes; the Holy Spirit's presence constituting his life as Son of God *and* his life reversing the very conditions of people's lives. Mary rejoices in praise that God has scattered the proud, brought down the mighty from their thrones, and sent away the rich with nothing (1:51–53). Conversely, she praises God that he has raised the humble, filled the hungry, and shown his people mercy (1:52–54). Zechariah, also filled with the Holy Spirit (1:67), prophesies that God was fulfilling what he had promised their ancestors; giving freedom, giving a savior from the line of David, and saving them from their enemies to serve God without fear (1:68–75). He prophesies that his son John would go before the Lord to prepare his way, making people know they would be saved by having their sins forgiven, that God was bringing a new day to shine on those living in darkness, to guide them in the path of peace, and freeing them from their enemies and from the power of those who hate them (1:76–79). These seem like two incompatible starting points. How does one born in the Spirit as a political, economic, and cultural outcast himself (in a Jewish peasant family from Nazareth) free Israel from their enemies, free people from their sins, or make people serve God without fear? Jesus' life as Son of God and receiver of the Spirit must be for Luke more of a relational sense of Jesus fulfilling his Father's calling and mission by way of reversal.[19]

18. Yoder, *The Original Revolution*, 21.

19. Neufeld, *Recovering Jesus*, 304. Neufeld explains the importance of seeing many references to "son of God" in the Gospels as signifying this relational aspect of *how*

This reversal is already being portrayed by Luke as affecting the social standings of all people; from the high and mighty to the lowly and weak. This is obvious when an angel of the Lord announces Jesus' birth to the socially despised shepherds, inviting them to be the first to see the messiah of Israel, the Lord.[20] They would find him wrapped in pieces of cloth and lying in a feeding trough (1:8–12, 16). This reversal is seen in Simeon's pronouncement over Jesus at the Temple when he, full of the Spirit, rejoices for seeing God's salvation before he dies as was promised him by the Holy Spirit. He rejoiced that he had seen God's salvation, "A light of revelation to the Gentiles, and the glory of your people Israel" (2:32). However, he tells Mary that her child Jesus "is appointed for the fall and rise of many in Israel, and for a sign to be opposed—and a sword will pierce even your own soul—to the end that thoughts from many hearts may be revealed" (2:34–35).

How could Jesus' life be both the result of the Spirit's presence and a life that causes division and rejection at the same time? Could Luke be describing Jesus' life in the Spirit as the reversing of such a deep-seated human condition that, due to its offensive nature, will be a salvation many will not accept?[21] If so, we must ask whether Luke is setting these two themes in opposition antithetically or reciprocally. Either way, how could two seemingly incongruous things co-exist in one person? Luke does not say; he only continues developing his narrative.

Jesus Received the Spirit at His Baptism as God's Beloved Son

The second constitutive event defining Jesus' life as the Son of God in the Spirit is his baptism by John. As the constitutive event of his birth was his reception of the Spirit's presence to fulfill his mission as the Son of God, his baptism begins his mission marked by his reception of the Spirit and by his Father's approval from heaven that he is his beloved Son. What was announced at his birth now begins to take shape. Jesus, as the Son of God in the Spirit identifies with "sinners," that is, those outside the margins

---

Jesus lived his life rather than a substantial nature of divinity, a relational trust seen in faithfulness to his Father in carrying out his mission. "First, it signifies a high degree of intimacy with God as father, an intensely close bond that finds expression in the character of the *righteous one*: his way of life shows what he is made of. Secondly, his bond with God also implies that he can count on God's protection or at least vindication beyond the suffering of the moment" (emphasis original).

20. Rowe, *Early Narrative Christology*, 49–55.

21. Tannehill, *The Gospel according to Luke*, 109–10.

of Israel's worship in Jerusalem according to Israel's own God-given laws of division. To be a "sinner" meant one was *already* outside the worship establishment by being poor, sick, lame, ethnically different, a woman, or otherwise illegitimate to participate in Israel's "pure" worship at the Temple. Seen in contrast to Israel's worship, John's baptism in the Jordan meant more of a claim to be right with God *apart from* the Temple ceremonies in Jerusalem than it was a claim to an inner spiritual condition.

By Israel's standards, John's baptism was illegitimate because it defied the Temple's religious monopoly as the "broker" of God's righteousness to the people based on the law. Since God had given the law through Moses and the Temple through King David to carry out Israel's worship based on the law, Israel's partitions and exclusions were held to be sacred, even inherently righteous. By bypassing Israel's Temple worship, John's baptism was claiming a right standing with God through a totally different means than the law; one of repentance from one's sins and entrance into God's kingdom of changed hearts and lives through, of all things, emersion in the Jordan River (Luke 3:3). How could emersion in the Jordan River make someone clean before God? Surely God was doing a new thing in Israel and was using John's baptism to prepare people for it. As the word of God came to John (3:2), he proclaimed Isaiah's prophecy as fulfilled in him; "Make ready the way of the Lord, make his paths straight"(3:4) in order to bring the day when "all flesh will see the salvation of God" (3:6). To prepare the way of the Lord, John's message was one of God's ability to raise up other children of Abraham (3:8), judgment upon those who do not produce good fruit (3:9), and justice, fairness, and mercy carried out by the likes of tax collectors and soldiers; Israel's most despised enemies (3:10–14). By Luke making all these connections between John's ministry and Jesus' future ministry, the narrative sets up Jesus' ministry to be one of greater intensity through his baptizing with the Holy Spirit and fire (3:16); gathering up the good grain into his barn but burning up the chaff in judgment (3:17). By bringing together these themes in the two constitutive events of Jesus' birth and baptism, Luke establishes Jesus' ministry to be both in the Spirit's presence and the carrying out of his Father's kingdom of peace and justice but also his judgment.

The Constitutive Events in Jesus' Ministry in the Spirit Elicit Rejection

We now turn our attention to the Spirit's presence at work in Jesus' ministry to bring about God's kingdom of peace and the rejection that he receives from those who refuse both him and his message. As we have already seen in Jesus being the receiver of the Spirit at his birth and baptism, he also bears the Spirit's presence in his ministry to carry out his Father's kingdom; ultimately being rejected for doing so. Beginning to emerge at Jesus' temptations and at his ministry announcement at the synagogue in Nazareth is this reciprocal pattern between Jesus' life as God's Son in the Spirit and the rejection that his ministry elicits. Jesus' ministry elicits rejection from those who refuse to believe he is from God and instead attribute his miracles to the power of Beelzebub (Luke 11:14–23). Luke places this passage within a wider context of Jesus' teaching; that his sonship with his Father must be revealed to people for them to understand his identity (10:21–24), his teaching on prayer to God as Father (11:1–13), and his call for repentance and judgment upon the Pharisees (11:29–54). Even from Jesus' temptation in the wilderness by Satan and his ministry announcement in Nazareth, Luke is setting the stage for this later development of rejection and suffering that Jesus receives for being God's Son in the Spirit.

Luke sets up this opposition to Jesus' life as the Son of God in the Spirit by describing the temptations in the wilderness as Satan's attempt to derail him from carrying out his Father's mission. Still filled with the Holy Spirit from his baptism, the Spirit leads Jesus into the wilderness to be tempted by Satan to use worldly means of being king and to usurp his Father's plan of being king. Satan tempted Jesus to use food to satisfy the people's physical hunger (4:3–4), to possess all the earthly kingdoms by bowing to him (4:5–8), and to survive the death penalty for blasphemy, being thrown off the Temple wall in Jerusalem (4:9–13).[22] By adding that Jesus returned to Galilee in the power of the Holy Spirit (4:14), Luke brackets the temptation passage with Jesus being full of the Holy Spirit, implying Jesus' sonship with the Father and his submission to his Father's will as defining for Jesus' life in the Spirit's presence. In the Spirit's presence Jesus resists Satan's temptations to renounce his mission as the Son of God (4:3, 9).

This antithesis between the Spirit' presence in Jesus as God's anointed Son and the opposition he receives from Satan for doing so anticipates, for the reader, the same antithesis just ahead between Jesus and the religious leaders. As Luke has already given some clues from Simeon's prophecy, now, from the beginning of Jesus' ministry, such opposition,

22. Yoder, *The Politics of Jesus*, 24–27.

rejection, and suffering are to be expected results of Jesus living in the Spirit and doing the will of his Father. However, making the connections between Jesus being rejected by the religious leaders and the Spirit's presence has not been a popular scholarly endeavor. Even less popular have been the connections of Jesus' rejection to both the Spirit's presence and his sonship with the Father within a Trinitarian framework. Recently, Martin Mittelstadt has explored Luke's connections between the Spirit and suffering in Jesus' life, even though his purpose was not to develop this theme within a wider Trinitarian framework.[23] Sánchez's framework allows us to use Mittelstadt's contribution to account for Jesus' rejection and suffering as a result of his relation as Son of the Father in the Spirit. This allows us to see the life Jesus lived as the Son of his Father in the Spirit's presence as what actually elicited rejection and suffering.

Beginning here at Jesus' ministry announcement at the synagogue in Nazareth (Luke 4:14–22), the rejection and suffering that Jesus elicits by living in the Spirit now come together in a reciprocal relationship that is beyond doubt. It is here that Jesus begins to establish his Father's kingdom of peace *through* humanity rejecting his peace and *through* peacefully accepting the rejection and suffering that result from it. In the same way his birth and baptism mark his life in the Spirit as bringing about a new existence for humanity, as the Son of God, his announcement at the synagogue inaugurates his ministry that both *performs* his Father's kingdom in the Spirit's anointing and *peacefully* accepts the rejection that his sonship elicits. As the one who bears the Father's Holy Spirit, he will preach good news to the poor, free captives, give sight to the blind, and proclaim the year of the Lord's favor; all things opposite human norms since they are done in the Holy Spirit for the will of the Father.[24] Jesus'

---

23. Mittelstadt, *The Spirit and Suffering in Luke-Acts*, 3. Mittelstadt has rightly identified this lack of perception even within his own Pentecostal tradition, saying "the Pentecostal tradition, at a scholarly and experiential level, has generally neglected to address and to apply the role of the Holy Spirit in contexts of suffering and persecution." Cf. ibid., 62–63. Mittelstadt provides a useful analysis of Luke's connections regarding the Spirit and suffering in Luke-Acts to correct Pentecostalism's narrow focus on speech and the prophetic. While his account does not place Jesus' sufferings and the Spirit within a larger Trinitarian framework, such was not his intent.

24. Rowe, *Early Narrative Christology*, 79. Rowe sees the Spirit's presence as constitutive for Jesus' existence at conception by Luke (1:35) to inform all his activities throughout his life, especially by the "programmatic" character of his Spirit-anointed platform announced in the synagogue at Nazareth. By doing so, "Luke continues his emphasis upon the inseparability of Jesus' actions from that of the Holy Spirit of the

ministry in the Spirit elicits rejection from the kingdoms of this world angered by his declaring their kingdoms fallen and replaced by God's kingdom. It is this judgment upon their views of God that angers them most as he declares himself to be the representative of the true God of Israel, one quite foreign to their preconceived notion of what kind of God Israel's God was supposed to be. Jesus is performing God "to them" and "upon them" as God's Son in the Spirit and they reject him for making such "blasphemous" claims. His ministry now begins to threaten their claim to be the sole "dispensers" of God.

However, they are not merely threatened by Jesus claiming to be a spokesperson for God, like all the true prophets in Israel's past, they are threatened by him *performing God* to them by ascribing to himself the fulfillment of Isaiah's prophecies. He says Isaiah's prophecy was being fulfilled while they were listening to him recite Isaiah (Luke 4:21). Jesus claims his life and ministry *as* the very words and works of God, not as merely a spokesman for God. To provoke them further, he compares himself to Elijah going to a Gentile woman instead of one in Israel, which sends them into a rage. They force him out of town to throw him off a cliff. Here is a real chance for Jesus to enact Satan's earlier temptation to survive being thrown off the Temple for blasphemy. He could *prove* his messiahship with such an indisputable sign. Instead, he accepts his Father's way of being a king and walks away peacefully through the crowd (4:28–30).

As Jesus carries out his mission of sonship, even the demons know he is the Son of God (Luke 4:34, 41). So why does he tell them to be quiet? What is it about his messiahship that must be hid from the crowds? Is it to be alone and pray or is it to resist growing popular (Luke 5:15–16)? Was his kind of messiahship threatened by fame? Luke does portray Jesus' messiahship to be at odds with the religious leaders who are threatened by his growing popularity. They are especially threatened by Jesus' ability to heal the sick and forgive sins (Luke 5:21–24), but why? Luke does not explain; he only shows Jesus refusing the political options available at the time,[25] which only brings about greater antagonism between Jesus and the religious leaders. The tension grows by Jesus telling his followers they

God of Israel, a theme which Luke consistently develops not only in Jesus' conception (1:35), but also in his baptism (3:22), entrance into the wilderness (4:1), and return to Galilee (4:13)."

25. Ibid., 79.

too will be hated, shut out, insulted, and called evil (Luke 6:22–23). He calls them to do the opposite of the powerful; to bless their enemies, to do good to those who do harm, to pray for those who are cruel, and to give without expecting any return (Luke 6:27–36). Doing these things will make them children of the Most High God, the same title Gabriel had told Mary that Jesus would have; "Son of the Most High" (Luke 1:32).

Now Jesus' peaceful response to those who oppose him begins to appear as another result of the Spirit. People opposing Jesus healing the sick and releasing people from sin is on a collision course with the Spirit's anointing that enables Jesus to do the healing and releasing. Luke weaves together several events that contrast Jesus performing miracles from the people's disbelief (Luke 9:7–9) and from the disciples' ideas as to what course he should take as a result of their disbelief (Luke 9:33, 45, 46, 54). Following Jesus sending out his apostles with power and authority to also *perform* God's kingdom (Luke 9:1–6), he tells them to only rejoice that their names are known by God. Luke clusters episodes together contrasting Jesus' miracles with people's lack of belief; from Peter's confession that Jesus is God's messiah (Luke 9:20) to those who refuse and reject Jesus (Luke 10:1–16). It appears that Luke is developing the idea that God's kingdom, with Jesus as his kingly Son, looks upside-down to human understanding, making it impossible for people to accept or believe it. Oddly enough, Jesus rejoices in the Spirit to the Father that people actually *disbelieve* in his messiahship (Luke 10:21). Jesus praises his Father for withholding "these things" from the wise and learned and for their Father-Son relationship being known only to them. Why does Jesus rejoice that their Father-Son relationship must be revealed *to* people in order for people to believe it? Is Jesus' messiahship, that is, being the Son of God, hidden from human understanding by virtue of its very nature?

This brings us to another constitutive event in Jesus doing the work of the Father in the Spirit's anointing and the subsequent rejection he receives for doing so. Having sent out the seventy who came back rejoicing that demons obeyed them simply by using Jesus' name (Luke 10:17), people later accuse Jesus of casting out demons by the power of Beelzebub, the prince of demons (11:14). In response, Jesus corrects their accusation saying it is illogical since a house divided against itself cannot stand (11:17–18), but he adds, "If I use the finger of God to cast out demons then the kingdom of God has come upon you" (11:20). That Jesus did not use any formulas but simply commanded demons to depart, using the "finger of God" as his source, implies that his command over demons was a "direct and unmediated act of God" so that the kingdom of God had come upon them.[26] Whereas Luke reduces the number of exorcisms from his sources, they point to a greater significance of Jesus' ministry of spiritual deliverance of those who are bound by Satan.[27] Edward Woods suggests "The most natural interpretation of the phrase 'finger of God' . . . is God's direct and immediate 'power' . . . involved in the release of Satan's captives."[28] By using the "finger of God" as his source for Satan's immediate expulsion from people's lives, Jesus is claiming sonship with the Father by the Father's power operative in and through his ministry, linked to God by "the Spirit of God" in the parallel passages (Matt 12:22–32; Mark 3:22–30). This demonstrates Jesus' relational unity with the Father. "Therefore on the basis of linguistic usage, the finger 'of God' at Luke 11.20 best interprets God the Father's activity in bringing about his own kingdom."[29] The claim Jesus is making is his unity with the Father by his Father's kingdom operative in his exorcisms of Satan. This makes the argument over Luke's use of "finger of God" versus Mathew's "Spirit of God" immaterial (Matt 12:28). The real dichotomy is between God's power (in the Spirit) and Satan's power.[30] Those who say Jesus uses the power of Beelzebub to cast out demons are denying Jesus' sonship with the Father. Ironically, the demons know what the religious authorities refuse to believe, that Jesus is God's Son and, as God's Son, his power is God's unmediated power. Therefore, rejecting Jesus is rejecting God.

26. Woods, *The "Finger of God" and Pneumatology in Luke-Acts*, 143.

27. Ibid., 148–49.

28. Ibid., 151.

29. Ibid., 152.

30. Dunn, *Jesus and the Spirit*, 46. "However, the point may be largely academic, since in fact the two concepts are synonymous. 'Spirit' and 'hand of the Lord' (= finger of God; cf. Exod 3.20; 8.19) are used as equivalent concepts on a number of occasions in the OT . . . its meaning is quite clear: Jesus claimed that his exorcisms were performed by the power of God." See also McDonnell, *The Other Hand of God*, 105. McDonnell, referring to the Cappadocians and especially Basil, emphasizes the Spirit as the Trinitarian mediation in which we experience God as God the Holy Spirit. "A double movement typifies the Spirit: The divine movement toward the fully transcendent God and the sanctifying movement toward us. But the sanctifying movement toward us is deceptive. The movement toward us is Father–Son–Holy Spirit. Basil does not want the Spirit separated from the Father and the Son. He is concerned to maintain the deepest union between baptism, creed, and doxology. Because we celebrate a trinitarian baptism we confess a trinitarian faith, which determines the form of the doxology."

The Constitutive Event of Jesus' Death a Result of Living in the Spirit

The tension builds as Luke weaves together these two themes; as Jesus lives in the Spirit to perform God's kingdom, enacting his kingly reign as Son of God, even his disciples increasingly *disbelieve* his kind of kingly reign. These two themes now can be shown to reciprocally coalesce in Jesus' death as the result of living in the Spirit as the faithful Son of God. As Jesus enters Jerusalem, Luke portrays the events surrounding his entrance as the culmination of Jesus' being controlled and consumed by his Father's will, from claiming authority over the Temple as the true Davidic heir to his submission to his Father's will in Gethsemane. This emphasis sets up Luke's portrayal of Jesus' death as *both* the submission to his Father's will and as a human failure. This brings us to an often neglected aspect of Jesus' death on a cross as the Son of God, its unbelievability on account of failure. Does Jesus claim his own messiahship as Son of God just at the point when it is *most* unbelievable?" If so, what would be the point of its unbelievability?

C. K. Barrett suggested such a notion; that Jesus' own claim as messiah comes into clearer view after his arrest while being questioned by the Jewish elders. "Jesus affirms that he is the Messiah and Son of God at precisely the moment at which it is inconceivable that anyone should believe him."[31] Robert C. Tannehill also observes how Luke weaves together these two seemingly incompatible themes of Jesus' life and God's purposes being fulfilled through rejection and suffering. "Since the outcome of events repeatedly conflicts with human calculations, the signature of this God appears in the human experience of irony."[32] God's purposes are thwarted by humanity rejecting them yet it is through humanity rejecting God's purposes that he fulfills his purposes through Jesus' death. Jesus' death on a cross will be the culmination of God's plan of humanity rejecting his plan. Now we must ask, "Would God work his purposes in Jesus' life and death *in spite of* humans' inability to perceive his purposes? Why would God fulfill his purposes *through* human inability to perceive it? Tannehill explains this necessity of human inability to understand God's purposes in Jesus' death.

> The narrator does not intend to suggest, however, that an arbitrary God is whimsically playing with human beings. Rather,

---

31. Barrett, *Jesus and the Gospel Tradition*, 23; cf. 58.
32. Tannehill, *The Gospel according to Luke*, 31.

there is something inherently difficult in understanding God's ways of working through the death of Jesus. God holds human eyes in the sense that God's ways *necessarily appear meaningless* to humans who understand events in terms of their own purposes and ways of achieving them.[33]

Tannehill helps us realize the difficulty in understanding Jesus' death as not only the end result of his messiahship but *as* his messiahship. Tannehill helps make the point even clearer concerning the need for Jesus to reveal his identity *to people* rather than people using their reasoning ability to know his identity.[34] Now the irony in Barrett's suggestion is truer than we wanted to or could have realized. The disparity between Jesus being messiah, the Son of God, and the human ability to believe he is God's Son is the most pronounced as he approaches his crucifixion. The closer Jesus moves toward his death the more his messiahship *appears* a complete failure. However, that Jesus' life *appears* a failure is just the point. As Yoder says, Jesus' cross is his kingdom come.[35] From a human perspective it was and still is a failure; from a human perspective any true Son of God *would save* his own life. How could one be the Son of God and not save himself?

This is the reason Spirit-Christology must begin with Jesus' death and resurrection; it views Jesus trusting his Father in the Spirit even though it was his Father who allowed wicked men to destroy him. In the Spirit's presence, Jesus trusted and submitted to the Father even in the kind of death that, by its very nature, was meant to inflict the most public shame, ridicule, and physical torture one could possibly receive. This aspect of the public shame and torture of Jesus' death is eclipsed by a Christology imbedded in and indebted to the Western understanding of inner individual guilt. However, this is the most crucial aspect of Jesus' death; in the Spirit Jesus trusted his Father in the midst of a most shameful death. By not justifying himself publically before all the people who were either inflicting the torture and shame or before those who refused to come to his rescue, Jesus justified God. This required Jesus to rely on his only option left; trusting his Father to resurrect him from the dead as vindication that, as the recipient of humans' most unjustifiable act, he justified God in complete selfless obedience and trust. This aspect is what

33. Ibid., 282; emphasis added.
34. Ibid., 238–39, 278–89.
35. Yoder, *The Politics of Jesus*, 51.

makes Jesus' death on a cross *most* unbelievable; that he claimed God as his Father, YHWH of Israel, to be a God who would not only destroy his life but that *this kind of death* would save others *because* he refused to save himself. This shows it to be true; believing Jesus to be the Son of God just when he refuses to save himself in order to justify God is not possible, since *that kind* of a God could never be believed to be God, much less a God one calls their *heavenly Father*. What kind of heavenly Father would do *that* to his only Son?

The Father Resurrected Jesus in the Spirit, Proving His Death Justified God

Since Jesus died in the Spirit allowing God his Father to destroy him, the resurrection becomes not only more significant, it becomes the very basis upon which Jesus' death is validated by the Father as justifying God. As Jesus' sonship with the Father is most fully actualized in his death on a cross, the Father's fatherhood is most fully actualized in raising his Son from the dead. Jesus suffered a torturous and shameful death claiming to be God's Spirit-anointed Son with total trust in his Father to resurrect him from the dead; trusting his Father to vindicate him in that his claim of sonship with God was true. Now, the resurrection can be seen as God the Father not merely putting life back into Jesus' dead corpse, but as the Father vindicating Jesus' denial of his own life in order to accept his Father's will of destroying his life on a cross, trusting his Father with his very breath of life. How was it that Jesus claimed to be the Son of God while the God he trusted as his Father would destroy him even while he claimed to be his Son? How could a God like that be trusted as one's heavenly Father? Such an idea is completely incompatible with any form of human logic or reasoning because the conclusion denies the very premise upon which it is based. As the denial of human logic, Jesus' death and resurrection is the greatest reversal of all; God reversing human reasoning by defying the very nature of cause and effect upon which human reasoning depends.

This shows Jesus' cross and resurrection as God's Trinitarian event of destroying Jesus' life and the raising up of that destroyed life as the vindication that his death justified God for all who would believe that it did. God the Father vindicated his son Jesus *as his Son* because he died in the Spirit justifying God rather than himself. Who else could allow God to abandon them to a death on a cross for doing God's will other than someone whose very life was constituted by the Holy Spirit's presence from beginning to end? This is what it meant for Jesus to live in the Spirit as the only Son of God, to die justifying God in a way inconceivable to human perception and contrary to human calculation. This more biblical view of his death also supplies his resurrection with more significance. It also provides a more biblical approach to faith as the work of the Spirit transforming a person into an adopted son who confesses Jesus as risen from the dead and Lord over all.

This brings us to asking an even more daunting question, "Since Jesus died on a cross for claiming to be God's Spirit-anointed Son and was raised in vindication that his claim was true, does believing Jesus to be the Son of God not also *equally* depend on the Spirit's presence? This is especially important now that we have seen Jesus' death on a cross and his resurrection to be *how* the Spirit worked in Jesus as the unique Son of God. If so, the Spirit's work of Jesus' cross and resurrection must be and can only be repeated, of sorts, in other people for them to not only know that Jesus' cross and resurrection is God's salvation but for them to be adopted as "other sons" of God by the Spirit's presence who *does the knowing within them intrinsically*, and that by a work of transformation. Otherwise, without the Spirit's transforming presence within the hearers, Jesus' cross and resurrection cannot be believed on as either one's salvation or as one's way of living.

Here we are at the most critical crossroads yet. If Jesus' life of sonship with the Father in the Spirit meant forsaking his own will in order to do the will of his Father, even though it meant his own death, how do we say that others attain sonship now that we have also seen that such a life defies human ability to either believe or live? In order for such an account of others attaining sonship with the Father to be consistent with what we have already seen concerning Jesus' life, death, and resurrection, the Spirit's presence must be shown to be equally significant for others *knowing* Jesus to be the Son of God and also for living the same kind of life Jesus lived that led to the kind of death he died. Such an explanation must be our next concern as we continue on in our task of showing the Christian life to be a life lived in the Spirit. Thankfully, the trajectories of Luke's description of the characteristics of Jesus' life and death in the Spirit given in his gospel can be traced into the cruciform lives of Jesus' disciples in his sequel of Acts. Showing the outline and contours of their lives will give us a solid biblical basis for describing both *how* others are adopted as sons of God by the Spirit and *what* shape and direction their lives take as adopted sons who live in the Spirit.

Jesus Gives His Spirit to Adopt "Other Sons" to Live in His Cruciform Life

Now that we have discovered the Holy Spirit as the "constitutive ingredient" in Jesus' life, *how* he lived and died as receiver and bearer of the Spirit, we are now at a place to explain Jesus as giver of the Spirit for others to both believe in Jesus' cross and resurrection as their salvation and by Jesus' life and death being their own way of life. For this Spirit-Christology to be coherent and consistent it first acknowledges the inability for anyone to live and die the way Jesus did because no one else possesses the Holy Spirit as the "constitutive ingredient" of their life. By being born without the Spirit, people must be given the Spirit to live and die in the same order of Jesus' death and resurrection. Jesus' life as God's *only* begotten Son from conception was unique: to die for the sins of others, to be raised from the dead as God's vindication, and to ascend to God's right hand in heaven. By virtue of his unique mission as the Son of God, Jesus being seated at God's right hand was the Father's glorification for Jesus to pour out his Spirit on others for them to live out a life of sonship to the Father in the same cruciform life as he lived and died. This can now be shown to be a more coherent reading of Luke-Acts by explaining how Luke continues his trajectory of Jesus' sonship, from Luke, by way of narrative description into the lives of Jesus' followers, in Acts. By Jesus pouring out his Spirit, Jesus' death and resurrection become the cruciform way of life for his followers who live in his same Spirit.

Our task now is to see if we can glean from Luke some kind of bridge from Jesus' life in the Spirit as the Son of God to other people being adopted as sons of the Father in the Spirit. This Spirit-Christology for the Christian life needs to show a consistency from Jesus' life in the Spirit as the unique Son of God, as described in Luke, to the Spirit's work in Jesus' followers for them to live out Jesus' death and resurrection as their own way of life in Acts. Since we have already considered Luke' narrative for what it meant for Jesus to live and die as the Son of God in the Spirit, Luke's narrative of Acts will serve as the basis upon which this bridge is constructed. Many have explained Luke's literary connections between Luke 24 and Acts 1–2, but I will confine my analysis to those aspects that support a Spirit-Christology that informs the Christian life as life in the Spirit in the following three areas. First, Jesus as giver of the Spirit is founded upon Luke 24:44–53, second, Jesus gives his Spirit initially in Acts 2, establishing his community of called out "other sons" who live in Christ's *koinonia* fellowship, and third, Jesus continues giving his Spirit in Acts 8, 10, and 19 in order to fulfill, through his disciples, the making of other disciples from all nations into *one koinonia fellowship*. These events will demonstrate not only that the Spirit given is the same Spirit in which Jesus lived and died, but that the pattern established by Jesus himself, by which he imparts his Spirit, *is* his life, death, and resurrection.

First, in Luke 24:44–53 we see Luke fashioning a literary pattern that becomes the shape of the narrative proclamation in Acts through which the Spirit works to make other sons of God. But this is not merely a literary pattern; it is Jesus narrating his own life, death, and resurrection *as* God's redemptive history; Jesus narrates his life as God's meaning of history. This is seen in how Jesus describes his life as the fulfillment of God's revelation of the law through Moses, the prophets, and the psalms; the fulfillment of all Israel's history (24:44). Luke adds that Jesus "opened their minds" in order for them to understand Scripture (24:45) and that it was written that he should suffer death and rise again the third day (24:46). Now that he had died and rose again, his death and resurrection require repentance and forgiveness of sins to be *preached* to all nations (24:47) and that his disciples were now *witnesses* to this truth (24:48). For them to be his witnesses, Jesus said he would now send the promise of his Father, the Holy Spirit, upon them while they waited in Jerusalem. With the Spirit they would be "clothed with power from on high" to carry out his mission as witnesses to his life, death, and resurrection (24:49).

While this serves as a literary pattern for Luke, to see it as only that deprives it of its main function; that of Jesus interpreting his own life, death, and resurrection as the bearer of God's Spirit, and now, as he nears his ascension and glorification, as the sole giver of the Spirit to make adopted sons of God. As adopted sons of God, endued with the Spirit's presence to live and even die, they would now be able to carry out his mission of making other disciples, fellow followers, in his community of "called out other sons" living in *koinonia* fellowship with each other. They would also be enabled to live a cruciform life that would do more than even Jesus did as performers and proclaimers of God's kingdom, but who would also likewise suffer just as he said they would (Luke 12:11, 49–53;

14:26–33) because they would now have the same indwelling Spirit in which he did the will of his Father in both word and deed. Luke's literary connection of Luke 24 and Acts 1 is lost if one fails to see his point that Jesus' ascension to the right hand of the Father is his glorification to the place of Spirit giver. In that he was bearer of the Spirit in his death that justified God, he attained his unique position as Spirit giver upon his resurrection, ascension, and glorification, giving his Spirit to reconcile people back to God as other sons of the Father.

Prior to the Day of Pentecost, Jesus' followers knew he was the Christ, but they were still blind to the true meaning of the kingdom of God because the Spirit had not yet been given inwardly for them to see it. Even their understandings of the true meaning of the *messiah* and the kingdom over which he reigned were skewed by their lack of the Spirit's presence necessary to perceive it. They asked Jesus about the restoration of Israel's kingdom because they did not yet understand the kingdom of God as the condemnation of and replacement to the kingdoms of this world, of which they were still very much indebted to in their thinking (Acts 1:6). The power they would receive by the Spirit's outpouring would change this self-seeking and self-preserving use of worldly power from the inside out. The Spirit's presence from Pentecost onward worked sonship *within* them, giving them the proper perspective of their Father's kingdom in which Jesus had lived and died in the Spirit. The Spirit's presence, from Pentecost onward, now exposes and condemns this desire for self-seeking authority (*exousia*) (Acts 1:7), giving Jesus' followers the same life of Christ's Spirit-indwelt power (*dynamis*) (Acts 1:8) that caused him to give up his will for the will of the Father. The Spirit's presence would also cause them to give up their wills for the will of the Father, allowing them to live in a community of fellowship in the Spirit. At Pentecost, Christ gives his Spirit to form his *ecclesia* of other sons who, with the Spirit's inner presence, now live in *koinonia* fellowship as Christ's body, doing the will of the Father. This fellowship in the Spirit appears unsettling to the world (Acts 17:6) just as Jesus' life and death also were by their reversing of the human condition upon which the world's order functions and by which it is sustained.

This unsettling reality of Christ's *koinonia* fellowship began on the day of Pentecost when Jesus Christ gave his Spirit for others to live as sons of God in the kingdom over which Jesus Christ now reigns. "When the day of Pentecost had come" (Acts 2:1) connects the Holy Spirit outpouring to the Jewish festival celebrating the first fruits of the harvest. What the Spirit did, by coming upon all 120 at once, was only the beginning of the "last days;" the age of "harvest" in which the Spirit would dwell within people in a way not possible before Jesus' ascension and glorification. The "last days" was now the age in which the Second Temple was replaced with Jesus and his followers as the new temple. The new temple was now a building made up of human stones, people indwelt with the Spirit's presence as Jesus had been, with Jesus as the head stone who the builders of this world rejected because he did not fit into their building plans. In establishing the new building of God's temple, the Spirit's presence manifested in physical forms of wind that filled the room and flames of fire over each of their heads (2:2–3), using the same forms as he had in the nation of Israel during their wilderness wonderings and in their Temple. However, this was a new age in which the Spirit dwells within people in an inner presence enabling each to speak languages as the Spirit enabled their utterances (2:2–4) and to carry the gospel message as witnesses to all nations (Luke 24:47; Acts 1:8). No human ability is more deep-seated than speaking a language or being a witness to Jesus' lordship. In this new age, the Spirit is now speaking new languages and witnessing to Jesus' lordship through people, not a building, showing his presence to be innately within people to both proclaim and perform God's kingdom over which his Son Jesus reigns forever.

These manifestations were now upon and within each person rather than in the physical temple building or exclusively upon ethnic Jews in Israel. As each of these had been God's manifestations to his people in Israel's history, they were now signs of the Spirit dwelling *within* the disciples as his new temple, a temple of witnesses from all nations and ethnicities. What God had done in the past to show Israel's exclusivity in the physical Temple, he was now doing in a new way to show how his New Israel would be a temple of inclusivity by being one *koinonia* fellowship that included every race, language, age, gender, and social standing. Peter, filled with the Holy Spirit, stood up and boldly proclaimed these manifestations of the Spirit as signs of the "last days" spoken of by Joel (2:16–21; Joel 2:28–32). This marked the beginning of a new reality of the Spirit's presence based on Jesus' life, death, and resurrection that not only justified God but brought people from all nations back together into one fellowship by breaking down all the barriers that even the Old Testament law had prescribed.

This new reality was already bringing together formerly estranged people to be one in a salvation available to all who call on the name of the Lord (2:21). According to Jewish law, the 120 disciples were already a diverse group of Jews, made of up men and women from Galilee no less. This was no doubt *already* the Spirit's work because the many languages they spoke by the Spirit's utterance were languages recognized by Jews staying in Jerusalem from every known country (Acts 2:5). Peter confirms this new reality of the Spirit poured out on all people as the "last days" by quoting Joel 2:28–32 (Acts 2:16–21). He says this new age is one in which the Spirit makes one community of worship out of groups previously distinguished by the laws of Israel's worship which make people more or less righteous insiders. Now the Spirit would equally be within and upon all; sons and daughters, old men and young men, male slaves and female slaves (Acts 2:17–18), in one community that makes no distinction by outward appearances or status, a reality due *only* to the Spirit's *inward work* of sonship. With the Spirit's presence residing in the community and within each member of the community as the new temple, there would be no prejudices between ages, genders, and social classes. In this new community of fellowship, sonship in the Spirit is marked with the same kind of life Jesus lived, a life of sharing, racial harmony, and social inclusivity out of a concern for one's neighbor over the natural human concern for one's own self.

Peter says this new reality is now possible for others because Jesus bore the Spirit and, having been raised and glorified to God's right hand, has now given this same Holy Spirit to others, causing what they had just seen and heard (Acts 2:32–33). Peter concludes his sermon by proclaiming that Jesus was the son of David but they, his hearers (Jews from every nation), had nailed him to a cross. Even this rejection and suffering was God's plan for his Son, however, God did this in Jesus for the purpose of raising him from the dead in vindication and seating him at his right hand as Lord and Christ (2:36). Through Peter's proclamation of Jesus' life as God's Son, the Spirit worked sonship in the hearers so that they cried out in guilt and shame, "What must we do?" Peter's response was for them to repent, be baptized in the name of Jesus Christ and that they too would receive the Holy Spirit (2:38). Those who believed Peter's message were baptized and added to the church that very day. People being added to the community was the result of the Spirit's presence in and through the proclamation of Jesus' life, death, and resurrection, by the Spirit doing

Jesus' "death" and "resurrection" in their lives as well. What the Spirit had done in Jesus' life as God's Son, through his death and resurrection, the Spirit was now doing in others as Christ gave his Spirit to work "death" and "resurrection" in other people for other sons to be born again of the Father. Here in Acts, Luke is showing that it is only through the proclamation of Jesus' death and resurrection that the Spirit works Jesus' death to and in people for Jesus' cruciform life to become the confession of those who call on his name for salvation. By the Spirit's presence, the Father works Jesus' cruciform life in others as they repent and are baptized into Jesus' life.

Throughout Acts the Spirit continues to be poured out, multiplying Jesus' new community of followers. Even the first deacons preached the good news of Jesus' life, death, and resurrection as the overcoming of human sin, estrangement from God and from others. Subsequent outpourings of the Spirit in Acts transform previously estranged groups into one community through the proclamation of Jesus as the Son of God raised to God's right hand from where he pours out his Spirit. Philip, one of the first deacons full of the Spirit (Acts 6:3–6), preached Christ and cast out evil spirits in the city of Samaria (Acts 8:5–7) so that many believed and were baptized, even Simon the sorcerer (8:8–13), who would later be rejected for wanting to make money by dispensing the Spirit (8:18–19). However, when Peter and John arrived, they laid hands on them and prayed for the believers to receive the Holy Spirit (8:14–17).

In similar fashion, Peter, called by God in a vision to go to the "unclean" Gentiles, goes to Cornelius's house in Caesarea and preaches to them that Jesus had been given the Holy Spirit by God and did good works because God was with him. But, even though the Jews had killed him, God raised him from the dead to judge the living and the dead. Now, whoever believes in Jesus' name would be forgiven of their sins (Acts 10:38–43). While they were hearing Peter speak the message of Jesus' death and resurrection, the Holy Spirit fell on those listening. The Jews who were with Peter were amazed that the Spirit had been given to the nations, the Gentiles, for they heard them speak in other languages as on the day of Pentecost (10:44–46). They were then baptized in the name of Jesus Christ, bringing them into the same community of fellowship as the Jewish Christians (10:47–48). This happened a third time after Pentecost when Paul travelled to Ephesus and found people there who had been baptized according to John's baptism (Acts 19:1–3). After telling them that Jesus was the one to whom John testified, they were all baptized in the name of Jesus (19:4–5). Following their baptism, Paul laid his hands on them and they received the Holy Spirit and began to speak with other languages and to prophesy as on the day of Pentecost (19:6).

In all these events of the Holy Spirit being poured out in Acts, Luke shows conclusively that the Spirit is given when Jesus' life, death, and resurrection are proclaimed as God's salvation for the nations. When Jesus' death and resurrection is proclaimed, the Spirit causes people to believe on his death and resurrection as God's reconciliation of people from all nations back into relationship with him as other sons, a relationship made possible only by the Spirit's presence. By Luke's accounts of Jesus' life as receiver and bearer of the Spirit in his gospel and of Jesus as giver of the Spirit in Acts, he accounts for the Christian life as life in the Spirit. However, for this account to be conclusive it must be fully consistent with Luke's description in Acts of how Christians lived out their lives as Jesus' followers. It must show that Luke not only describes how the Spirit is given when Jesus life, death, and resurrection are proclaimed, but how the disciples in Acts live out the same cruciform life as Jesus lived also in the same Spirit. Can this account of the Christian life as a life lived in the Spirit, as described by Luke, show it to be a life constituted by Jesus' cross and resurrection in a way that defines the Christian life as a cruciform life? Asked another way, can it be determined from Acts that Luke is describing both the Christian life and the Spirit's presence in a Christian life as synonymous with a cruciform life?

Luke Describes Jesus' Disciples as Living Christ's Cruciform Life in the Spirit

A feature of Luke's account in Acts that is largely marginalized to insignificance in many Western accounts of the Christian life is his description of the disciples living out Jesus' cruciform life as their own. After Christ pours out his Spirit on the day of Pentecost, Jesus' followers begin living out Jesus' life of cross and resurrection as their own, doing what they were previously unable and even *unwilling* to do before they received the Spirit. Ironically, even Pentecostal scholars, who should at least remember the sacrificial lives of the early Pentecostals, often elevate the prophetic dimension of the apostles' and deacons' lives in Acts to the neglect of the cruciform lives they lived, lives that mirror the life Jesus lived and died in the Spirit as previously detailed by Luke in his gospel. Why such a glaring omission or disconnect? Why are the obvious connections ignored in favor of less obvious ones? Why do many Pentecostals no longer describe their own movement as the "29th chapter of Acts" as their founders did in the early years of the twentieth century? While answering these questions will be more to the point in chapter 5, raising them here gives us a basis upon which to examine Luke's narrative of Acts as to how the Spirit's outpouring caused the apostles and deacons to live cruciform lives in the same manner in which Jesus lived.

An interesting feature of Luke's depiction of their cruciform lives is how he tells about them almost in passing. Luke is rather nonchalant about the hardships, persecutions, and even deaths suffered by those whom Christ had called and empowered with his Spirit to carry out the mission of making other disciples of Jesus' gospel. Luke describes their lives so matter-of-factly as willing sufferers for the gospel, who even considered it an honor to suffer shame for the name of Jesus Christ (Acts 5:41). It is as if Luke himself believes that suffering persecution for preaching and living as a follower of Jesus Christ is only the natural result of Christ's gospel invading the principalities and powers of this world and announcing their defeat. If so, this view of Acts would mean the Spirit's outpouring is for the express purpose of proclaiming the victory of Christ over the powers of this world, a proclamation that inherently receives rejection, scorn, suffering, abuse, and even death from those powers. Who, living in the same Spirit in which Jesus lived, would question any suffering they might receive for speaking forth the message that humanity's estrangement from God has been conquered by Jesus' life, death, and resurrection?

Such estrangement from God in sin is the very core element of the innate human condition of violence upon which the powers of this world are sustained. That Jesus' death and resurrection has declared this estrangement from God in sin as condemned and awaiting its final judgment is to incite rejection as a natural result. As such, the disciples' message following Pentecost is that Jesus' death, resurrection, and ascension to God's right hand was the dawning of the "last days;" a time when Christians would live "between the times" of God's declaring the powers of this world defeated by Jesus' resurrection and the Last Day when those powers would receive their final judgment with Christ's physical return to earth to set up his Kingdom. This living "between the times" that Luke describes in Acts is none other than the Spirit's presence that now enables Jesus' disciples to live like Jesus did, as sons of God who have taken on cruciform lives of "cross" and "resurrection" as their own that mirror Jesus' cross and resurrection. This new life is a life of dying to this world and a resurrection to live in Christ's life in the Spirit.

Right away, beginning at Pentecost with the Spirit's outpouring, Luke emphasizes the boldness of the apostles and deacons in the proclaiming of and living within God's story of his Son Jesus as their own way of life. Like Jesus, they show no concern for what consequences await them, just rejoicing that they are found worthy to suffer like Jesus had (Acts 5:41), even praising God while in prison for proclaiming the gospel of Jesus (16:23–25). By weaving together the proclamation of the gospel of Jesus Christ and the lifestyles they live, Luke emphasizes the Spirit's empowerment for witness that led the first Christians to suffer this same rejection, abuse, punishment, and even death as Jesus had on account of his life in the Spirit.

None other than the impetuous Peter boldly stands up to proclaim the event of the Spirit's outpouring on Pentecost as that prophesied by Joel. Peter tells the crowd that since the Father had given the Spirit to Jesus and now Jesus had given his Spirit to his followers (2:33), Christ's lordship over all was confirmed; fulfilling what David had prophesied about Christ receiving honor and power to rule over all his enemies (2:34–35; Ps 110:1). Peter, full of the Spirit, boldly proclaims that Christ now sits at the right hand of the Father from which he gives his Spirit, confirming that "God has made this man Jesus, the man you nailed to the cross, both Lord and Christ" (2:37). Jesus' death, resurrection, and ascension now not only *require* both repentance and baptism but the proclamation of these events of Jesus' life *cause* repentance and baptism for others to receive the Spirit (2:38). He says "this is that" sign of the last days, which God fulfilled in Jesus' life, death, and resurrection and about which king David had prophesied; God's holy one being raised from the dead (Acts 2:25–32). Peter boldly tells them they were responsible for nailing Jesus to a cross (2:23, 36) and that they must repent and be baptized for the remission of their sins. However, with repentance and baptism, they too would receive this same Holy Spirit indwelling (2:38) for the promise is "for all who are far off, as many as the Lord our God will call to himself" (2:39). Going even further, Peter warns them with many words to save themselves from the evil ways of their generation (2:40), calling them out of this world and its evil.

Was Peter calling them out of the same evil of the world that not many days before was responsible for killing Jesus? If so, the proclamation Peter gave that day fell right in line with the proclamations of John the Baptist, Jesus, and all of Israel's prophets before them who suffered the same rejection for calling people to repent. Peter proclaimed Jesus' death and resurrection as not only God's salvation but also as the very form of the proclamation itself and, going one step further, as the form of the Christian life. In other words, Jesus' cross and resurrection become both the content of salvation, the nature of the proclamation by which people are saved, and the form by which Jesus' followers live their lives within Christ's cruciform life. Jesus' life, death, and resurrection are now not only *what* one believes, but *how* one believes, and, having been adopted as another son of God in the same Spirit, Jesus' life is also the way one lives their own life as one of his disciples. By way of narrative, Luke describes the Christian life in the same way Paul does by way of propositions; as one who lives out Jesus' cruciform life as a son of God in the Spirit.

That *how* one believes and lives a cruciform life as a follower of Jesus in the Spirit is made nowhere more evident by Luke than how he portrays Stephen's horrific death by stoning. Notice the parallels between Stephen's trial and death and that of Jesus' death. The church had chosen seven men full of the Holy Spirit to carry out the main duties of the church, which was making sure the food was evenly distributed to those most culturally despised among them—Greek speaking widows (Acts 6:1-3). Stephen was not only one of these men but is described further by Luke as "full of faith and the Holy Spirit" (6:5). Although Jewish leaders were against him doing great miracles and signs among the people (6:8), the Spirit was helping Stephen speak boldly with wisdom so that his words were too strong for his critics to refute (6:10). As a result of the leaders conspiring to have some accuse Stephen of speaking against the Temple and Moses (6:12-14), the high priest brought him in for questioning where he boldly proclaimed the message of Israel and Jesus, telling them they were stubborn and always against the Holy Spirit and that now they had killed Jesus, the "One who is good" (7:52). At this they became furious, but Stephen, full of the Holy Spirit, looked up to heaven and saw the "Son of Man standing at the right hand of God" (7:56). Upon hearing this, they took him out and began stoning him, but he prayed, "Lord Jesus, receive my spirit" (7:59) and "Lord, do not hold this sin against them" (8:60), two of the same prayers Jesus had prayed to his Father while dying on a cross at the hands of evil and lawless people (Luke 23:46, 34). "Having said this, he fell asleep" (Acts 7:60).

Throughout Acts, Luke continues weaving together both the proclamation content of Jesus' life, death, and resurrection and *how* Christians are living out the gospel and receiving rejection and suffering for doing so. Both of these elements in Jesus' life, as seen earlier in this chapter, are in Peter's message on Solomon's portico at the Temple in Acts 3. Peter says in both speeches, first to the people and then to the leaders, that Jesus was God's faithful servant, that they had him killed, but that God raised him from the dead (3:13–15; 4:10). God's vindication of Jesus, by raising him from the dead, continues to necessitate repentance, just as his message had during his ministry (3:19). What is most evident in this passage is how Luke identifies these episodes of boldness and rejoicing with the Holy Spirit's presence. Peter, full of the Spirit, speaks boldly to the Jewish leaders (4:8), the people rejoice that the Holy Spirit had spoken about this through king David concerning the nations' anger against God's messiah (4:25–26), and they were all filled again with the Holy Spirit to speak God's word without fear (4:31).

Luke shows this same two-part aspect in Peter and the other apostles' arrest in Acts 5 where again they perform miracles on Solomon's portico at the Temple, are arrested for doing so, and, being led out of prison by an angel during the night, go right back to the temple to do it all over again only to be arrested again (5:12–39). A remarkable aspect of this account is Peter's address to the authorities that it is the Holy Spirit, given to all who obey God, who proves these things to be true concerning Jesus Christ as God's anointed servant (5:32). Being full of the Spirit who gives this "proof," the apostles, having just been beaten, leave the meeting full of joy for being counted worthy of suffering disgrace and shame on account of Jesus' name (5:40–41). So courageous are they that they continue going to the temple daily and in people's homes preaching the good news that Jesus is God's messiah (5:42). How can Luke so casually describe the apostles' lives in Acts as both full of the Spirit *and* as being persecuted for it? Does Luke's methodology in writing his account of the spread of the gospel conform to the very content and proclamation of the gospel itself, that the Spirit's presence elicits rejection from this world just as Jesus' life had? Luke does not say; one can only follow how he narrates the story.

Following Stephen's arrest and martyrdom in Acts 6–7, Luke shows the news about Jesus Christ spreading not only in spite of its rejection but *because* of it. The true gospel of Jesus Christ not only causes rejection, it thrives on account of rejection; demonstrating that the Spirit establishes and builds Christ's *ecclesia* in Acts in *opposition* to the kingdoms of this world, certainly not upon them. The rejection and persecution of the apostles' in Jerusalem *cause* them to be scattered to other part of Judea and Samaria (8:1) and to other places beyond (11:19), thus propelling the church to fulfill its mission of making disciples from all the nations, beginning with Jerusalem but also in all Judea, in Samaria, and to all nations as commanded by Jesus (1:8).

The most unlikely candidate to take the gospel of Jesus to the farthest parts of the world was Saul of Tarsus. Following his dramatic conversion on the Damascus Road (9:1–9), he receives the Holy Spirit when Ananias lays hands on him (9:17) and is baptized (9:18). Saul then changed his name to Paul and became the model of the Holy Spirit's power to both proclaim the gospel and live Christ's cruciform life as his own. As God's messenger to the Gentiles and their kings, Paul was told by Ananias how much he would suffer for the name of Jesus, even from his own Jewish people (9:15–16). As evident from Luke's narrative, even Paul's sufferings and persecutions were for the spread of the gospel, the preaching of which was the very cause of his eventual trip to Rome as a prisoner. Being under arrest, he was enabled to carry the gospel message to the center of the ancient political, economic, and cultural world, even to the very center of the Roman military guard.

In the midst of this vast and varied spread of the gospel, the church suffered tremendously but, according to Luke, such suffering was the expected result of the message of Jesus' life, death, and resurrection invading the world's condition of estrangement that naturally rejects Jesus and his messengers. Luke discusses this opposition to the gospel almost in passing, as though the Spirit's presence that gives them boldness and comfort is equal to and opposite the rejection and suffering they receive. Luke writes only two sentences about King Herod having John's brother James killed by the sword (Acts 12:1–2), but he describes the opposition to the gospel message itself in virtually every place the apostles preach. Paul and Barnabas suffer rejection in Cyprus (13:8–11), in Antioch (13:50), in Iconium (14:5–6), and in Lystra (14:19–20). Luke even attributes the apostles' inability to preach in Asia and Bithynia to the Holy

Spirit (15:6–7). They are also rejected, beaten, and thrown in prison in Philippi (16:19–34) and are rejected in Thessalonica (17:5–9). Paul's message in Athens, of Jesus being raised from the dead, causes some of the philosophers to laugh at him in ridicule (17:32), his message in Corinth causes several to say evil things about him (18:6), he is taken to court over saying things against the religion of Southern Greece (18:12–16), and is rejected in Ephesus for turning people away from worshipping Artemis (19:23–41).

It is here in Ephesus that Paul attributes to the Holy Spirit the guidance that will get him arrested in Jerusalem, which was the same message the Holy Spirit had been telling him in each of these previous times of rejection and suffering (20:22–23). It is Luke who says that Paul identifies his own life by the cruciform life of Jesus; not caring for his own life but only for completing the mission to which the Lord had called him—to preach the good news of God's grace (20:24). Can Luke really not know that much about Paul's theology, as some suggest? Is Luke's Pneumatology that different from Paul's? Or, is Luke providing, by way of narrative description, what Paul describes elsewhere in propositional description, a theology of the cruciform life in the Spirit?

If so, we are encountered by the continuity between the gospel message and the messenger. This would suggest that the messenger of the gospel be conformed to the message of the gospel itself. This leads us to ask, must the messenger of the cruciform life of Jesus also live the cruciform life in the Spirit in order to call others to believe it? Luke certainly portrays this as a reality in Paul's departing message to the Ephesians. Here, Paul connects his own proclamation of the gospel of Jesus Christ to the way he lived before them for three years in the same manner of Jesus' cruciform life; continually praying for them and often crying over them (20:31), not wanting any of their money or fine clothes for himself (20:33), but by working to provide for his own needs and those under his care (20:34). By living the cruciform life, Paul endeavored to teach them to care for the needs of the weak because Jesus taught that it was more blessed to give than to receive (20:35).

Conclusion

We are now left with possibly a greater dilemma than when we started. Now that we can see how Luke weaves together the content of Jesus' life, death, and resurrection as the content of the gospel with the cruciform lives of those proclaiming the gospel, we are faced with the question of how the Spirit makes other sons of God to both perform and proclaim the kingdom of God in the manner in which Jesus lived out his sonship with the Father. We must now venture into a deeper investigation of how Luke portrays this happening after Christ gives his Spirit at Pentecost and following, when Christ begins pouring out his Spirit upon Galileans, Samaritans, and Gentiles. Could there be something inherent about the relationship between Christ and his Spirit that requires an adequate presentation of Christ's cruciform life in the Spirit in order for the Spirit to transform others into adopted sons of God who, as sons of God, live in Christ's image? At the very least, this would require a complete transformation of the very core element of the human condition, a work only accomplished by the Holy Spirit through the message preached.

4

God Gives His Spirit by Working Jesus Christ
in Others

Introduction

The basic difficulty in giving the kind of account presented here is the fact that much theological reflection on the Christian life discounts the life of Christ as determinative for the Christian life. As I discussed earlier, Yoder took up this problem especially in *The Politics of Jesus*, in which he argued that the Incarnation implied that Christ's life must inform the life of the Christian. But Yoder's account does not adequately attend to the question of *how one is made a disciple* of Jesus, what Adolf Köberle called the "energy" question,[1] because he does not adequately account for the Spirit in the life of the Christian. The reason for this lies in the Christology that Yoder adopted: a two-natures Chalcedonian Christology. This Christology implied *that* the life of Christ should inform the life of the Christian, because Jesus Christ himself was as fully and truly human as he was fully and truly divine. But this Christology could not explain how the life of the Christian was at once and the same time lived by the presence and power of the Holy Spirit, because it accounted for Christ in terms of his personal constitution. A complementary account of Christ was necessary to give an adequate explanation of *how* a person becomes a Christian and, in the Spirit, lives the kind of life Jesus lived. This called for a different account of the person of Christ ("Christology" in the strict sense) and for this I turned to a "pneumatological Christology" that accounts for Jesus Christ in terms of his relationship to God the Father in

---

1. Köberle, *The Quest for Holiness*, 84.

the Spirit's presence. This account of Christ not only makes sense of his person but also his mission by the constitutive events in his life, including his baptism, ministry, crucifixion, and resurrection. By clearly showing how Jesus lived his life by the Holy Spirit, we also gain clarity on how others are adopted sons of God by the same Spirit's indwelling presence.

This view of Jesus' life in the Spirit presents yet another difficult question to be dealt with in this chapter, "How is this Spirit-transformed life actually attained? Or, "How does one's life become a life lived in the presence of the Spirit in which Jesus lived as one of God's adopted sons?" The answer shared across confessional and ecclesial lines is: "Through the ministry of the Church, the body of Christ." I will retain this answer rather than question it or propose an alternative. However, we should be clear that this means conceiving the ministry of the church as the work of God. This understanding of the church's ministry has been questioned and denied, at least in effect, in many contemporary American churches, not least, I fear, among those of my own Pentecostal tradition. Therefore it will be helpful to indicate *how and why* the ministry of the church may need to be reimagined before offering my own concrete proposal.

Reimagining the Ministry of the Church That Believes in Life in the Spirit

I began this discussion by observing along with Yoder that much reflection on the Christian life does not take the life Jesus lived seriously for how one is to live. This neglect of Jesus' life eclipses any need for Spirit transformation. We can see this not only in accounts of the Christian life, but also in those accounts of Christian ministry that, in effect, also deny transformation as necessary because it does not aim for transformation.

As might be expected, post-Constantinians have a criticism along these lines.[2] For example, Stanley Hauerwas and William Willimon have criticized Christian *ministry* that is conducted in ways that ignore or deny the necessity of transformation in accounting for a faithful ministry. Of course, few Christians would say this about themselves, or even think it, but, as the saying goes, "actions speak louder than words." The actions in

---

2. Although I have criticized Yoder and Hauerwas for not giving a detailed account for the Spirit in the life of the Christian, I did acknowledge that they recognize the significance of transformation. See above, chapter 1, 23–27.

this case bespeak a "practical atheism" in that it is undertaken without the conviction that God is essential to its genuine success.[3]

Such a situation calls for a thorough reimagination of the church's ministry. What, then, does a "reimagined ministry" look like or believe in? About preaching, Willimon says:

> We must learn to preach again in such a way as to demonstrate that, if there is no Holy Spirit, if Jesus has not been raised from the dead, then our preaching is doomed to fall upon deaf ears. Our preaching ought to be so confrontive, so in violation of all that contemporary Americans think they know, that it requires no less than a miracle to be heard. We preach best with a reckless confidence in the power of the gospel to evoke the audience it deserves.[4]

The anthropological parallel to the practical atheism that Hauerwas and Willimon identified is belief in "free choice," as Gerhard Forde noted in *Theology Is for Proclamation*.[5] A corollary for the proclamation of the gospel is the "bondage of the will," not the freedom of the will.[6] But "the usual manner of thinking," Forde points out, is to "assume that if there is no freedom of will, proclamation is pointless."[7] But this is to be mistaken about the proclamation of the gospel. It is not a mere explanation of the true state of affairs, but the Word of God that brings deliverance to the captives by being "the invasion of the house of the 'strong man armed' who hopes to keep control of things."[8] This notion of the ministry, of course, recognizes the centrality of the transforming work of God, where "the proclaimer hopes and thus proclaims in the expectation that through the proclamation the 'Spirit of the Lord' is at work to set captives free."[9]

As this chapter will bear out from Luke's account in Acts, faithful preaching depends on the Spirit to transform its hearers into faithful disciples of Jesus Christ by it intruding into people's lives; working repen-

---

3. Hauerwas and Willimon, *Resident Aliens*, 120; cf., 19–24. See also Willimon, *The Intrusive Word*, 18–22.

4. Willimon, *The Intrusive Word*, 22.

5. Forde, *Theology is for Proclamation*, 42–44.

6. Ibid., 42. By "proclamation" Forde meant "explicit declaration of the good news, the gospel, the kerygma" (1).

7. Ibid., 42–43.

8. Ibid., 43.

9. Ibid., 43.

tance and new life through "cross" and "resurrection" in baptism. This shows the Christian life to be *intrinsically* life in the Spirit.

What I am calling for is a return to a view of the church's primary ministry of proclaiming the gospel of Jesus Christ in which the Spirit is active to work repentance and baptism, thereby giving the Spirit to transform unbelievers into believers.

A clear and concrete example of this kind of ministry may be seen in the preaching of the late David Wilkerson, a Pentecostal who became widely known through his preaching to street gangs in New York City beginning in the late 1950s.[10] Even though his later years led to an increasing marginalization from those who thought a more "respectable" or "popular" style of preaching was needed to reach "high-culture" Americans, Wilkerson stayed true to his convictions and consistent in his approach. He continued to preach Jesus Christ to all, from prostitutes to Wall Street bankers, founding Times Square Church in New York City to do so. Wilkerson's preaching was notable not only for its content but also for the form in which it evoked and required the Holy Spirit to work repentance and faith. His preaching drove hearers towards contrition and repentance because it announced the eschatological reign of Jesus Christ and judgment upon all unrighteousness—especially America's.[11]

One reason Wilkerson was marginalized was his conviction that salvation was not about a person "choosing" Christ but rather all about God choosing us through Christ. "God chose us. Our salvation—our *being chosen for Christ*— was done by the Lord."[12] Wilkerson's preaching relied on Christ's work, not in human ability. Preaching reveals the "vastness" of Christ that "swallows up" all of life's problems by knowing that "Christ is bigger than it all."[13] However, preaching Christ depends first upon the Spirit revealing Christ.

> To preach nothing but Christ we must have a continuous flow of revelation from the Holy Spirit. Otherwise, we will end up repeating a stale message. If the Holy Spirit knows the mind of God and searches the deep and hidden things of the Father, and if He is to well up as a flowing water within us, then we must

10. Wilkerson, *The Cross and the Switchblade*.

11. Wilkerson, *Racing toward Judgment*; *Set the Trumpet to Thy Mouth: Hosea 8:1*; *The Vision*.

12. Wilkerson, *Hungry for More of Jesus*, 98.

13. Ibid., 68.

be available to be filled with that flowing water. We must stay filled up with a never-ending revelation of Christ. Such revelation awaits every servant of the Lord who is willing to wait on Him, believing and trusting the Holy Spirit to manifest to him the mind of God.[14]

In contrast to this dependency on the Holy Spirit, Wilkerson was rightfully critical of those who preached only to bring glory to their own flesh and, in doing so, grieved the Holy Spirit.

How the Holy Spirit must grieve as He beholds pastors and evangelists today turning His ministry into a circus! The Spirit cannot bear the manipulations and fleshly showmanship, all done in His name. I have heard recently about phenomenal gimmicks that have been used to try to create a sense of His presence. How grievous that must be to God's heart! Moreover, it is blasphemy against the Spirit of God.[15]

The departure of ministers from depending on the Holy Spirit and trying to substitute the Spirit with human manipulation was, for Wilkerson, the result of preaching not calling for repentance.

Much Gospel preaching today contains no mention of the cross, no doctrine of suffering, no reproof, no repentance, no hatred for sin, no demand for separation or purity, no call for unconditional surrender to the Lordship of Christ, no daily death to self, no crucifixion of the fleshly lusts, no self-denial, no rejection of the self-life, no warnings of coming persecution and imminent judgment. And, most tragic of all, many Christians now prefer to hear about their rights in Christ—and ignore *His* claims on *us*![16]

Self-denial and repentance in a Christian's life was, for Wilkerson, not an option, because self-denial is what the Holy Spirit works; transforming and conforming a person to Jesus Christ's life.[17]

In his later years, Wilkerson articulated this self-denial aspect of salvation even more clearly as death to one's self. In *The New Covenant*

14. Ibid., 69.
15. Ibid., 102.
16. Ibid., 77; emphasis original.
17. Ibid., 132.

Unveiled, he describes the Christian life as death to even one's own faith in the flesh and receiving new life in Christ's faith.

> Death—it is the only way out of the Old Covenant and into the New. Flesh faith has to die. No more striving to believe. If I am to have faith—true faith, the faith of Christ—he has to give it to me. We have been given a measure of faith—yet if it's true that I can do nothing of myself, then this includes having his faith. That's why the scripture calls it "the faith of Christ."[18]

It is in this understanding of death that the meaning of the cross in the life of the Christian also is found. Wilkerson revealed how that, after years of preaching about the cross, he failed to understand the way of Jesus' cross as the true meaning of the Christian's life because, as he says, the Lord revealed to him, "You must experience the cross before you can understand it."[19] This led him to distinguish between God *working* the cross and only *knowing about* the cross. Most know about the cross, "but few have experienced and understood the real spiritual meaning of the crucifixion of Christ, let alone our personal cross, and what it means to die with Christ."[20] Self-denial is the work of the Holy Spirit, so learning in the "school of the Holy Spirit" brings us to the end of ourselves and makes us realize suffering is either God's judgment upon sin or it is God's purpose through which Christians "learn Christ" through "death" to one's self in repentance (Eph 4:20–21). Thus, Wilkerson thought suffering to be a good thing because through it the Spirit works the sufferings of Jesus Christ in us, "filling up" the sufferings of Christ, as Paul says in Col 1:24. However, suffering only makes sense in light of the resurrection, so that God's glory, *not ours*, might be revealed in us at Jesus' coming. "Those who have suffered and died holding strongly to their faith have received a true healing; it was Christ for them. Peter said they 'partake of Christ's sufferings, that when His glory is revealed, [they] may also be glad with exceeding joy' (1 Peter 4:13). Their faith, demonstrated here, will bring great honor to God *in glory*."[21]

The upshot of Wilkerson's preaching is that many times it fell on deaf ears, but he never wavered. He kept pointing faithful preachers and

18. Wilkerson, *The New Covenant Unveiled*, 54.

19. Ibid., 48.

20. Ibid., 49.

21. Wilkerson, *Hungry for More of Jesus*, 139–40; emphasis original.

Christians in the right direction, towards an account of the Christian life that makes Christ's life *one's own life*. Even though Wilkerson's preaching was lost on many in his later years, his preaching was nothing new among Pentecostals. It only sounded different in comparison to contemporary Pentecostal preaching, and that was only a measure of how far Pentecostalism in America had traveled away from repentance and baptism as the sign that God has adopted people as his sons. It was more typical of Pentecostal preaching of the early twentieth century that emphasized the Spirit's main purpose to be that of giving Christ's life so that the "fullness of the Spirit" was the result of being put into Christ's life through repentance from one's own life.

The realization that Pentecostalism, and many other church traditions, have developed faulty notions of the church and its ministries, especially preaching and baptism, calls for not only a reexamination of preaching in Acts but for the task of placing preaching within the context of the church's overall mission of making disciples from all nations.

The Ministry of the Church in Acts as Christ's Ecclesial Body in the Spirit

As Wilkerson's preaching shows, preaching Jesus Christ in the Spirit gives the life of Jesus Christ to its hearers. And as Willimon and Forde have reminded us, this requires the active presence of the Spirit for the message to not fall on deaf ears. We see this in Acts, where Luke describes the ministry of the church to be the proclamation of the gospel in which repentance, faith, baptism, and the Holy Spirit are always coordinated. Appropriating the church's model of ministry from Acts is essential for a post-Constantinian and Trinitarian understanding of the Christian life, for it establishes the paradigm for ministry in an unbelieving culture, which requires a miracle of transforming faith and not simply approving agreement. In Acts, the church ministered Christ in such a way that brought either belief or rejection. Today's post-Constantinian world requires the church to do no less.

The basic features of this paradigm for ministry are clearly present in Luke's account of Pentecost. Here, as I have just suggested, we find the proclamation of the gospel, repentance, faith, baptism and the gift of the Holy Spirit all present and coordinated. On the day of Pentecost onlookers ridiculed the effects of the Spirit's work and others were amazed and confused, saying, "What does this mean?" (Acts 2:12–13). Through Peter's proclamation concerning the life, death, resurrection, and exaltation of Jesus, the Spirit "cut to the heart" many who listened, causing them to cry out, "What shall we do?" (Acts 2:37). To this question, Peter answered, "Repent, and each of you be baptized in the name of Jesus Christ for the forgiveness of your sins; and you will receive the gift of the Holy Spirit. For the promise is for you and your children and all who are far off, as many as the Lord our God calls to Himself" (Acts 2:38–39).

Pentecost is not a one-day event. This same pattern is repeated in the narrative of Acts as the church carries out its mission. Following the Samaritans' baptisms, the Holy Spirit is poured out on them when Peter and John lay their hands on them to receive (Acts 8:14–17). The Holy Spirit is also poured out on all those in Cornelius's house as they are listening to Peter's sermon; they all speak in other languages and all are baptized (Acts 10:44–48). At Ephesus, Paul proclaims Jesus to them, they are baptized, they receive the Holy Spirit when Paul lays his hands on them, and they speak in other languages and prophecy (Acts 19:1–7). The coordination of these events reveals a pattern if not a consistent chronology: the Spirit is poured out when Jesus' lordship is proclaimed and people are baptized in Jesus' name. In Luke's account the Spirit is poured out through the proclamation of the gospel and baptism, working an intrinsic transformation that leads to a holistic life as a member in Christ's unified body. The church's ministry of preaching, through which the Spirit does these works has distinguishing features that are common throughout Acts, suggesting a specific manner in which the church ministers the gospel and baptizes believers into Christ's *ecclesia*.

Later in this chapter I will look in more detail at the features of this ministry, but first I want to draw out the features of the Spirit's work through the church's ministry according to Acts. Returning to the story about Pentecost, we find that Peter's command for them to repent and be baptized in order to receive the Holy Spirit shows proclamation of the gospel to be a holistic transformation of one's entire existence by people believing a scandal to be their salvation, the Spirit's work of *reversing* people's thinking. Peter's command also shows proclamation of the gospel to be *unifying* in that not only do all people have an equal opportunity to the transforming work of the Spirit but that all who do believe become one ecclesial fellowship of *koinonia* ("sharedness"), a clear and distinctive theme throughout Acts.

These two features of the Spirit's work in Acts, holistic transformation and unifying fellowship, work reciprocally together to give the church its ecclesial identity as God's new political, economic, and cultural community. They also supply meaning to proclamation, baptism, and the Lord's Supper as activities that convey and evoke the Spirit's presence by *giving* people Christ's life to be *their own*. Through these activities, the identity of Jesus Christ, known by the constitutive events in his life, becomes the believer's identity by the Spirit's transformation and unification into Christ's body. Luke's narrative in Acts reveals these aspects to be God's mission through the church's witness to Jesus Christ as Lord of all in the Spirit.

The Spirit Works Holistic Transformation through the Church's Ministry

Acts describes the church fulfilling God's mission of establishing his ecclesial community in Christ by the Spirit transforming unbelievers into a holistic existence of faith in God. In Luke's account, the Spirit is the divine agent who transforms sinners, taking them out of their ignorance, unbelief, and disobedience and putting them into Jesus' Trinitarian life of sonship with God the Father through the proclamation of the gospel and being baptized into Christ's life. The church's proclamation and baptizing of believers *are* the work of the Spirit in and through the community as the Lord adds to and strengthens his church as God's new political, economic, and social order that witnesses in and to the world of Christ's reign over all.

It should be stressed that Luke's account of the Christian life as Christ's life is holistic and unifying. The presence of the Holy Spirit makes Christians one people. In the one Spirit there is diversity: there are apostles, prophets, and teachers (Acts 1:15–26, 13:1–3), there are healings (Acts 5:12–16; 9:32–42; 28:8–9), miracles of deliverance (5:17–21; 16:25–40) and protection (27:39–8:6), speaking in tongues (2:4; 10:46; 19:6), and casting out of demons (5:16, 19:11). But this diversity serves one God the Father, sustains one confession ("Jesus is Lord"), moves along one Way, and builds up one people, the church. Acts itself provides no explicit reflection on this theme, but Paul does, and his teachings read as a commentary on the life of the church that Acts portrays by way of narrative. Since there is only one Spirit of God (Eph 4:4), the body of Christ receives its unity in the Spirit by already existing as one body as

Christ's new *ecclesia*. As one body, Christians are to live as they *already are*; as transformed by the Spirit in believing the gospel of Jesus Christ (Gal 3:2–3). As Paul says, "There is one body and one Spirit, just as also you were called in one hope of your calling; one Lord, one faith, one baptism, one God and Father of all who is over all and through all and in all" (Eph 4:4–6).

However, Christ's *ecclesia* does not always live out the unity in the Spirit that Jesus' life and death procured for his body. One example of this disunity is how various readings of Acts highlight only one view of the Spirit's work and neglect the others. How could this be Luke's intent when such modern dichotomies were unthinkable for him; such as the one between the Spirit's outpouring for prophetic speech or for the establishing of the church's mission, or the dichotomy between the outward working of miracles and the inner working of faith in Christ? The only dichotomy Luke narrates is the one between the Spirit of Christ and the spirits of this world that rule through its Caesars and the people who worship them.

In terms of the church's ministry, one significant dichotomy concerning the Spirit's work can arise when the Spirit's work is understood as sometimes prescriptive—to be expected for all times—and sometimes as descriptive—not to be expected in all times. This dichotomy and its significance are illustrated by an ongoing debate between Robert Menzies and Max Turner, a debate that was initiated by James Dunn in 1970.[22] While Menzies emphasizes the prophetic utterances of speech and other tongues as the sign of Spirit empowerment for witness,[23] Turner takes a middle approach that emphasizes the ethical conduct within the community following the Spirit's outpouring on the Day of Pentecost.[24] This ongoing debate is the result of disparate readings of Luke from within and from outside Pentecostalism.[25] Traditionally, Pentecostals have seen the first four verses of Acts 2 as prescriptive (for all times) while the last four verses of Acts 2 (2:44–47) are merely descriptive (only for the early church). On the other hand, many non-Pentecostals reverse this order by finding the last four verses prescriptive while holding that the first four verses are merely descriptive. This latter view sees the Spirit being poured

22. Dunn, *Baptism in the Holy Spirit*.

23. Menzies, *Empowered for Witness*.

24. Turner, *Power from on High*.

25. For a recent and concise summary of this debate, see Mittelstadt, *Reading Luke-Acts*, 46–63.

out on the church to fulfill its mission of uniting Jews and Gentiles into one fellowship, fulfilling Jesus' programmatic imperative to his disciples to be his witnesses to the ends of the earth (Acts 1:8), while the former sees the Spirit's empowerment as the impetus of bold proclamation and prophetic utterances. Can two disparate but legitimate readings both be right?

I have raised a vexing question, but I have no intention of trying to settle it here. I have brought it up merely as an important example of a dichotomous view of the Spirit's work in Acts. But I would suggest that, as much as Pentecostals believe that non-Pentecostals have overlooked the prophetic as normative for the church and Christians, it may be possible that Pentecostals have likewise overlooked a central truth of Luke's Pneumatology that has been right in front of them, namely, the Spirit's holistic and unifying work in and through Christ's *ecclesia* of God's adopted sons. Moreover and more importantly, the possibility itself opens up an opportunity to reflect on the Spirit's work as bringing about and enlivening the body of Christ, the church, and in this way to also see the Christian life in the world from an ecclesial (and not merely an individual) standpoint.

The Spirit Works Unity in Christ's One Body of Koinonia Fellowship

The Spirit's outpouring to establish Christ's unified body of fellowship always intrigued me growing up in a Pentecostal minister's home. Coming from humble beginnings themselves, my parents reached out to the socially despised, poor, handicapped, uneducated, and otherwise ostracized people in small towns in Kansas and Missouri. This resulted in scorn from those who thought such people should be ignored, or worse. In churches that emphasized the Holy Spirit transforming lives *and* giving spiritual gifts to believers, I often wondered which came first; the outpouring of the Spirit that unified quite diverse people or did the Spirit's unity result in fresh outpourings of the Spirit? Or, were both working reciprocally together? The years since have only increased my first inclinations; witnessing the Spirit transforming *and* imparting spiritual gifts as Christians gathered in unity and prayed in anticipation for Christ to be exalted, just as the Spirit was poured out anew on the believers in Acts; "when they had prayed, the place where they had gathered together was shaken, and they were all filled with the Holy Spirit and began to speak the word of God with boldness" (Acts 4:31). It is my belief that Pentecostals have largely neglected this unifying aspect of the Spirit in Luke, even though many have identified the unity that existed in Pentecostalism from the Azusa Street Revival in Los Angeles, but which was lost because it buckled to the pressure to conform to American culture rather than to the gospel.[26]

However, some Pentecostal scholars have begun to recognize this neglect within the movement. We find one important response in the recovery of a holistic reading of Luke by Roger Stronstad who began to see the need for a holistic account of the missiological emphasis of Luke's charismatic Pneumatology by pointing out the methodological fallacy that dichotomizes between didactic and historic narrative.[27] Stronstad shows Luke's account of the Spirit as both missiological and charismatic, God calling people to further Christ's mission, for which he transforms and equips his *ecclesial* fellowship with the Spirit to carry out.

> If Luke's record accurately reflects the teaching of Jesus about the purpose of the gift of the Holy Spirit, then the result of receiving the Spirit will be consistent with the purpose . . . Whether the Spirit is given to John as an unborn infant, to Jesus at the Jordan, to the disciples on the day of Pentecost, or to Saul in Damascus, the pattern is consistent: the gift of the Spirit always results in mission . . . Though we may look to Luke in vain for directives for the so-called normative Christian experience, we do encounter an invariable pattern for the gift of the Spirit in the unfolding record of the *inauguration and extension of the gospel*: the gift of the Spirit always precedes and effects mission or vocation.[28]

Even as Stronstad says the charismatic aspect of God's mission in Acts has been looked upon with suspicion by those who reduce the Spirit's work in Acts to strictly baptism/salvation or holiness/sanctification,[29] his account has also been seen, like Menzies, as too restrictive.[30]

Even so, Stronstad issued a challenge concerning this contemporary impasse over the doctrine of the Holy Spirit. "The charismatic charac-

---

26. Hunter and Robeck Jr., eds., *The Azusa Street Revival and its Legacy*; Robeck Jr., *The Azusa Street Mission and Revival*; Bartleman, *Azusa Street*; Hjalmeby, *A Rhetorical History*.

27. Stronstad, *The Charismatic Theology of St. Luke*, 2–9.

28. Ibid., 80; emphasis added.

29. Ibid., 83.

30. Penney, *The Missionary Emphasis of Lukan Pneumatology*, 28–35; Turner, *Power from on High*, 62–66.

ter of the Church makes it imperative that all traditions in the Church reassess their doctrine and experience of the Spirit in the light of Luke's charismatic theology."[31] Stronstad's challenge must include a reciprocal examination of the Pentecostal traditions regarding the gift of the Spirit upon the church through its preaching the gospel and in its administering of baptism. This does not need to nullify Luke's charismatic theology. Rather, as Stronstad mentions, these elements of salvation, sanctification, and service, each one being primary for the various Protestant traditions, are "interdependent and complementary."[32] Each must learn from the others if unity in the Spirit is not only the goal of the church but constitutes its very essence as the one body of Christ in one Spirit.

Even Pentecostal scholars recognize the very center of Luke's charismatic Pneumatology to be the fulfillment of the church's mission of bringing salvation to the nations; the eschatological fulfillment of God's promise to Israel by Christ pouring out his Spirit. Frank Macchia suggests the present reality of Spirit baptism *and* its continual eschatological unfolding, only completely fulfilled at the Eschaton, must be seen together in light of Lukan Pneumatology.

> [T]he experience of new life in faith, hope, and love in the context of the gospel, the sacraments, and the Pentecostal experience of prophetic consecration (with charismatic signs following) allows one to participate *already* in a Spirit baptism that is yet to come. It is *always present and coming*, emerging and encountering.[33]

This eschatological and ecclesiological dimension to the Spirit's work in Acts is also brought out by Matthias Wenk and John Michael Penney.[34] Wenk, following Max Turner, believes Luke's Pneumatology to be emphasizing the restoration of covenant Israel, not for kingship but for servanthood. This aspect of servanthood is seen in the sharp contrast of Acts 1:7 between the disciples' request for worldly power and Jesus' promise of the Spirit's power for them to be his witnesses to all nations.[35] The Holy Spirit coming upon them would make them "witnesses to the fact that God has

31. Stronstad, *The Charismatic Theology of St. Luke*, 83.

32. Ibid.

33. Macchia, *Baptized in the Spirit*, 87.

34. Penney, *The Missionary Emphasis of Lukan Pneumatology*, 64–77.

35. Wenk, *Community-Forming Power*, 240; see also Turner, *Power from on High*, 301.

given the promise and restored the kingdom (cf. Acts 3.18–26)."[36] This covenant restoration theme is inclusive of the entirety of Acts 2, bringing together 2:1–4 and 2:42–47 by way of a chiastic structure[37] that shows the latter to be a summary that ties together the disciples' unity (Acts 1:14 and 2:1) and Jesus' command to not leave Jerusalem, but to wait for the gift his Father had promised (1:4).[38] As Wenk suggests, "The summary [of 2:42–47] prevents the unity prior to Pentecost from being singled out as unique. . . . This underlines the normative character of the church's unity and sharing of possessions."[39] In this way, Wenk holds together what scholars have separated; the prophetic and the ethical.

> In the case of Acts 2.42–47, the individual experience is the Pentecostal event as part of Jesus' liberating work, defined in terms of a charismatic socio-ethical experience . . . The "particular Pentecostal experience" is generalized in Acts 2.42–43: Jesus' liberating and cleansing work, as encountered at Pentecost, generally leads to a community renewal in one way or another *and* to charismatic experiences (expressed by the reference to signs and miracles).[40]

Wenk applies his theory that Acts 2 is programmatic for the Spirit's work of unity to the later "crisis moments" in Acts when the church is threatened with disunity. This establishes a strong connection between ecclesiological unity and the Spirit's subsequent outpourings, especially upon the Samaritans. Wenk suggests, "Peter and John are the bonding element between Jerusalem and Samaria" that accounts for the delay between the Samaritans' conversions and their reception of the Holy Spirit (Acts 8) and, as such, shows how the "Spirit-manifestation not only testifies to but realizes the inclusion of the Samaritans into the renewed Israel; the Samaritans now have a share in Israel's salvation."[41]

Wenk's holistic account shows the Spirit's outpouring in Acts as forming a community existing in *koinonia* fellowship. This holistic account not only gives meaning to the prophetic for strengthening the

36. Wenk, *Community-Forming Power*, 241.

37. Classen, "To You is the Promise," 28–31; See also Wenk, *Community Forming Power*, 261.

38. Wenk, *Community-Forming Power*, 264.

39. Ibid., 264–65.

40. Ibid., 270; emphasis added.

41. Ibid., 293.

community, as Paul explains (1 Cor 12:4–11, 27–31), but it also accounts for the "clustering" or "complex" of the Spirit's activities of conversion, baptism, and reception of the Holy Spirit through and on account of the church's proclamation of Jesus Christ.[42] Luke's "clustering" of the events surrounding the Spirit's outpouring in Acts causes one to recognize the Spirit's reception in Acts to be transformative, holistic, and unifying at its core. As holistic, this life begins with repentance and baptism, which serves as one's initiation into the community of Jesus' followers much like it did for the Essenes, only probably more radical in that it applied to both Jews and Gentiles entering God's eschatological reign in Christ, showing Jews to also be sinners.[43] Craig Keener also believes Luke's view of baptism to be holistic in that it was administered "in Jesus' name," connoting initiation into a life of confessing Jesus' lordship over all other lords on account of his exaltation.[44] This foundational and primary work of the Spirit transforming unbelievers into believers through repentance and baptism is the basis for not only the prophetic but for the Spirit's presence in the church's Christ-given authority to *make disciples* of Jesus Christ from all nations (Matt 28:18–20). But if the Spirit-indwelt life is a transformed life, what is transformation?

The Spirit Works Unity through Holistic Transformation

Seeing Luke's emphasis on the Spirit's activity as holistic transformation elevates the church's proclamation and baptizing *in Jesus' name* to its essential calling of making disciples out of all the nations. This is already evident in Acts 2 where Jews from 15 regions, with their own languages, are unified into one fellowship by Christ sending his Spirit upon them (Acts 2:5–12). The Day of Pentecost marks the Spirit's "first fruits" of unifying disparate groups into one ecclesial fellowship in Christ. Peter's sermon captures this unification from Joel's prophecy; which is not about the Spirit being given merely to individuals, but that, in Christ, all individuals now exist as one ecclesial fellowship (Acts 2:16–21; Joel 2:28–32). This also happens when the Spirit is poured out on the Samaritans and on Cornelius's household just as he was upon the Galilean Jews in Jerusalem (Acts 8:14–17; 11:1–18; 15:8). Luke gives this more significance by de-

---

42. Ibid., 275–76; see also Turner, *Power from on High*, 352–78.

43. Keener, *Introduction*, 977.

44. Ibid., 982–84.

scribing the Jerusalem council which was called, ironically, to deal with the Jewish Christians' *confusion* caused by the Spirit's *unification* of such disparate people as Samaritans, eunuchs, and Pharisees into one fellowship with the Jewish disciples (Acts 8:14–17; 10:44–48; 15:1–32; see also Gal 2:11–16). Could it be that the Spirit's outpouring has more, or at least an equal amount, to do with God creating a new eschatological community of *koinonia* fellowship than with an *individual* power for witness?

There is no mistaking that Luke is more concerned about the purpose for which the Spirit is poured out upon the church to fulfill its mission than he is about the individuals who receive the Spirit. In fact, one could argue that the Spirit's work in Acts makes the individual people merely willing participants in God's mission of the church bringing salvation to the nations, a case that Tannehill makes following the model provided by Luke Timothy Johnson.[45] This is evident in how Luke arranges the material to emphasize that the Spirit's outpourings are for the church to carry out the advancement of the gospel of Jesus Christ into the Gentile regions: beginning at Jerusalem (the disciples at the Temple, Acts 2:1–4), Judea (those gathered for Pentecost who heard Peter and were baptized, Acts 2:41), Samaria (Acts 8), and to the uttermost parts of the earth, such as Ephesus (Acts 19) and finally to Rome itself (Acts 27–28). This was according to Jesus' prophecy that, in order to fulfill Scripture, "repentance for forgiveness of sins would be proclaimed in His name to all the nations, beginning from Jerusalem" (Luke 24:47) and that, after his disciples had received the Holy Spirit in Jerusalem, they would *be his witnesses* "both in Jerusalem, and in all Judea and Samaria, and even to the remotest part of the earth" (Acts 1:8).

This emphasis upon the Spirit being poured out on the church for it to take the gospel of salvation to the nations and baptize the nations in Jesus' name is also evident by how Luke emphasizes the holistic transformation that happens to people when they believe in the gospel, are baptized, and receive the Holy Spirit's indwelling than he is about the specific sequencing of events surrounding the Spirit's transformation. It should come as no surprise that Luke is unconcerned with modern issues in Lukan Pneumatology! We see this in his lack of precision in detailing the sequencing of the Spirit outpouring events. In Acts 2, the Spirit comes upon the disciples and they speak with other languages (2:1–4), those

---

45. Tannehill, *The Acts of the Apostles*, 32–33; Johnson, *Literary Function of Possessions*, 38–40.

who hear Peter's sermon repent, are baptized, receive the Spirit, and are included in the church (2:37–42). In Acts 8, the Samaritans believed on Christ, were baptized, but did not receive the Spirit until Peter and John came and began laying hands on them, praying that they would receive the Spirit (8:5–8, 12–17). In Acts 10, Cornelius's household all receive the Holy Spirit *while* Peter is proclaiming Jesus Christ to them and they begin speaking in other languages, then they are baptized in the name of Jesus (10:48). And, in Acts 19, those at Ephesus who believed in John's baptism were baptized in Jesus' name following Paul's instructions, then Paul laid his hands on them and they were filled with the Holy Spirit and spoke in other languages and prophesied (19:1–6).

What Luke is conveying in these episodes is not only the unity of Jews, Judeans, Samaritans, and Ephesians, but a transformation by the Spirit's reception that is the impetus for this reconciliation between such disparate people; making one fellowship of adopted sons of God by faith, whose ancestry is traced back not only to Abraham but to God himself (Luke 3:34, 38). This brings us to examine a question various Lukan Pneumatologies have neglected in their attempt to establish a theology of the Third Article, "How is one transformed by the Spirit to be an adopted son of God in Christ's ecclesial fellowship?" Whether one believes the Spirit's reception is for the ethical or the prophetic should not hinder one from recognizing the church's primary ministry in Acts to be that of preaching the gospel and baptizing new believers into Jesus' name. In Acts, the constitutive events in Jesus' life that we saw in Luke are not only the content of belief in Christ but they become the form by which the Spirit adopts other sons of God.

The major obstacle to seeing Luke's Pneumatology as holistic and unifying is that the work of faith and the gift of the Spirit are seen as distinct, as if faith were possible without the Spirit or as if faith operated like a "substance" all to itself, apart from God or the human recipient. The Spirit of God works faith in God, which manifests itself in repentance, baptism, and living lives of faithfulness as adopted sons of God. This is most clearly seen in Peter, Paul, and Barnabas's address to the Jerusalem council concerning God's acceptance of the Gentiles by giving them the Spirit, which Peter says was the result of them believing the gospel and by God accepting them just as he had the Jewish believers. In God's sight, these people were just like the Jews and so, when they believed, God made their hearts pure (Acts 15:8–9). As F. D. Bruner said, this text shows God to be the subject and humans to be the recipients of salvation.

> The giving, the cleansing, the faith are all described as his work. This must come as a relief to those who discover it and who learn that God does not demand their accomplishment of these momentous realities before he will give himself, but that, typical of grace, God gives himself by giving these realities.[46]

The realization that God works transformation of unbelievers into believers through the proclamation of the gospel that engenders faith in the gospel (Acts 2:37–42; 10:44–48; 15:7–9) shows the Spirit being given by Christ to reproduce his life, death, and resurrection in others as adopted sons of God. Therefore the constitutive events of Jesus' life become the activities through which his Spirit works both initial faith and continual faith. Jesus' baptism, preaching, miracles, offering forgiveness of sins, his conduct, and his death on a cross become the very activities which the Spirit works in others through God adopting them as his sons. Furthermore, these activities become the primary ministries of the church as Christ's ecclesial body as the Spirit's new temple. The Spirit's presence in and through the church's preaching, its baptizing, and its partaking of the Lord's Supper all work faith by their being signs of Christ's work of reconciling estranged humanity back to the Father as his sons. Not only are they works of Christ and his Spirit of faith, they evoke faith by requiring faith. As Wilkerson explained, they are the Spirit's work that "kills" one's own flesh faith and "raises" one up by giving Christ's faith. Now we must turn our attention to how faith is given by the Spirit being present in the church's preaching of Christ and in baptizing new believers into one fellowship of Christ. This will provide a basis for describing the shape and direction of the Christian life as life in the Spirit, the subject of the next chapter.

Preaching Jesus' Cross and Resurrection Gives the Spirit

Now that we have traced out the work of the Spirit as bringing and sustaining the Christian life, especially as portrayed in Acts, we are in a position to answer more concretely the question of the chapter: "How is the Spirit-filled life actually attained?" As I have already acknowledged, the answer

---

46. Bruner, *A Theology of the Holy Spirit*, 201.

here will be in line with the catholic answer: "Through the ministry of the Church, the body of Christ." But given what we have noted about the state of the ministry of the church today, reimaging this ministry is in order.

In Acts, Luke shows that preaching is the *initial* activity of the church's ministry. In other words, according to Luke's account of the early church, the ministry of the church begins with preaching the Gospel of Jesus as Christ and Lord. Preaching precedes repentance, baptism, faith, and the gift of the Holy Spirit on Pentecost, just as it does for the Ethiopian eunuch (Acts 8) and with Cornelius and his house (Acts 10). To be sure, preaching the Gospel does not always result in repentance, as it did with Peter and John before the Sanhedrin (Acts 4) or Paul on the Areopagus (Acts 17). But it is the *initial* activity in the church's ministry. It comes first in the ministry of the church because it is the message that sets forth the situation for hearers; in common parlance, it "establishes the context," or "tells people how things really are." Moreover, because it conveys that "Jesus is Lord" and indicates the coming of God's judgment and salvation, preaching puts hearers into a critical situation. Preaching puts hearers "on the spot," as it were, leaving them with this choice: either of turning from themselves, their idols, their own conceptions of life and security, and turning towards God, seeking his grace, or turning away from this God in continued unbelief. On Pentecost, thousands heard this message, repented, and sought forgiveness and the Spirit in the waters of baptism (Acts 2), but not long after that, the rulers of the Jewish people heard the same message and turned away from Jesus (Acts 4). It was the same with Stephen and the Jews, Philip and the Ethiopian eunuch, Peter and Cornelius, and Paul on Mars Hill: each time they are engaged they begin by preaching. Sometimes there is repentance, faith, baptism, and the gift of the Spirit and at other times there is rejection and unbelief, but in all cases first comes preaching.

But what does it mean to have "faithful preaching" and to be "faithful preachers"? As we have already observed, at the very least there is no general consensus over the answers and so it is necessary to work out some answers.

Preaching Christ Faithfully Requires the Holy Spirit to Work Faith

As the previous section brought out, the ministry of the church that gives the Holy Spirit begins with the Holy Spirit in the ministers and their preaching. So, specifically in terms of preaching, "preaching Christ" should be understood as "preaching in the Spirit." From Acts we have already developed an account of the church that preaches, an account that might be called a "pneumatological ecclesiology." But just as the ministry of the church calls for those who preach *in the Spirit*, it also calls for those who preach *in expectation of the Spirit*. Willimon on this point is worth repeating: "We must learn to preach again in such a way as to demonstrate that, if there is no Holy Spirit, if Jesus has not been raised from the dead, then our preaching is doomed to fall upon deaf ears."[47]

Willimon's claim could be easily construed as a conclusion drawn from Acts, for this is exactly how they preached. The sermons in Acts show how necessary Jesus' resurrection was by showing it to be God's vindication of the identity and mission of Jesus Christ as his Son. Paul's sermon at Athens in Acts 17 is one example, where he takes what the Athenians know about religion, especially their "knowledge" of an unknown god, and turns it on its head by describing the *man* Jesus as God's final judge of the world and that he proved it by raising him from the dead. Therefore, Jesus and his resurrection do not affirm their lives or their false gods, but demand repentance *from them*. Paul condemns the Athenians' religious desires as idolatrous by showing their gods to be human fabrications.[48] If religious desire must be repented of then it can certainly not provide a footing upon which one can agree with Jesus' life, death, and certainly not his resurrection.

Today however, one can readily find preaching that does not depend on the Holy Spirit and, as a result, only asks people to agree with the gospel, an "adding on" of Christ to their own narratives as merely a fulfillment of their religious desires. This was the kind of message that David Wilkerson criticized and opposed, but it continues to be touted. For example, the popular pastor and author Rick Warren does this in his best-selling book *The Purpose Driven Life*. Warren espouses Christianity to be the best of what people naturally desire, based on humanity's fall

---

47. Willimon, *The Intrusive Word*, 22.

48. This called for their repentance of all they had known and worshipped prior (17:30–31), causing three responses: scornful laughter, interest, or belief (17:32–33). It is noteworthy that Paul's discussion of Jesus and the resurrection did not condemn their polytheism directly, however (17:18), since their gods could include other gods yet to be discovered. Jesus and the resurrection could be simply two more gods added to their pantheon of gods. What took a miracle for them to believe was that God resurrected a crucified man, Jesus, from the dead and glorified him in heaven as future judge of the world, a belief which condemned their prior gods as false (Acts 17:31).

into sin as a *partial loss* of God's image and likeness. He says "all people, not just believers, possess part of the image of God; that is why murder and abortion are wrong."[49] This is most confusing since he asserts that other religions and New Age philosophies promise the lie that either we are or can become gods, but then goes on to use Satan's promise to Adam and Eve that they would be like God (Gen 3:5) to explain these false claims of other religions. However, in doing so, Warren also applies it to Christians. "This desire to be a god shows up every time we try to control our circumstances, our future, and people around us."[50] But if this is true, did not God's curse at Eden instill a *permanent desire* to be like God in all people? If so, the remedy is *not* a desire to be like God but the desire to let God *alone* be God. Warren adds more confusion by using a paraphrased version of Ephesians 4:24, saying, "The Bible says, '*You were . . . created to be like God, truly righteous and holy.*'"[51] This is the exact opposite of how the Greek reads, which is more accurately translated, "and put on the new self, which in the likeness of God has been created in righteousness and holiness of the truth."[52] Here, as well as Col 3:10, Paul is talking about the Christian continually *putting on Christ's life* (Col 1:15), *not becoming* like God in one's nature but putting on Christ's person to *replace* one's sinful nature, one's former self.

This message reflects *extrinsicism,* that is, it shows that an underlying conviction in Warren's theology is that Christ and his Spirit are "added on" to a person's life. This explains why repentance appears very little in his account of the Christian life, and when it does, it amounts only to changing "the way you think by *adopting* how God thinks—about yourself, sin, God, other people, life, your future, and everything else."[53] If all repentance entails is *adopting* God's ways of thinking onto how one already thinks then one need not deal with *how* Jesus lived and died as the

49. Warren, *The Purpose Driven Life*, 172.

50. Ibid.

51. Ibid. Warren takes this verse from God's Word Translation.

52. Ibid., 175. Warren uses for Ephesians 4:24 here the New International Version. However, even though this is more accurate with the Greek, he uses it in a context of becoming, in our inner character, like Christ "by developing new, godly habits. Your character is essentially the sum of your habits; it is how you *habitually* act" (emphasis original). Elsewhere, Warren explicitly states, "God has done the work of *changing my nature*. Now I need to cooperate with His efforts and work at letting His goodness fill me." Warren, *The Power to Change Your Life*, 94; emphasis added.

53. Warren, *The Purpose Driven Life*, 182; emphasis added.

Son of God. This keeps the person as the subject with God as the "object" that human reason only needs to "adopt," a view opposite of God adopting people as his object of salvation. For a Christian to remain the subject of their own life does not take a miracle. Anyone can believe "the purpose of your life is *far greater* than your own personal fulfillment . . . or even your wildest ambitions."[54] Moreover, that seems to be exactly the point, a belief that is only *greater than* what one is capable of believing with one's own natural and rational abilities.

What does take a miracle is repenting of the *desire to have a purpose* in life and taking on Christ's life as one's purpose (Rom 8:28–29). This means that repenting by one's acceptance or agreement is a contradiction. Repentance is turning away from that which one already agrees. This is why Paul calls the gospel foolishness to the Greeks and a stumbling block to the Jews (1 Cor 1:18–25). Neither Jew nor Greek has a narrative into which the gospel fits for agreement to be possible. Repentance is the Spirit's work within a person renouncing and denying one's self and its desires. Willimon explains this central aspect of the gospel as a peculiar experience.

> The gospel is not a set of interesting ideas about which we are supposed to make up our minds. The gospel is intrusive news that evokes a new set of practices, a complex of habits, a way of living in the world, discipleship. Because of its epistemological uniqueness, we cannot merely map the gospel onto our present experiences. The gospel is not an archaic, peculiar way of naming our typical human experiences through certain religious expressions. The gospel means to engender, to evoke, a peculiar experience that we would not have had before we met the gospel.[55]

According to Willimon, preaching that does not engender discipleship is a result of a kind of atheism running through it that renders God unnecessary. It is Willimon's belief that the atheism lurking behind much preaching today "is the conviction that the presence and power of God are unessential to the work of ministry, that we can find the right technique, the proper approach, and the appropriate attitude and therefore will not need God to validate our ministry."[56] This preaching is "success-

---

54. Ibid., 17; emphasis added.

55. Willimon, *The Intrusive Word*, 39.

56. Ibid., 22.

ful" because it does no more than validate the lives of many Christians who live as "practical atheists" who go about their daily lives as if God does not exist.[57]

The sermons in Acts show preaching the gospel as framing the world by Jesus and his resurrection (conceptually rather than merely chronologically). Therefore, it begins with Jesus' death and resurrection as "God's grain of the universe" that requires the same miracle of the Spirit to believe as it did for the Spirit to raise Jesus from the dead.[58] Preaching the gospel requires a certain form for the Spirit to "raise the dead," a miracle of belief, as Willimon explains.

> Easter is an embarrassment the church can't get around. Yet in this embarrassment is the engine that drives our preaching. It is only because Jesus has been raised from the dead that I have the confidence in preaching. It is only on the basis of the risen Christ's return to his disheartened followers after Easter that I presume that he has made me an agent of gospel subversion through preaching. . . .
>
> I don't preach Jesus' story in light of my experience, as some sort of helpful symbol or myth that is usefully illuminated by my story. Rather, I am invited by Easter to interpret my story in the light of God's triumph in the resurrection.[59]

As we have already seen in Paul's sermon at Athens, this dependence on the Spirit to work a miracle of belief in Jesus Christ is also evident in Peter's sermon at Pentecost in Acts 2. Peter says that on account of Jesus' death, resurrection, and ascension, all history is reinterpreted. Now are the "last days" marked by the Spirit "poured out on all flesh" (Acts 2:17) by the risen and exalted Christ who received the Spirit from the Father to pour it out on others (2:33). Peter gives the reason for why Jesus has poured out his Spirit upon all peoples to be the verification that salva-

---

57. Gay, *The Way of the (Modern) World*, 9–28.

58. This presupposes that all people are already living in death. Paul makes clear in Romans 8 that the human sinful self of the flesh is already living in death but that the Spirit of God is life in the resurrection of Jesus Christ (8:1–17). However, there is no life without death, no resurrection without a cross, which is the realization that one is already as good as dead, requiring death to the sinful self which mistakenly thinks one's life of dying is true living. True living only begins when one's self is "drowned" by sharing in Christ's death in baptism (Rom 6:3–4).

59. Willimon, *The Intrusive Word*, 25.

tion has been uniquely given in the scandal of Jesus Christ's death and resurrection.[60]

The Spirit's presence working belief in the hearers renders Jesus' death and resurrection no longer a scandal as it is for those who refuse to believe.[61] For those who do believe, they are salvation in not only *what* one believes but in *how* one believes, being attested to by the Spirit as the inner witness to the veracity of its truth (Rom 8:18).[62] As Marion Soards points out, in the same fashion that these events of the Holy Spirit being poured out (all of them speaking praises to God in unknown languages, 2:6, 11) "demonstrates the reality of Jesus' resurrection and exaltation, so this psalm text [Ps 110:1 in 2:34–35] documents the truth of Peter's claim that God raised Jesus and exalted him."[63] The Spirit's outpouring at Pentecost, and at the other subsequent times in Acts, not only supplies the inner activity for the outward signs ("as the Spirit was giving the utterance" Acts 2:4), but are given as veracity to Jesus' death, resurrection, and exaltation.

60. Soards, *Speeches in Acts*, 36. "The idea of resurrection is expanded in these verses [2:32–33] by the introduction of the idea of God's exalting Jesus . . . Here Peter declares (A) that Jesus is exalted at the right hand of God, (B) that he received the Holy Spirit from God, (C) that from his exalted position and in possession of the Spirit he bestowed the Spirit on the disciples, and (D) that the marvelous events transpiring before the crowd are now evidence to them of Jesus' resurrection, exaltation, and bestowal of the Spirit. The 'evidence' of the veracity of this argument is the Holy Spirit. In several speeches one observes the tendency to understand the Holy Spirit as the ultimate 'evidence' or 'witness' to God's will and work (2:33; 5:32; 7:51 [?]; 11:15–17; 15:8; 20:23 [?]; 21:11)."

61. This realization shifts the focus of repentance and faith off the individual's desire for forgiveness due to forgiveness (release from sins) *being what God does* within a person based on their belief that God has done his definitive work of judgment and redemption of the world through his Son Jesus' death and resurrection. Because of Jesus' resurrection, these "last days" are days of repentance. Therefore, in "this present age" the Spirit works repentance through the proclamation of the scandal of Jesus' death and resurrection (1 Cor 1:18, 20–23, 27–28) to change his death on a cross from a scandal into the very power of God's salvation through one's faith in it (Rom 1:16:17; 1 Cor 1:18, 21, 24). This change can only be affected within a person by the Spirit revealing its truth through the proclamation of it, not only its content but in its form taking on and doing the same "death" and "resurrection" in its hearers that the Spirit did in Jesus (1 Cor 1:10–14).

62. This shows not only the content of salvation to be Trinitarian, as we discovered in the previous chapter concerning Jesus' life, but it shows *how* one believes to be also Trinitarian in that the Holy Spirit is the very "witness" given to the hearers of the gospel as to Jesus' death and resurrection being God's plan for the world's redemption.

63. Soards, *Speeches in Acts*, 36.

Paul's sermon at Antioch in Acts 13 makes this idea most explicit when, by citing Ps 2:7, Isa 55:3, and Ps 15:10, he shows God's promises to Israel now making sense by Jesus' resurrection from the grave to no longer see corruption. Soards explains how "Paul's speech frames these texts in the context of the story of Jesus, especially in relation to his resurrection."[64] With the coming of the Spirit who, in himself, is the veracity of Jesus' cross as the "fracture" of human understanding, God's resurrection of Jesus can no longer be seen as validated by the Old Testament prophecies but, in the greatest reversal of all human interpretation, is itself God's interpretation of the protological, as Soards explains.

> The logic of this section is to demonstrate the truth of christological claims by arguing that one finds God's promises fulfilled in Jesus and one knows this by viewing God's actions in relation to Old Testament texts. The idea of divine promise and fulfillment is itself an interpretation of Jesus' resurrection . . . The use of the Old Testament in this context is not along the lines of prophecy-fulfillment or a proof-from-prophecy scheme; rather the texts serve as explanation of the veracity of the promise-fulfillment interpretation of Jesus' resurrection.[65]

Here we see one of the best explanations of how the Spirit works through the proclamation of the gospel of Jesus' death and resurrection to work faith in not only what one is to believe as their salvation but in *how one believes it by faith*. It is only God's resurrection Spirit that validates the veracity of the gospel message as truth. Hence, there is no "foundation" for the gospel to rest upon besides its own proclamation.

The Spirit serving as the veracity to the gospel is evident by how Luke weaves together the form and content of the sermons in Acts. For Luke, the Spirit is the consistency between Jesus and the constitutive events of his life being given to others for their salvation. Soards has helpfully identified this inner consistency in Acts by showing the connections Luke makes between the content of the message preached and the form by which it is preached, what he calls Luke's narrative intention of the preaching achieving the unity it seeks.[66]

---

64. Ibid., 86.
65. Ibid., 86n225.
66. Ibid., 11–16.

The speeches in Acts are more than a literary device, or a historiographic convention, or a theological vehicle—though they are all of these; they achieve the unification of the otherwise diverse and incoherent elements comprised by Acts. Through the regular introduction of formally repetitive speeches, Luke unified his narrative; and, more important, he unified the image of an otherwise personally, ethnically, and geographically diverse early Christianity. This is no mean feat: Luke crafted from events and words a history that was coherent and, moreover, ideologically pointed—a tradition it repeated and thereby deliberately advancing its causes.[67]

Soards confirms our earlier thinking about Luke's holistic Pneumatology. The form and content of the gospel work reciprocally together to enact the constitutive events of Jesus' life in others, adopting them as sons by the Spirit working "death" and "resurrection" in those who hear.

The Spirit Acts in Preaching Done in Christ's Authority to "Kill" and "Make Alive"

In this section I am offering some answers to the question "What is preaching?" that will help the contemporary church to understand and conduct the preaching ministry in ways that will foster rather than hinder the giving of the Spirit and the making of "other sons" of God who lead faithful lives in the power of the Spirit. This goal implies that an important way to answer the question is to show *what preaching does*.

The same power and authority that Christ received from his Father he gave to his apostles, the authority to preach repentance, make disciples by baptizing, and by teaching them all he had commanded (Matt 28:18–20; Luke 24:46–49). In Christ's authority, the apostles preach with boldness due to the Spirit's outpouring at Pentecost. Preaching and acting in Jesus' authority provides the crucial link between Jesus' life in the Spirit, his giving the Spirit to his disciples, and how the church's gives Christ and his Spirit in and through its ministries.

As Sánchez suggests, connecting Jesus as receiver and bearer of the Spirit to the exalted Christ giving his Spirit to others leads to proclamation, exemplified in Acts. In contrast to views that identify the Spirit as "religious desire" in all people, Sánchez's Spirit-Christology helps us see the Spirit as the unrepeatable indwelling presence in Jesus' life as identi-

---

67. Ibid., 12.

fied by the constitutive events in his life.[68] Jesus as bearer of the Spirit shows Jesus' mission to be *discontinuous* with sinners, that is, Jesus *against us* works death to the old self, while Jesus *for us* brings about a rising or resurrection into a new identity as sons of God, a new life by the presence of the same Spirit who dwells in Jesus Christ. This account sees Jesus anointed by the Spirit at his baptism to carry out the Father's *mission of fulfilling all righteousness* (Matt 3:13–15; see also 8:16–17; Luke 3:22; 4:18–19; Acts 10:38), righteousness *for us* that brings death to the sinful persons we are and life in God's freedom in Christ's own righteousness. By Christ's authority in the Spirit, the preacher not only preaches about Christ, but "does" Christ's life to the hearers by speaking God's judgment upon and forgiveness of sin.

This explanation of preaching as speaking for God in the authority Christ gave the church has been the legacy of Gerhard Forde. The preacher of the gospel, according to Forde, not only explains the word of God, he *does* the word of God by the authority Christ gave his church.

> The proclaimer must so announce the forgiveness to those gathered here and now as to amaze them by the audacity of it all. Perhaps they will even glorify God once again. The proclaimer must, on the authority of Jesus, have the guts to do again in the living present what was done once upon a time . . . to do the deed authorized, not merely explain the deeds of the past . . . The deed is to be done.[69]

This "doing of the deed" changes proclamation from merely the preacher's own words into the words of God in the Spirit. Likewise, preaching

---

68. Sánchez M., *Receiver, Bearer, and Giver of God's Spirit*, 189. "Although Jesus is like one of us, we cannot forget that he is also 'without sin' (Heb 4:15). The Holy Spirit makes the child in Mary's womb 'holy' and the incarnate 'Son of God' from conception (Luke 1:35). This unrepeatable indwelling of the Spirit in Jesus surpasses God's presence in humans not merely in degree but *in nature*. The Son's incarnation by the Spirit of God stands as the historical side of the eternal Son's unique hypostatic or personal openness to the Father in the same Spirit. It is not merely the culmination in history of the Spirit's general work in creation whereby all human creatures are given a partial disposition or affinity towards God. Theologians of the cross acknowledge that since Eden they have lost all inclination to live in the Spirit and thus according to God's will. . . . Jesus' unique reception of he Spirit of God from conception allows for the fulfillment of the Father's original plan for his creatures frustrated by their rebellion, for it serves as the unparalleled condition for the Holy Spirit's gracious indwelling of the saints as gift from the Father through his anointed, crucified, and risen Son" (emphasis added).

69. Forde, *Theology is for Proclamation*, 157.

that "does the deed" takes the responsibility for making disciples off the preacher and onto the Spirit, which explains Paul's reason why it needs no human eloquence to support it (1 Cor 1:18–2:5).

Forde's description of preaching is in stark contrast to much preaching today that is non-authoritative in an effort to appease the autonomous individual. Fred B. Craddock has been most influential in this kind of preaching. In *As One without Authority*, Craddock regards preaching as an inductive narrative in dialogue with the audience that affirms rather than exhorts.[70] Craddock did see the demise of Christendom as a turning point for the church, but he only moved preaching closer into alliance with American culture by advocating that it begin with human experience since the "inductive process is fundamental to the American way of life."[71]

Essential to Craddock's method are the lived experiences of preacher and audience. The "everydayness" of life's experiences are prioritized by an existentialism that places greater weight on life as a journey than on the gospel as truth. Craddock says truth of the sermon and hearer are equally important,[72] but he preferences the hearer's existential moment of decision over the gospel itself. He says, "It is, therefore, pointless to speak of the Gospel as Truth in and of itself; the Gospel is *Truth for us*."[73] This affirms the individual choosing their own destiny, even if a wrong one.[74] However, as Willimon says, Craddock's choosing individual elevates one's *own* freedom. Craddock's freedom "is not freedom to choose or reject Christ, or the freedom of all the baptized to wrestle together over the implications of the gospel. Freedom, in *As One without Authority*, is freedom of the individual, apart from Scripture or community, to draw his or her own democratic conclusions."[75]

---

70. Craddock, *As One without Authority*, 58.

71. Ibid. Craddock identifies authoritative preaching with Christendom, which allowed for the deductive method (from the general truth to the particular) of preaching due to authority given to the church and its preachers by the surrounding society. As such, authoritative preaching could only prevail as long as Christendom prevailed.

72. Ibid., 70. In an attempt to overcome the artificial dichotomy between objective and subjective, Craddock appeals to Buber, Heidegger, and Sartre to conclude that "at least two persons are essential to the transaction [of a word], and neither is secondary."

73. Ibid., 70–71; emphasis original.

74. Ibid., 73–74.

75. Willimon, *Peculiar Speech*, 48–49.

This elevation of human freedom is rooted in Craddock's belief that each person "is equipped with a set of senses with which he experiences the world about him, and [the preacher] addressing those senses will *awaken that experience* anew."[76] Craddock's non-authoritarian method of preaching is at least consistently non-authoritarian by leaving both the content and method of preaching open-ended for preacher and hearer alike to decide how to appropriate their own aesthetic experiences as they so choose.[77] This approach allows the hearer of sermons and the reader of Scripture to remain an "objective interpreter." For Craddock, "most of the New Testament can be viewed as interpretations and reinterpretations of the tradition . . ."[78] Even many of Jesus' sayings "are better understood as conclusions about Christ reached by disciples than his assertions about himself."[79] This allows Scripture to remain a text from which meaning is to be "exegeted" rather than the avenue through which God "reads us," keeping God at a safe distance from infringing on human freedom.

Missing from Craddock's approach is the preacher standing in for God to "do the text" to the hearers in Christ's authority. Sánchez has pointed out just how difficult is for modern Westerners to understand the difference this performative function of the Word makes for preaching Jesus' cross.[80] This is due to, as Willimon says, Westerners, but especially Americans, being "people whose story is the claim that they are individuals who have not been formed by a story,"[81] which has, ironically, become its own story. The "American story" promises freedom but only binds us tighter to "the authoritarianism of liberal democratic societies which destroys human community by fragmenting us into a herd of isolated

---

76. Craddock, *As One without Authority*, 93; emphasis added.

77. Ibid., 69–73.

78. Ibid., 120–21.

79. Ibid., 94.

80. Sánchez, *Receiver, Bearer, and Giver of God's Spirit*, 183–84. "The written word informs about the past, the spoken word transforms in the present. Yet this insight seems difficult enough to get through the mind of an educated middle-class Westerner. . . . For Luther, both the written and spoken forms of the word are ultimately authoritative because through them the Spirit points to Jesus Christ, the enfleshed Word; but the reformer also teaches that the written word exists for the sake of the spoken one. How difficult it is for the children of modernity to recall the words of Paul: 'So faith comes from what is heard' (Rom 10:17)."

81. Willimon, *Peculiar Speech*, 52. See also Hauerwas, *Wilderness Wanderings*, 26.

units."[82] Thus, the need for the Spirit to transform the individual in order to hear the story of Jesus does not "fit into" the story of the autonomous individual. "Any suggestion that in order to even begin understanding the sermon would require transformation of our lives, particularly our economic and political habits, is considered *unthinkable*."[83] This is why Craddock's approach is so compelling; it makes Scripture fit into the ideals of Western democratic culture so that any infringement upon the individual's "right to choose" is itself seen as "heretical" since the autonomous choosing individual is culturally "orthodox." Peter Berger described this phenomenon of Western culture as the "heretical imperative," being "condemned to freedom" by which one must "take a choice" (*hairesis*) even in regards to religious preference.[84] In contrast to Craddock's method, Scripture's narrative shows us the Spirit's work of *making a community* of God's people shaped by the story of Jesus.

The church as the community shaped by the story of Jesus serves as the basis for Gerhard Forde's description of preaching as the minister "doing Jesus" to the hearers in place of God. Since "Jesus Christ incarnate is what the Father and Holy Spirit have been after throughout history" and since the "law ends when Christ arrives, in his person no less,"[85] the person of Jesus Christ is what God is still doing in the world today through preaching. Without the Spirit of Christ no one can understand that what God is up to in the world is exactly the life of Christ, especially his dying at the behest of his Father God. Therefore, the preacher's responsibility is not to find a "meaning" in the text and then "apply" it," the preacher is to use the text to show what God is up to today through his Son Jesus, asking, "*How does it work* and *what does it do?*"

> Doing the text, furthermore, involves paying attention to the text in a quite specific manner: looking to see what the text actually *did* and is supposed to do, and therefore what it authorizes

82. Willimon, *Peculiar Speech*, 52.

83. Willimon and Hauerwas, *Preaching to Strangers*, 9; emphasis added.

84. Berger, *The Heretical Imperative*, 30–31. "Modernity multiplies choice and concomitantly reduces the scope of what is experienced as destiny. In the matter of religion, as indeed in other areas of human life and thought, this means that the modern individual is faced not just with the opportunity but with the necessity to make choices as to his beliefs. This fact constitutes the heretical imperative in the contemporary situation. Thus heresy, once the occupation of marginal and eccentric types, has become a much more general condition; indeed, heresy has become universalized."

85. Mattes and Paulson, Introduction to Forde, *The Preached God*, 10–11.

you to do. One must see what it did and then re-aim it to do the same thing in the present to the assembled hearers. Usually the text gives you the clues. The text usually involves highly charged dramatic situations in which the Word of God is cutting into people's lives. It will tell you they were amazed, shocked, incensed, or even took up stones to kill, or marveled, or glorified God, and so on. Jesus got killed for saying those things. Doing the text again should provide a rather interesting agenda![86]

Seeing the text as "God cutting into people's lives" or that "preaching of the law is the use of the text to cut in upon and slay old beings"[87] is a hermeneutic that rightfully sees God as God and humans as humans, a theology "from below" that sees humans cursed by God in a constant state of rebellion whereby we desire to be God, what Forde terms an "upward fall."[88]

Forde's parallel concept of a theology of the cross helps us understand preaching as that which implicates all people in Jesus' death. Jesus' death on a cross is not only *what* to believe, the cross is *how* God works belief in people.[89]

> The move to doing the Word in that fashion involves the recognition that the proclamation must be a Word of the cross. That does not mean only that there is lots of talk about the cross. The point is that the proclamation itself ought to bear the form of the Word of the cross. It is to do the cross to the hearers. The proclamation is to kill and make alive. It purposes to make an end and a new beginning. What makes proclamation the Word of the cross is not the fact that the cross is always the direct subject or the only subject of the address, but that the words themselves have the *form* of the cross, presuppose it, drive inexorably to it, and flow from it. To be a Word of the cross, the proclamation must cut in upon our lives to end the old and begin the new.[90]

86. Forde, *The Preached God*, 94; emphasis original.

87. Forde, *Theology Is for Proclamation*, 154.

88. Ibid., 48–49.

89. Sánchez M., *Receiver, Bearer, and Giver of God's Spirit*, 184. Conversely, theologians of glory are those who "see themselves as sinners who have fallen to some degree from God's scale of perfection," but in tending "to focus on their *partially lost* goodness and innate freedom to receive God's favor, they will not hear Jesus' story if that implies their *complicity in his death* and their irreversible rejection of God's mercy through him" (emphasis added).

90. Forde, *Theology is for Proclamation*, 157; emphasis original.

Proclamation is ultimately God's word to us that declares us sinners in need of repentance and faith but which also, by the Spirit's work of repentance and faith, declares us released from sin.

The Spirit Acts in Preaching That Is Tragic to the Individual

Many have traced the progression in Western culture of the autonomous individual without describing its most deceptive aspects; its *unquestionable presuppositions* of democracy and capitalism that prohibit its critique from Scripture.[91] With little or no critique, nationalistic pride and economic prosperity go unchecked as simply "God's blessings" on the nationalistic aspirations of the collective whole or on the economic aspirations of the individual. For many Christians, the control these narratives wield over their lives are as invisible as they are powerful, eclipsing their ability to see the constitutive events of Jesus' life in the Spirit as their own.[92]

These competing narratives of "freedom," the most notable being American culture, calls for a re-assessment of what Christian preaching is if it claims to offer true freedom in Jesus Christ rather than simply therapy. John Wright, in *Telling God's Story*, critiques this prevalent therapeutic form of preaching as "comedic," resembling a comedy that fuses the horizons of Christian's lives and the biblical text into one narrative.[93] Wright explains how this comedic style of preaching gives priority to the hearers' experiences over that of the biblical narrative.

> The basic task of preaching is to ensure relevance by translating the biblical text into the horizon, convictions and experiences that each member possesses. The end result is to provide a biblically based answer to the questions and needs that an individual brings into the sanctuary/auditorium through fusing the biblical text into the experience of the hearer.

91. Bellah et al., *Habits of the Heart*; Taylor, *Sources of the Self*.

92. Gay, *The Way of the (modern) World*, 131–79. Basing his views on Max Weber's critique of rationalization that drives modern market capitalism, Gay believes economic concerns override any concern institutions might have once had for religious ends. "Far from being incidental to the process of secularization, the modern economy is one of its chief institutional culprits. Indeed, the economy underwrites much of the plausibility of practical atheism in the contemporary situation . . . the *market economy* is one of the most significant 'carriers' of secularity and practical atheism in contemporary society and culture" (132; emphasis original).

93. Wright, *Telling God's Story*, 36.

... Therefore, preaching must translate the biblical language into the horizon of the audience so that they might understand their experience in Christian terms. The fusion of horizons takes place in the melding of the translated biblical conceptuality into the previously existing horizon of the hearers, Christian and non-Christian alike. The sermon seeks to reinforce and uphold each attendee's basic convictions, bringing in an experience of "the Christ" in order to enrich the lives of all present as they struggle through their daily existence. Preaching here is characterized by the fusion of horizons. It therefore has the structure of a comedy.[94]

Comedic preaching eclipses gospel proclamation by fitting the gospel into the narrative of the larger society to which many Christians are more allegiant than they are to Christ or his church.

Comedic preaching never opens the hearers to the genuinely new, the possibility of a different narrative in which they can live their lives outside a certain Christianized version of the standard story that sustains the society at large, that of an autonomous individual searching for their personal good.[95]

Wright identifies the prevailing Christian narratives that give legitimacy to North American culture as the "federal covenant" and "covenant of grace," which together form the greatest obstacle to the church existing as God's people due to their narratives that offer *upward mobility* to the nation collectively and to the person individually.[96] Both result from a Constantinian compromise that keeps the church functioning as a mediating agency that supports nationalistic supremacy and individualistic consumerism.[97]

Many Christian preachers promote these American ideals of national progress, individual prosperity, or both. Christian television talk-show host Pat Robertson has promoted both by asserting Christianity as the highest form of American values. In *The Secret Kingdom*, Robertson offers conflicting statements about Christianity, saying one "must start with the crucifixion and the resurrection, but we must follow through with the

94. Ibid., 35–36.
95. Ibid., 38.
96. Ibid., 66–76.
97. Ibid., 74.

practice and principles, the laws of life."[98] He proceeds to equate Jesus' teachings with Old Testament laws and natural law, going so far as to say "the truths of Jesus have the characteristic of the 'truths' of the American Declaration of Independence—they are 'self-evident.'"[99] Such blatant misrepresentation of Jesus could only be attributed to a compromise that sees the Kingdom of God as the invisible kingdom that will eventually take over the world. Conspicuously missing in Robertson's account is the life Jesus lived that led to suffering and death. By also leaving out repentance, baptism, and a biblical view of the church, Robertson, simply "adds Jesus on" to an American life, making it the good life.[100]

The good life is also how Chuck Colson, former aide to President Nixon, describes the Christian life. In *The Good Life*, Colson reflects back on nearly thirty years since his Watergate conviction and prison term brought him to the end of himself and his turn to Christianity.[101] Living in a culture going the wrong direction, he believes we need to "seek the true picture of how the world really works and what we need to live well."[102] Through riveting stories of heroism, courage, and perseverance, Colson paints a picture of the Christian life as the highest moral, natural, and just life. He says that when one accepts "the idea of a created order, a world with intention and design, a world that comes from a Creator, then certain things come into focus, and you discover that the natural order gives us the key ingredients of the good life."[103] Both Robertson and Colson confirm John Wright's notion that this type of Christianity is merely an "enriching perspective to enhance participation within the North American society at large, . . . [but that] such a church can only exist deeply assimilated to the contours of its host society . . . and will always be captive to the role that the host society will permit it to play."[104]

Especially difficult is uncovering the methodology of this kind of preaching that keeps Christianity serving as a "chaplain" to its host society. Wright's answer is simple; the true gospel is tragic to both the hearer and to the false narratives of death in which the societies of this

98. Robertson, *The Secret Kingdom*, 55.

99. Ibid., 57.

100. Ibid., 69, 74, 93–94, 104–5, 150.

101. Colson, *The Good Life*, xv.

102. Ibid.

103. Ibid., 254.

104. Wright, *Telling God's Story*, 38–39.

world inevitably live. Using Alasdair McIntyre's description of an "epistemological crises," Wright says preaching should cause a "tragic hermeneutical moment by constructing a new, more adequate narrative."[105] The adequate narrative for preaching a tragic moment is God's story of calling to himself a new community of people, the church, established in the faithfulness Jesus lived.

> This church would be defined by Jesus' faithfulness to God in the world, faithfulness seen ultimately on the cross. It would understand that conversion is more than a personal experience of a personal relationship with God; conversion requires the incorporation of an individual into a new people, a new family and developing the necessary virtues to live as aliens and exiles in this new transnational community. Such a congregation will live by the Word proclaimed that redirects and re-forms the lives of those who would live faithfully as the people of God in the world.[106]

Wright's assessment of preaching calls for people to repent from the status quo of North American culture. He says preaching today needs "more radical turnings" due to the gulf that exists between North American culture and the biblical narrative.[107] This gulf requires preaching to shift the hearers' narrative horizons from the world to the biblical narrative to "form the church as a peculiar people, living within the biblical narrative as a sign of God's redemptive intent for all creation."[108]

In Acts, these "radical turnings" in the sermons bring about repentance and baptism on account of God's eschatological judgment that has already begun. Peter says these are the "last days" (2:17) in which God has now established both the necessity and the possibility of repentance on account of Jesus' life and death (3:18–19, 24).[109] In Peter's sermon at Pentecost (2:14–38), at Solomon's Portico (3:12–26), and at Cornelius' house (10:28–47) and in Paul's sermon at Antioch (13:16–47), Jesus'

---

105. Ibid., 41–42; cf. 21–25. In contrast to this prevalent method built upon Friedrich Schleiermacher's quest to find a universal objective method of hermeneutics that splits interpretation from preaching, Wright proposes its alternative of a "tragic hermeneutic" that, following Hans-Georg Gadamer, sees preaching "as the normative guide to understanding the very dynamics of interpretation itself" (29).

106. Ibid., 75; cf. 95, 102, 109–10.

107. Ibid., 92.

108. Ibid., 91; cf. 44.

109. Soards, *Speeches in Acts*, 42, 107.

death and resurrection are proclaimed to be God's acts in history that not only establish his plan of repentance but the proclamation as the means through which repentance and faith are now given, just as Jesus gave repentance and faith in his life.[110] These speeches make clear that God's eschatological judgment are on account of Jesus' death, resurrection, and exaltation, which demand repentance as the only human response.[111]

Paul also connects God's final judgment to Jesus' death and resurrection in his sermon at Athens (Acts 17:22–31), the assurance of which he gave by raising Jesus from the dead (17:30–31, see 24:25). Soards says Paul's "explicit reference to the resurrection . . . brings the notion of resurrection into close proximity with the idea of judgment . . . [and] registers the second half of the familiar christological contrast scheme (see 2:23–24), which often follows the mention or implication of an audience's guilt."[112] A "sinner is not compelled to repent because it is the appropriate response to sin; instead, the sinner is compelled to repent because *a new period in history has begun*."[113] God's new period in history requires a new political community entered only by rebirth by the Spirit. The sermons in Acts describe baptism as being the one sign through which one enters this new life in the Spirit.

---

110. As Jesus' stated mission in Luke was "to preach the gospel to the poor . . . to proclaim release to the captives" (Luke 4:18) and "to preach the kingdom of God" (Luke 4:43), the other Synoptic Gospels describe the eschatological nature of the kingdom of God as requiring repentance. In Mark, Jesus connects all four elements: "The time is fulfilled, and the kingdom of God is at hand; repent and believe in the gospel" (Mark 1:15).

111. Nave, *The Role and Function of Repentance*, 132. The coming of the kingdom of God in the person of Jesus inaugurates the reign of God as the fulfillment of time and, as such, "marks the decisive intervention of God into human history, and has created a situation that demands repentance." Peter at Pentecost quotes from Joel concerning God's judgment ([Acts] 2:19–20); on Solomon's Portico he speaks about the restoration of all things as was spoken by the prophets since the world began (3:21); and at Cornelius's house he tells them it was Jesus who was ordained by God to be the judge of the living and the dead (10:42).

112. Soards, *Speeches in Acts*, 99–100.

113. Nave, *The Role and Function of Repentance*, 131–32; emphasis added. In Jesus' resurrection, everything is new (2 Cor 5:17). This world is old and passing away, awaiting judgment (Rom 8:19–22; 2 Pet 3:7–12). Thus, only by faith in Jesus' death and resurrection can one have a proper view of creation, nature, history, and reality.

The Church Baptizes Believers into Christ's New Life in the Spirit

The concluding section of this chapter will describe baptism as the sign God has given to show the Spirit's work of adopting others sons into a life of sonship to God as members of Christ's ecclesial body of *koinonia* fellowship, a Trinitarian and post-Constantinian life respectively. As we have seen by Luke's description in Acts, baptism properly understood is a result of proclamation that transforms by the Spirit's presence working "death" and "resurrection" in those who hear, making believers out of unbelievers. Where preaching fails to require the Spirit to transform people into believers, other versions of baptism also prevail, rendering it merely as a requirement of following Jesus' command (which makes it a law) or of following Jesus' example (which makes it a work). Both are the result of preaching that is agreeable with human reason, as already discussed, by failing to see baptism as a *political* work of the Spirit by which God *concretely* works the constitutive events of Jesus' life in those who hear and believe. In line with preaching that depends on the Spirit to work Christ's life of sonship in others, this section will explain baptism as both Trinitarian, as the sign that God has done Christ's life of sonship in others, and as post-Constantinian, as God's work of "death" to one's political allegiances in "this world" and of "resurrection" into the politics of one's new identity in Jesus Christ by being added to his body, the *ecclesia* of *koinonia* fellowship of the church. This will give us the necessary link between proclamation of the gospel that gives the Spirit and the shape of the Christian life as life in the Spirit as explained in the next chapter.

Baptism as the Sign of God Adopting Other Sons in the Spirit

As a new community whose existence in is the Spirit, baptism is the sign God has given to his church to verify his adoption of others as his sons. As Jesus' baptism marked the beginning of his mission to fulfill all righteousness in obedience to the Father completed in death, baptism marks the beginning of one's life of sonship unto God with the gift of the Holy Spirit as the seal of promise that one is a chosen son of God. Jesus' baptism was the *public* inauguration to his life of sonship for which the Spirit's anointing would lead him in his divine mission to be a servant, even unto death on a cross (Phil 2:6–11). A Trinitarian view of Jesus' baptism for understanding the Christian life concerns itself more with the connection between the Spirit's anointing on Jesus to fulfill all righteousness, as

God's calling to a task, than it does with changing one's status or nature. The latter has difficulty connecting Jesus' baptism with the believer but the former sees Jesus' baptism as paradigmatic for the believer in how it makes sense of the Christian life as God's *claim on us* to be his witnesses as adopted sons. Baptism is God's public claim on those he has called to be his servants in Christ's body to fulfill his purposes.[114]

Therefore, a Christian's baptism not only takes faith in the gospel proclaimed, which supplies its meaning by defining faith itself, but the preaching of the gospel and baptism work faith reciprocally together by the Spirit's presence in them.[115] Faith in the preached gospel makes baptism effectual, that is, "faith alone makes the person worthy to receive the saving, divine water profitably. Because such blessings are offered and promised in the words that accompany the water, they cannot be received unless we believe them from the heart."[116] Thus, faith in the gospel and baptism cannot be separated, for baptism is not only the sign of God's work of faith but is also the external object of faith in that God declares sonship through it. It evokes faith by one knowing that, in baptism, they have been adopted by God and given all the responsibilities and privileges that being made a son of God entails, as it did in Jesus' life and death.

First, God's claim on his own in baptism entails the responsibilities of sonship as it did in Jesus' life, that of learning obedience through the things he suffered (Heb 5:8). Jesus' baptism not only brought the Father's good pleasure and the Spirit's anointing, it was the beginning of a life of sonship leading to death on a cross (Mark 10:38; Luke 12:50).

> Jesus' own baptism was the beginning of an obedient ministry which would not be fulfilled until he was obedient even unto the cross. Baptism was the beginning of his death, the first visible indication of the radical quality of his servanthood.
>
> It was at the cross and the tomb that Jesus' "baptism" was finally accomplished.[117]

114. Willimon, *Remember Who You Are*, 38.

115. Kolb and Wengert, eds., *The Book of Concord*, 461. "In baptism, therefore, every Christian has enough to study and practice all his or her life. Christians always have enough to do to believe what baptism promises and brings—victory over death and the devil, forgiveness of sin, God's grace, the entire Christ, and the Holy Spirit with his gifts."

116. Ibid., 460.

117. Willimon, *Remember Who You Are*, 97.

This is how Paul sees the Christian life, a "drowning" and "burial" in the "tomb" of the waters of baptism in which God claims one for his own and anoints them with his Spirit to accomplish the life of "death" and "resurrection," one's own life lived as a witness (martyr) to Jesus' death and resurrection. Just as the Spirit 'kills' the enmity of death itself in the hearers through preaching, Paul describes baptism as God putting to death the old man of the flesh and raising up the new man to live in Jesus Christ's resurrected life, as he says in Romans 6:3–7.

> Or do you not know that all of us who have been baptized into Christ Jesus have been baptized into His death? Therefore we have been buried with Him through baptism into death, so that as Christ was raised from the dead through the glory of the Father, so we too might walk in newness of life. For if we have become united with Him in the likeness of His death, certainly we shall also be in the likeness of His resurrection, knowing this, that our old self was crucified with Him, in order that our body of sin might be done away with, so that we would no longer be slaves to sin; for he who has died is freed from sin.

In baptism God unites the believer with Christ in the likeness of his death, working in them and giving to them the constitutive events of Jesus' life by the Spirit's intrinsic presence in which Jesus lived and died. As chapter 3 described how God dealt with his Son Jesus, a Christian's baptism is God's way of dealing with humanity. It is the way God works Christ's life in others.

Second, through baptism the believer has all the privileges of sonship that the Spirit's indwelling presence brings, the seal of promise that provides hope that God will finish making us his children (Rom 8:23) so that Jesus might be the "first born" of all those who believe in him and have been called to be conformed to his likeness (Rom 8:29–30). When Christians remember their baptism it means they are living in the *reality* that their old sinful self has died by their sharing in Christ's own death (Rom 6:1–7). By living in the reality of Jesus' death and resurrection in the Spirit, Christians also have the hope of their future resurrection that will free them ultimately from sin and death in the life to come (Rom 8:11, 17–25). By being adopted by God in baptism, the Spirit gives the believer hope in the future resurrection of their bodies from the grave just as Jesus was raised from the dead by the Spirit (Rom 8:11, 23; 1 Cor 15:3–57).

In baptism, not only are the constitutive events of Jesus' life and death given to be the life of the Christian by the indwelling Spirit, the events of his resurrection and even ascension back to the Father are given by way of "down payment" on God's eschatological fulfillment of his promises to his adopted sons (Rom 8:18–25; 1 Pet 1:3–4). Even the rest of creation groans in anticipation for the complete glorification of God's sons (Rom 8:19) and, through us, the Spirit speaks to God with groans unable to be expressed with known words (8:26). Baptism then is eschatological in that it is God's sign that, by his Spirit, he is actively re-creating humanity in the image of his Son Jesus, the New Adam. God's re-creation of humanity through the death and resurrection of Jesus means a complete reversal of nature itself and the laws that God gave to Israel. Now they are assigned a merely typological role[118] and even creation itself is now seen in the new light of Jesus' life and one's faith in his life.[119] This newness in Jesus Christ's identity brings about a complete reversal in how one interprets life itself. This new hermeneutic of the Spirit is due to the eschatological nature of Jesus' resurrection, which interprets the world as fallen and awaiting its final judgment. Jesus' death and resurrection is properly seen in proclamation and baptism as God having broken into the human situation of death to give life.

At a time when many Christians and even preachers are giving up all hope in the believer's future physical resurrection of the body from the grave in favor of a more appealing hope in one's life here in this world, making this connection in Paul's theology between the cruciform life in this world and one's true hope being in the world to come is one of the most critical aspects for understanding the believer's life as life in the Spirit. For Paul, being in Christ by the Spirit means putting one's hope in the future and literal resurrection from the grave just as Jesus hoped in his Father to rescue him from the grave. Having already explained the Christian life as one who has died to this world in baptism (Rom 6:1–11), Paul explains the Christian's cruciform life depending upon the future resurrection from the dead. This dependency upon the resurrection allows the believer to trust in their Father God with everything in this life, but especially ones' own death, a trust that comes from the Spirit working Christ's resurrection within, which is opposed to the Old Adam's desire for self-preservation.

118. Harrisville, *Fracture*, 68, 98.

119. Forde, *Theology is for Proclamation*, 144.

Paul explains this connection best in Romans 8 and in 1 Corinthians 15. In Romans 8, he says that what people could not do by following the law, in that we are controlled by our sinful selves, God did by sending his Son Jesus in the likeness of sinful flesh to destroy sin (8:3). God did this "killing" of sinful flesh so that his children could be the kind of people who could do the law by the Spirit's indwelling (8:4). Believing in Christ makes one free from the penalty of the law, which is sin and death, to live in the freedom of the Spirit by being controlled by life and peace (8:6). However, contrary to many Western notions of freedom, freedom that comes from being in Christ and having the Spirit living within means being ruled by the Spirit and being dead to one's self and its will (8:9). Such freedom is only attained by being bound to Christ to live under his Spirit's rule and such life is only attained by being dead to one's body of sin (8:10).

This freedom and life is only in Christ, who the Spirit raised from the dead, and is only attained by dying, both spiritually and physically. One's spiritual death (to their self in this world) is in baptism, which gives the Spirit of Jesus' resurrected life to live within. One's physical death is also ultimately necessary in order for the mortal body to be sown in the ground and then to be raised in immortality in the life to come (1 Cor 15:35–38, 42–57). With Jesus' resurrected life of sonship living within by his Spirit (Rom 8:14–16), the believer lives in the hope of their future resurrection from the dead by the same Spirit (Rom 8:11), their being raised at the Last Day in immortality just as Jesus was (1 Cor 15:35–50). Because Jesus was physically raised from the dead to be given an immortal body (1 Cor 15:12–19), those who believe that Jesus is Lord and was raised by God from the dead *will be* saved (Rom 10:9–10). Here in 1 Cor 15:42–49, Paul explains the Christian's life of sonship with God from this larger picture of God's plan of redemption, from creation to the Eschaton, revealing the only true dichotomy to be between the spiritual/heavenly and the sinful/earthly.

> So also is the resurrection of the dead. It is sown a perishable *body*, it is raised an imperishable *body*; it is sown in dishonor, it is raised in glory; it is sown in weakness, it is raised in power; it is sown a natural body, it is raised a spiritual body. If there is a natural body, there is also a spiritual *body*. So also it is written, "The first MAN, Adam, BECAME A LIVING SOUL." The last Adam *became* a life-giving spirit. However, the spiritual is not

first, but the natural; then the spiritual. The first man is from the earth, earthy; the second man is from heaven. As is the earthy, so also are those who are earthy; and as is the heavenly, so also are those who are heavenly. Just as we have borne the image of the earthy, we will also bear the image of the heavenly (1 Cor 15:42–49; emphasis original).

Such a holistic account of God's all-encompassing plan for creation is only known by the Spirit of Christ because it is only in and through Christ that God has brought about his plan for creation. For Paul, not only is the natural/spiritual dichotomy the only one, it is a dichotomy that God has made known to humanity by Christ's resurrection from the dead, showing the world and all humanity that creation now exists only in the natural that awaits its final judgment. This passage, possibly clearer than any other, brings together the Spirit's work in raising those dead in their natural state through the proclamation of Christ's gospel and the Spirit's future raising from the dead those who have died believing in Christ's gospel (1 Thess. 4:16). Those whom the Spirit has raised with Christ in baptism will be raised by the Spirit to live eternally with Christ in God.

This is the blessed hope, that the Spirit now living within is the one who *will raise* one's own life from the dead at the Last Day (Rom 8:11) just as he has already raised those who believe in him from their lives of death in this world to live in Christ's resurrected life in the Spirit. Life in the Spirit places one's affections, desires, and hopes in the life to come and diminishes one's attachments to things in this life, transferring one's allegiances to the Spirit who raised Jesus from the dead. Without Jesus' resurrection as the basis for the Christian's life in the Spirit and hope in the life to come, a Christian would only have hope in this world and, therefore, should be the most pitied of all (1 Cor 15:19) by placing their hope is what is already passing away (2 Peter 3:10–12).

Through the Spirit's presence in proclamation and baptism, God's hermeneutic of Jesus' cross and resurrection becomes the Christian's way of interpreting humanity and the world, "dead in its trespasses and sins" and in need of a "fracture" of new life. As life in the Spirit, the Christian's life is not only a new creation in Christ's resurrected life, but all things are new by the Spirit being the lens through which the believer is able to see the world as God does (2 Cor 5:17). The old does not fit into the new nor the new fit into the old anymore than old wineskins can hold new wine, else they fracture. This "new wineskins" approach to Paul's christological hermeneutic of the cross "describes a move from the event of Christ to the Old Testament cultus"[120] by its *qualitative* newness. Christ's life is not new in time but new in nature.

> But "newness" in the New Testament is never an exclusively chronological designation . . . Its truest definition concerns what is *qualitatively* new, a characteristic adhering to it by virtue of an inherent dynamic. Translated in terms of the Pauline language and conceptuality, the event of the cross is the theme throbbing throughout the apostle's work, and the character of his work needs to be discerned in that light. With Paul, that event has a life of its own. It exists outside him, an object toward which his feeling, thinking, and willing are directed.[121]

Paul's description of this qualitative newness of Christ's life is a completely new way of conducting one's life according to the obedience to God in which Jesus lived, humbling himself to not only the lowest place of humanity as a servant, but even unto death on a cross (Phil 2:6–11). This way of thinking is a cruciform life that sees suffering for the sake of Christ not as despised but as an honor, just as the apostles in Acts viewed their suffering even to the point of being stoned to death or taking a beating for confessing Jesus as Lord (Acts 5:40–41; Phil 1:29). This element to baptism only comes into clear view when being called by God to be a follower of Jesus means living in a contrast *polis* to the politics of this world and that suffering public disgrace for Jesus is now an honor that will receive its due reward in the future sharing in Christ's resurrection in glory (Rom 8:17; 1 Cor 15:35–57). In the Spirit, a believer rejoices in their baptism as God's sign that he has called them into his new *polis* of Christ's *ecclesial* fellowship until he returns.

Baptism as the Sign of the Spirit's Creation of God's New Polis in Christ

Paul describes the Christian life as a new alternative *polis* to the very way people live in the world, a whole new creation (2 Cor 5:17). His main concern was for Christians to conduct their lives (*politeuomai*) worthy of the gospel by which they had been called into God's new creation (Phil 1:27) with their citizenship (*politeuma*) being in heaven (Phil 3:20). People who do not think of Christ's life and death as their own are enemies of the

---

120. Harrisville, *Fracture*, 68; cf. 73–77.

121. Ibid., 103; emphasis original.

cross. They will be destroyed because they conduct themselves according to the flesh; glorifying their own bodies, being proud of their shameful acts, and only thinking about earthly things (Phil 3:18–19). Their *politics* is of this world according to the flesh, but the Christian's *polis* is in heaven, governed by an order opposite of this world. Entrance into heaven's *polis* is not by flesh and blood (by human works) but by Christ's Spirit (by God's work) that puts one's life and its former allegiances to death and raises them to life in Christ. Re-birth as God's adopted son is by water and Spirit, as Jesus told Nicodemus (John 3:5–8). It is God's calling of people into his eternal Kingdom, a *polis* of the Spirit that begins with one's death and resurrection in repentance and baptism. Entrance into this new *polis* of Christ' body is by God's Spirit so it can only be by faith, not of works, so that no person can boast in themselves but must boast only of Christ (Eph 2:7–9; 2 Cor 10:17), which means Christians are not to boast of their strengths but only of their weaknesses (2 Cor 11:30; 12:5–10). Therefore, repentance and baptism are not only the entrance into Christ's body, the *ecclesia*, but constitute the very political order in which Christians conduct their lives in the Spirit. The Christian life is God's new *polis* in Christ, meaning the church's worship, the community's life together, and its mission are in stark contrast to all the ways in which the world does its politics.

Baptism is God's sign that he has caught people up into Jesus' death and resurrection as their own story, making the church his *polis*, which makes disciples by baptizing people into not only Jesus' Trinitarian life of sonship but into his ecclesial body. This brings our various themes into one, showing the church's first order worship of preaching as baptismal in that baptism is God's sign that he has called us into the story of Jesus' death and resurrection. Willimon explains how all of the church's acts of worship come together in baptism.

> The worship of a church does not merely reflect the church's faith but actualizes it concretely in a sustained manner across the generations and in an irreducible way. Worship is the scripture's home rather than its stepchild. The Bible is the church's first liturgical book. Preaching is best conceived of as an act of worship, the precedent of and commentary upon baptism.
>
> To speak among the baptized, those who are dying and being raised (Romans 6:4), is to enter into a world of odd communication and peculiar speech. Baptismal speech need not conform to

> the reasons of this world (Romans 12:2). Conversation among
> the baptized is ecclesial in nature, political. A peculiar *polis* is
> being formed here, a family, a holy nation, a new people where
> once there was none (the images are all baptismal, 1 Peter 2:9).[122]

Lest Willimon's last sentence here be misconstrued as saying political language is derived from baptism rather than baptism actually being God's
political event of reversal, he goes on to say that the story of Jesus as a
baptismal story requires a "community that makes it make sense."[123] In
other words, baptism is political by it identifying a people God has called
to form a contrast society to all the nations of this world, which, by being
blinded by the god of this age (2 Cor 4:4), cannot see it or understand it.
Until preaching calls people out of their nation and into God's new *polis*
of the church then baptism likewise suffers from labels and descriptions
that only help lend credence to one's other allegiances to this world and
its fallen structures.

For Willimon, preaching, baptism, and the church are only sustain-
able across time when viewed as God's calling of a people to himself "out
of nothing."

> The church was called into being, as if out of nothing, as a people
> in dialogue with Scripture. Unlike conventional forms of human
> organization, the church had no ethnic, gender, or national basis
> for unity. All it had were these stories called Scripture. These
> Scriptures yielded a person, a personality, Jesus. For this new
> and distinctive community called the church, Jesus of Nazareth,
> as the Messiah, became the interpretive framework for all reality,
> the organizing principle for all of life. And it is so easy to forget
> how odd, how countercultural and potentially conflictive is such
> baptismal speaking.[124]

Willimon reminds us that baptism is God's work of death and resurrection in us, which turns the mere text of the Bible into Scripture, God's
word to us and for us. "'Scripture' suggests that authority has shifted
from ourselves to Scripture's use of us."[125] As we saw earlier in chapter
2, hermeneutics that begins with one's cultural context turns Scripture
into just another text from which to exegete meaning upon the basis of

122. Willimon, *Peculiar Speech*, 4; emphasis original.

123. Ibid., 11.

124. Ibid., 20.

125. Ibid., 13.

the interpreter's cultural context. As Willimon explains, this is a result of the church lacking a baptismal identity in Jesus Christ. "Where baptismal identity is lacking, listening is done from a cultural context—usually the therapeutic—other than that of a counter-cultural community called the church."[126]

On the first day of Christ's new community, Pentecost, the church was such a contrast-society to the firmly-held cultural norms that it required the Lord to add to the church daily those who were being saved (Acts 2:47). In such an environment, baptism would have been seen not only as imperative, due to Jesus' baptism and his life of suffering and death, but it would have been inconceivable to think one could enter such a contrast-society with anything less than death to all of one's former allegiances in this world. To enter such a politically *subversive* community, living on the wrong side of the political powers, would have required a public renouncement of one's allegiances to those powers. Actually, baptism *was* a public renouncement to those powers. Only baptism could capture this renouncement of one's allegiances to the powers of this world and entrance into God's new community of Jesus' disciples by it being the Spirit's work of "killing" all former allegiances and "raising" one to live in Christ's allegiance to God his Father.

Conclusion

This chapter has demonstrated the church to be God's assembly of those he has called to live in the cruciform identity of his Son Jesus in the Spirit through proclamation and baptism. I explained how the Spirit is active in proclamation of the gospel in three ways: in preaching that requires a miracle to believe, in preaching done in Jesus' authority that "kills" and "makes alive," and in preaching that is tragic to the individual by requiring repentance and baptism. As the Spirit's presence in Jesus' life led inevitably to a cross, trusting God to raise him from the dead, the Spirit's work of sonship in others is through repentance with baptism as its sign. As people who have been indwelt by God's Spirit to put on Christ's new identity through the death of their old selves and resurrection into his life, Christians are one body with Christ as the Head (Eph 1:10, 22; 4:15; 5:23). With Christ as the Head of his Body, the church, his followers have

---

126. Ibid.

their identity in Christ who fills the church (Eph 1:23) in order to equip it to serve, to mature it, and to perfect it in Christ's image (Eph 4:12–16).

This now leads us to the task of giving a more tangible explanation of the shape and direction of the Christian life as a life in the Spirit as a member of Christ's new political *ecclesia*, the actual political, economic, and cultural embodiment of the constitutive events in Jesus Christ's life as they are lived within and before the world. This brings us full circle back to describing what it means for Jesus' life to provide the shape and direction of the Christian life as life in the Spirit.

5

The Shape and Direction of the Christian Life

Conformed to Christ's Cruciform Life in the Spirit

Introduction

Now that we have seen how the Spirit transforms a person by the proclamation of the gospel of Jesus Christ into adopted sons of God, we are at a place where we can define the shape and direction of the Christian life. Since life in the Spirit is having been transformed by the Spirit into Christ's life in the Spirit, whose own life was cruciform, Christ's cruciform life is the shape and direction of the Christian life as well. This brings us to our final question asked here in chapter 5, "What does the Christian life look like today for those adopted by God to participate in Jesus' cruciform life?"

Life in the Spirit Is Living in Christ's Cruciform Life of Sonship

As we have seen in chapter 4, Luke and Paul show, in their respective styles, the Christian life to be the Spirit's cruciform work of "cross" and "resurrection" in one's life: the killing of one's old life of self-preservation and the raising to life one's new life of self-denial and repentance found only in Jesus Christ. This shows the gospel of Jesus Christ as particular in that Jesus, by virtue of being the only Son of God who received and bore the Spirit of the Father, is now the only giver of his Spirit to others. Therefore, the Spirit works salvation *only* through the proclamation of Christ's life, death, and resurrection (Rom 6:1–11) and in baptism through which one is transformed into Christ's cruciform life. As such, life in the Spirit is not only being put into Christ's cruciform life but is, likewise, always continually and finally conformed to his cruciform life and into his image (Rom 8:29), who is the image and likeness of God (Phil 2:6; Col 2:9; Heb 1:3). As God's adopted sons, the Spirit is ever present within believers, continually working Jesus' cross and resurrection in them. This is the same Spirit's work by which they were made participants in Jesus' Trinitarian existence in their repentance and baptism, a work of creation in which the Spirit makes a whole new person (2 Cor 5:17). Just what it means for the Christian life to be life in the Spirit is now coming into clearer focus by seeing how God adopts other sons by his Spirit working the constitutive events of Jesus' life of sonship intrinsically within people through proclamation and baptism, making the Christian life a cruciform life in the Spirit.

An account of the Christian life as a cruciform life shows clear trajectories beginning in how Jesus lived his cruciform life of sonship to the Father and running into the lives of his disciples in Acts who live full of the Holy Spirit. These trajectories continue on into how Paul and the other New Testament writers explain how Christians are to live their lives in the Spirit even today. Following these trajectories gives us a solid framework by which to describe the shape and direction of the Christian life as the same cruciform life in the Spirit that Jesus lived. These trajectories will be outlined in three areas: 1) loving God by living a life of non-violence, allowing a person to not retaliate against one's enemies, 2) loving others by being content with what one has from God, allowing a person to share material possessions with those in need, and 3) being content with how one is made by God, allowing a person to love people of other ethnicities with racial unity. In each of these areas, we will first revisit our test case of the early Pentecostals in America to see how they lived in the Spirit. They will serve as a more recent example by which to show how these three trajectories of the Spirit's work in Jesus' life and in the Christians' lives in Acts give shape and direction for the Christian life today.

Re-examining Our "Test Case" of the Early Pentecostals Who Lived in the Spirit

By way of Yoder's post-Constantinian framework, the Pentecostal movement in America can be understood as the loss of the pre-World War II post-Constantinian stance in the areas of politics, economics, and culture and the "gain" of succumbing to a Constantinian compromise to the more popular quest for attaining the American Dream. This account could very well be applied to other Christian traditions or even to Pentecostal traditions in other cultures, but, especially for our purposes here, possibly no other tradition over the past century exemplifies such a fast and drastic move away from an earlier post-Constantinian way of living to the contemporary Constantinian compromise than does modern Pentecostalism in America. However, this is a generalization that certainly does not apply to all Pentecostals or to all Pentecostal churches.

A contributing factor in this development within Pentecostalism is its quite common stance of looking at its past with nostalgia, a view many Christians today have toward the history of their particular tradition, or toward any tradition for that matter. Certainly many Pentecostals in America are nostalgic about the lives of their founders; but, by taking such an approach, they distance themselves from any significance the early Pentecostals might have for gaining a *theological* understanding of how Christians are to live today. By being nostalgic about their past, Pentecostals actually diminish the lives of the early Pentecostals for what it meant *theologically* for them to live lives of faithfulness and contentment in the Spirit. This diminishing of their lives for what it means to live in the Spirit today can be seen in two related ways.

First, nostalgia embellishes certain aspects of their lives only to reinforce the importance or legitimacy of the tradition itself but in no way uses those aspects for what it might have meant *for them* to live lives in the Spirit as faithful disciples of Jesus *in their time and to their world*. This approach uses certain ways they lived as only a means to validate the contemporary status of the movement itself in its quest for growth and popularity but not for what those aspects meant for them *living the kinds of lives they lived*. As such, the growth of the movement worldwide serves as more like a "cover" to legitimate its own departure from the ways in which the early Pentecostals actually lived sacrificial lives. Their sacrificial lives of faithfulness and contentment only serve as a reason for how the movement gained such fast momentum, being good for them but in no way reasonable enough for how Christians are to live today. As a result, the theological reasons for their faithfulness and contentment are either ignored or lost. This aspect of nostalgia is ironic in that it is charmed by how they lived but does not actually take their lives seriously for *why* they lived the way they did. One can hear this charm in how many Pentecostals today relate stories of the lives of early Pentecostals as if they were so naïve, poor, or uneducated that if these aspects of their lives were taken seriously for what it means to live faithful lives today it would be embarrassing. Nostalgia helps eliminate their embarrassing lives by opening up more "space" between their lives and ours. That this view patronizes those who sacrificed all they had for their faith in Jesus Christ, often in scorn and derision from their local culture, is lost on those who use them only to legitimize their own place within the movement that increasingly desires to be culturally and politically legitimate in the eyes of this world. Ironically, many now desire approval from the same "cultured despisers" their founders sacrificed to resist.

Second, a nostalgic view of their lives helps galvanize the increasing Constantinian compromise of the Pentecostal movement by reinforcing a sociological and psychological critique of what was a *theological reason* for those who were living the kinds of lives they lived. In that the earlier Pentecostals did little to develop an adequate theological account for why they lived the way they did, this lack provided an open space for other accounts to "fill the gap." This lack still provides much open space for scholars to explain the movement's beginnings and their own Pentecostal lives today with other competing non-theological forms more acceptable to a secularized American culture. This is why much reflection on the Pentecostal movement is largely sociological, historical, or even psychological, as if these were the reasons why people sacrificed their lives, some ultimately, for taking the gospel to the far reaches of the globe or in the face of ridicule here at home. That this methodology among Pentecostals is antithetical and detrimental to its own legitimacy works to further solidify non-theological reasons and to keep theology itself relegated largely to insignificance. This reciprocal relationship between the lack of a theological understanding and the apathy towards theology has been the single most determining factor in the downward spiral away from biblical preaching and the loss of focus in preparing ministers and missionaries among Pentecostal fellowships during the past fifty years in America.

There could be other factors, especially in more recent years, that contribute to this distancing of Pentecostalism from its powerful and intriguing past, but, for this account, we must confine our focus to simply an overview of this Constantinian development to provide a background for our discussion of the shape and direction of the Christian life as life lived in the Spirit. Up until now, our single focus has been one of providing the theological reasons for why followers of Jesus at any time and in any Christian tradition live their lives in conformity to the life Jesus lived.

This chapter will now apply our earlier post-Constantinian account to the Pentecostal movement by looking at its development over the past century to give greater clarity to the trajectories of our Trinitarian Spirit-Christology for what it means to live life fully in the Spirit today.

In order to demonstrate how Pentecostalism has been nostalgic about its past we will examine a few assessments of its beginnings and later developments by historians and sociologists most accepted as standard accounts. While there have been theological works concerning Pentecostal beginnings, they have not provided the necessary theological reasons for why they lived their lives the way they did, as stated above.[1] They tended to keep their doctrine "spiritual" and "experiential" without making many theological connections to the actual concrete ways they lived, other than the dominant one that their lives were ones of holiness separated from this world. However, even holiness remained largely in the realm of the "spiritual" with the main connection to their lives being in the area of individual and personal morality rather in the realm of community and social justice. Many Pentecostals still think of the Christian life as something entirely "spiritual" without any solid theological reasons for living a life of faith and faithfulness in the real world. This lack of explicit theological support within Pentecostalism is an obvious reason why other *non-theological* reasons have been given such credibility, even to the point that theological answers are viewed as suspect, or worse.

In order to provide a real appreciation for the lives of the early Pentecostals from a theological perspective, other non-theological typologies that have become widely accepted as "standard accounts" will be referred to throughout in regards to our three areas of interest. To lay some groundwork, we will look at some of these general works for how they establish certain typologies that have become generalized assessments of the Pentecostal movement in America and its influence on the larger Pentecostal movement around the world.

Probably the most standard works on the sociological and religious elements of the early Pentecostals have been those by Grant Wacker, Robert Mapes Anderson, and Harvey Cox. Grant Wacker, in *Heaven Below*, gives a candid look at the movement by examining what he calls the pragmatic mode of operation that gave the movement its initial impetus.[2] He says pragmatism gave these early pioneers the ability to

1. Dayton, *Theological Roots of Pentecostalism*.
2. Wacker, *Heaven Below*.

spread their message literally around the world with the smallest amount of resources imaginable. They operated on little money and even less education or strategy, yet they used what they had available to its greatest potential. In that Wacker attributes their effectiveness to pragmatism, his methodology claims that these elements of sacrifice lost out over time due to their minority status among the rank and file. The ways they lived were simply expedient for them out of necessity since most of them were poor, uneducated, and socially underprivileged in the first place. Many of them had no other options available so they had to make the most of what little they had. Wacker helps explain these elements in their lives, but his methodology also shows the need for a theological view to understand *their own reasons*, not ours, for living the kind of lives they lived and for why they took for granted that people would live the same way when filled with the Spirit. Whether they lost out because they were a minority or whether they gave in because of pragmatic concerns does not even begin to explain *theologically* why these elements were there in the first place. Even so, Wacker's assessment has made an immeasurable contribution to understanding their lives.

Another helpful assessment of the early Pentecostals is Robert Mapes Anderson's *The Vision of the Disinherited* in which he shows the cultural aspects of their lives as important as their theology for their community's identity.[3] Whereas Anderson gives a sociological account of the lives of the early Pentecostals, his account, like Wacker's, shows that certain aspects of their lives cannot be fully explained with merely a sociological typology, especially if one desires to appreciate how the early Pentecostals saw their own lives.

Another example of this dominant typology is Harvey Cox's *Fire From Heaven*, in which he also gives a religious and sociological look at the Pentecostal movement around the world but from an admittedly outsider's perspective.[4] In line with Wacker and Anderson, Cox believes their marginalization and community cohesiveness fueled the growth, especially in the larger cities of Latin America and Asia where displaced people look for belonging and community. Cox's sociological assessment, albeit religious, looks at the more recent phenomenon of Pentecostalism's explosive growth world-wide and is helpful in identifying these elements

3. Anderson, *The Vision of the Disinherited*.
4. Cox, *Fire From Heaven*.

even though Cox does not address the theological reasons underlying Pentecostal's desire to live out these strong community traits.

These mostly sociological assessments only serve to further legitimize nostalgic views of the lives of the early Pentecostals and to diminish what *they* believed to be theological reasons for why they were living the way they did. What is needed for an honest appraisal of their lives is a theological methodology that explains such phenomenon as what the Spirit does in the community of faithful disciples of Jesus. The methodology used here does this by inverting this current dominant typology that gives priority to sociological interpretations. These methods tend to "run backwards" by starting from today's sociological or historical perspectives as a place from which to view their lives. This is the same perspective that we saw in chapter 2 with theological approaches that construct theology from one's own cultural situation as a way to make the text "fit into" the interpreter's world. By contrast, the approach used here is theological. As such, it can only "run forwards" from the narrative of Jesus' life as the Son of God, into his disciples' lives in Acts, into the explanations of the other New Testament writers, and, finally, into the present. This chapter builds upon the methodology already developed in chapters 3 and 4 to explain these trajectories of the political, the economic, and the cultural for the shape and direction of the Christian life today as a life lived in the Spirit.

As the early Pentecostals lacked this kind of an explicit theological explanation for why they lived the kinds of lives they lived, we have seen here how this theological lack continues by Pentecostalism's reluctance to provide a "thick" theological description for the Christian life as life in the Spirit. If any group should have capitalized on this it was the early Pentecostals. They not only claimed they were living in the Spirit, but, even more important, they actually lived the kind of faithful lives that defy any other reason than the Holy Spirit. If they were naïve, at least by today's standards, it was in thinking that their *whole* lives were theological, that being a Christian was a life that had been bought and set apart for God's purpose and not for one's own purpose. They just thought that anyone who lived in the Spirit would live like Jesus lived and that the Spirit was necessary to live such a life. In this regard, they were right but certainly not naïve. So then, did the early Pentecostals, by living in the Spirit, live theologically-informed lives far better than they realized or than they could have even expressed? If so, their faithful lives demonstrate how nostalgic views are both theologically naïve and, even worse, unfaithful accounts of how they lived in the Spirit. What this chapter attempts to demonstrate is how the Pentecostals of the early twentieth century lived theologically in the Spirit far better than they realized, even far better than what sociological or cultural accounts have recently attempted. This theological account will be given by tracing the trajectories from Jesus' life in the Spirit, as explained in chapters 3 and 4, into the Christian life today.

Each one of these three trajectories will be traced from Jesus' life into his followers' lives by using the following sequence. First, I will examine the lives of the early Pentecostals. Second, I will discuss these traits in Jesus' life. Third, I will trace them into the lives of his followers in Acts. And fourth, I will then describe the shape and direction of the Christian's life today for what it means to live in the Spirit. As such, we will be able to move beyond a merely nostalgic view and gain a theological understanding of the Spirit's indwelling presence of peace as the reason for not only why the early Pentecostals lived the kind of lives they did, but, more importantly for today, give us the reasons why we are to live lives of faithful trust and obedience to the Father with tangible love for God and others in our time and before our world.

Life in the Spirit Is Peace with God: The Cruciform Politics of Non-violence

The first question we will investigate is whether or not Jesus lived a life that affirms the basic human assumption that one has the right to defend themselves with violence towards those who are violent, especially violent towards one's own person. Certainly anyone even partially familiar with Jesus' life and death by crucifixion would know the obvious answer to this somewhat rhetorical question. This shows the real problem to be not so much whether Jesus lived a life of non-violence but in being able to see his life of non-violence as a distinguishing feature of his life as one lived in the Spirit and, as such, one's life in the Spirit today. Even Pentecostals, who should know something about the connection of the Spirit to non-violence from their early beginnings, do not go far enough in developing a perspective of non-violence as the active work of the Spirit in Christians' lives; a result of not making the necessary connections in Jesus' own life. One Pentecostal scholar, Martin Mittelstadt, has recently contributed to this endeavor by showing the connections between Jesus' sufferings and the Spirit for Christians today in his study of Luke-Acts. However, he does not go far enough in showing the Spirit's work of non-violence in Jesus' life from a Trinitarian perspective, although this would have gone beyond his intent.[5] As a result, he does not go far enough in explaining Jesus' life of non-violence as the result of the Spirit's presence for either Jesus or the disciples. For Mittelstadt, the Spirit still remains too much like a static object of human knowledge about the Spirit rather than the Spirit as the *active subject* of God's Trinitarian relational reconciliation of adopting people as other sons of God.

> Thus, a Lukan pattern is unveiled, namely, Spirit-led ministry is a pathway to conflict with those who oppose Jesus and his message. To be sure, this message has relevance for Luke's readers, original and contemporary, including Pentecostals. Readers are exhorted to continue in their proclamation of Jesus despite opposition. In fact, reflection on the life of Jesus and his disciples would encourage them not only to continue but persevere in the midst of rejection and persecution. Contemporary Pentecostals, while continuing in the rigorous pursuit of the Holy Spirit, must also be prepared for and even expect opposition on account of association with Jesus.[6]

As such, Jesus' life of non-violence is described more as a passive circumstance of suffering rather than the Spirit's active and intentional work of making peace. However, Mittelstadt does make overtures to Jesus' life increasingly bringing about resistance due to the programmatic platform of the Spirit's anointing being carried out in his mission, even though he does not draw out the fuller theological dimensions of the relationship of Jesus' mission in the Spirit to people rejecting Jesus and bringing about his ultimate death. For Mittelstadt, Luke is simply "careful to highlight the inevitability of persecution derived from the necessity of proclamation."[7] What seems to be missing in Mittelstadt's analysis is an active and reciprocal relationship between the Spirit's work of peacemaking in Jesus performing and proclaiming the kingdom of God and people rejecting his claim that his life was doing God's will.

As helpful as Mittelstadt is in showing the relationship between suffering and the Spirit in the lives of Jesus and his disciples, suffering

---

5. Mittelstadt, *The Spirit and Suffering in Luke-Acts*.

6. Ibid., 65.

7. Ibid., 81.

remains too passive; much like an accidental result of Jesus and his disciples proclaiming the message rather than an inherent result of the Spirit's work in the message itself. His perspective would benefit by going a step further in showing the reciprocal nature between Jesus' life in the Spirit and the natural rejection the Spirit's work elicits; helping us see Jesus' life of peacemaking as an active, intentional, and truly inevitable outcome of living in the Spirit. It would also help us to see violence as the basic element *intrinsic* to the human condition that the Spirit reveals when the gospel is proclaimed rather than how it normally is, as only a trait of the most evil and violent. Seeing violence as the result of all people's estrangement from God, without the Spirit, helps us rightly understand Jesus' death at the hands of violent humanity as God's indictment on human estrangement from God and the violence which results as deserving his wrath.

There is certainly no mistaking that non-violence is a point of heated debate among Christians. Although scholars such as Hannah Arendt have suggested violence to be the most basic element of the human condition no matter what the religious persuasion,[8] some Christians are not so easily convinced. Even John Howard Yoder's work on non-violence, while quite compelling, must not be very convincing since it remains largely marginalized or even ignored by mainstream Christianity in America. Even with a growing number of Christian scholars addressing the issue of non-violence within ethics and biblical scholarship, their views remain largely marginalized as well.

The very fact that these kinds of views based on Jesus' life remain marginalized by many Christians should cause us to wonder why Jesus' life of non-violence is seen as such a threat to our lives. Where else should Christians look to formulate a view of human violence, especially since Jesus met a violent end to his own life and that his violent end constitutes what Christians claim as their salvation? Yoder has rightly distinguished non-violence as one of the major themes in Jesus' life, but without an explicit account of the fuller pneumatological dimension as the reason for Jesus living non-violently.[9] But, would Yoder's account be more convincing if Jesus' life of non-retaliation and non-violence was explained as a feature of the Spirit's indwelling? If so, this would allow us to say Jesus' life of non-violence most clearly identified him as the Son of God, and,

8. Arendt, *On Violence.*

9. Yoder, *The Politics of Jesus,* 162–211; *Nevertheless.*

as such, is most clearly seen just at the time when, most unbelievably, humanity crucified him and he refused to defend himself against their violence. This would solidify the argument that a life of non-violence is a distinguishing feature in Jesus' life as the Son of God in the Spirit and that, by extension, is also a main feature that distinguishes God's adopted sons who live in the Spirit. But first, let us examine our test case of early Pentecostalism to see how they lived lives of non-violence and peacemaking.

The Politics of Peacemaking among the Early Pentecostals

With Pentecostalism as our background, we will first sketch the development of the Pentecostal movement in America as it transitioned away from its earlier post-Constantinian stance of non-violence toward its more recent Constantinian acceptance of violence seen most clearly in its stance toward the nation and its wars. Early Pentecostal worship and preaching had a more general focus on the Christian life being one of peace made possible by the life, death, and resurrection of Jesus, but which, over time, lost out to the contemporary focus on inner subjectivism that strives for inner peace. This transition from an earlier focus on the objective reality of Jesus being Lord over the nations to a subjective striving to gain an inner awareness of an "absent Jesus" is the cost of this Constantinian loss of a proper distinction between the church and the nation's culture, especially the church's stance toward the nation and its wars.

As detailed by Paul Alexander, the Assemblies of God, America's largest predominantly white Pentecostal denomination, made the transition from its initial church position of peace and non-violence against war (1927) to the toleration of participation in war (1947) to its current position of encouraging participation in war (1967) within a span of only 40 years.[10] As also pointed out by Jay Beaman, the official doctrine of the major Pentecostal fellowships was an official stance against participating in war due to their proper distinction between the church and the nation state of America.[11] The argument could be made that such a stance was not the majority of Pentecostal believers but only the church's official stance adopted by its leaders that lost out due to being the minority

---

10. Alexander, *Peace to War*.

11. Beaman, *Pentecostal Pacifism*, 21–32.

position. Grant Wacker, while espousing this minority status view, also gives a telling appraisal of the early Pentecostals' overall attitude toward world events that shows the underlying reason for Pentecostals' personal detachment from the nation's wars.

> If outsiders were to glance at the headlines of some of the leading pentecostal periodicals, especially in the 1910's, they might conclude that converts found the war in Europe, Jews in Palestine, and natural disasters everywhere intensely interesting. But close inspection would show that those stories really had nothing to do with actual events. Rather world affairs for Pentecostals functioned as biblical antetypes, scenes in a vast cosmic drama planned from the beginning of the time. Prudent Christians studied such events in order to know where they themselves stood in the grand scheme of things, not to come up with constructive politics for the here and now.[12]

What Wacker is really observing is not simply a lack of concern for world events as much as it is the early Pentecostals' belief in God's purposes known in and through the church rather than in and through the world, a feature Yoder attributes to the early church before the Constantinian compromise.[13]

Wherever one places the blame for such a drastic shift away from its earlier stance toward the nation's wars and other world events, any sociological reason still does not explain theologically why church leaders and pastors moved the official church stance toward a Constantinian position behind the "leading" of its members. But even a sociological reason would show the cultural pressure upon church members to be stronger than the official church stance against it, and, more importantly, stronger than the theological reasons for the church's stance, even if it was a minority position. These other reasons at least show a lack of theological explanation strong enough to resist the cultural and sociological pressures working against it. Sociological accounts gained dominance over theological ones even for the church's explanation of its own essence and mission, ironically, even for Pentecostals who have generally insisted the Spirit to be responsible for everything they do. This dearth of theological explanation for how they lived their lives can only be overcome by a theological account that begins with Jesus and shows his life as transforming for the

---

12. Wacker, *Heaven Below*, 222.

13. Yoder, *The Royal Priesthood*, 54–64; *The Priestly Kingdom*, 96–101, 135–47.

early apostles and for his disciples still today. Only theology can explain why a Christian would live faithful to Jesus' life, death, and resurrection and only a theological reason can explain why one does not.

What follows here is an attempt to retrieve this aspect of peace found only in Jesus Christ by highlighting those themes discussed in the previous two chapters. This will trace the trajectory from Jesus' life of peace, through the lives of his followers in Acts, and into the lives of Christians today for what it means to live lives fully in the Spirit. As we saw earlier, Jesus' life as the Son of God was a life lived in faithful obedience to the Father by the indwelling presence of the Spirit. As such, his life was one of social non-conformity to the fallen structures of the world that use violence to ensure their continued existence. Post-Constantinianism helps us see Jesus' life for *what* peacemaking means for his followers and Spirit-Christology helps us see the indwelling presence of the Spirit as *how* he lived his life of peace.

Jesus Lived Non-violently in the Spirit

We now see that Jesus not only died *because* he lived obediently to his Father, he died obediently with the Spirit's presence intrinsically *as* his obedience to the Father. Not only did he passively endure death, he actively entrusted his life to his Father in the Spirit. Jesus trusted his Father knowing he would resurrect him even if he would not save him, a definite work of the Spirit and not his own will. Even Jesus' own will wanted to avoid death, but, in the Spirit, he surrendered his will to the will of the Father. This shifts the focus from his own ability to do the Father's will to the Spirit doing the Father's will intrinsically within him, showing his death as a Trinitarian event, not an individual one. As a Trinitarian event, God used human circumstances, especially rejection and violence, to demonstrate Jesus' non-violent trust in his Father as a work of the Spirit's presence. Bearing the Spirit, Jesus would not save himself. Rather, he would justify his Father by not justifying his own life. To do so, he refused violence as a means to circumvent his Father's plan, living what he taught: those who justify their self before God are rejected by God and those who justify God rather than their self are accepted by God.[14]

Jesus justifies God by identifying with sinners at his baptism and from his ministry announcement to fulfill his mission in the Spirit ac-

---

14. Johnson, *Literary Function of Possessions*, 110–11.

cording to Isaiah (Luke 4:18–19; Isa 61:1–2; 58:6). Both of these put Jesus at the wrong end of the political, economic, and cultural establishment by identifying with those rejected by the establishment. From the initial point of his ministry, his baptism and ministry announcement in Nazareth, Jesus became one of the despised by doing the work of the Spirit for and among the despised. At the end of his life, Jesus identifies with society's most despised, as a criminal, in that his disciples have two swords, but only two, which "are enough" (Luke 22:36–38; Isa 53:12).[15] This ensures that Jesus enacts his Father's intention to be identified with the despised and rejected so as to suffer their same fate even while being innocent of any violence himself. In refusing to participate in society's violence, Jesus' non-violence elicits their shame and rejection back upon himself. By provoking their rejection with non-violence, Jesus' life threatens their structures that require violence to continue their existence. As a result, they shame and reject Jesus in retaliation, thereby proving Jesus' teachings that their own deep-seated condition is one of violence against the most vulnerable—the righteous.

By refusing to defend himself, Jesus identifies with the most helpless of all, those helpless to defend themselves against the power of the religious and politically powerful who use their structures as weapons against any who do not conform to their dominating structures. Jesus refuses to use either their violence or even his Father's power to overthrow them, rejecting both insurrection and quietism.[16] He refuses to be quite about both forms of violence; the religious and political acts of violence of the rich and powerful against the poor and powerless. But it is just this refusal to conform to violence, or especially to overlook it, which identifies him with those most despised by the culture: those who barely had enough means to exist and even less of a say in determining the conditions of their own existence. By being one of these most culturally despised, Jesus refused to save his own life, that is, to be approved by society's elite who could save his life from the violence it perpetrated upon the vulnerable. Contrary to the elite, Jesus refused to be violent toward those whom the elite of culture despised, even giving his own life in place of the criminal Barabbas who the crowd wanted to save at Jesus' expense. Jesus could have saved his own life but, instead, entrusted it to his Father and those who hated him for claiming that, in doing so, he was

15. Yoder, *The Politics of Jesus*, 45.

16. Ibid., 36.

God's true Son, the rightful heir to David's throne. And, since no man is hailed a king who refuses to use violence to save himself, no one called Jesus God's kingly Son while he suffered the most shame and rejection of all; that of dying on a cross.

This can be seen in how Luke weaves together reciprocally the religious and political leaders' desire for violence upon Jesus and his peaceful submission to their violence. However, in taking the shame and rejection as one of the most despised, Jesus goes further than passively enduring it; he actively prays for his Father to forgive his killers, telling his Father they are doing it in ignorance (Luke 23:34). Jesus actively overcomes violence by submitting to it and then forgiving the violent while they are killing him. Nothing else in Jesus' life demonstrates such God-likeness as this act of praying for God to forgive those who were the most unrighteous of all—the ones murdering him for being God's righteous Son who bears the Spirit. Jesus' non-violence toward his violent murderers is the very demonstration of his own Father's character, loving those who despise and reject him. This shows Jesus' death to be the one constitutive event that truly justifies God because, in it, Jesus allowed God to be God even though it appeared to all people everywhere that he was cursed by God.

Jesus was not only cursed because he was God's king, he was God's king because he was most cursed and that he claimed to be most righteous *while* he was being most cursed. Jesus was most righteous because he accepted his Father's curse and even went so far as to say that his own cursed condition provided life for others. How could Jesus' refusal to save his own life, from what appeared to be God's curse, save the lives of others? This is a reversal of conventional human wisdom of the greatest proportion, a scandal, which Paul describes in 1 Cor 1:21, "For since in the wisdom of God the world through its wisdom did not come to know God." This can be seen already in Jesus' death as his acceptance of God's curse *as* his claim to be righteous; that death, even as the very curse of God, is the only way to attain true life. Does this mean that accepting God's curse of death is the way to life for others? If so, this means securing one's own life to be idolatry since it is the greatest result of God's curse of sin and death upon humanity. This certainly corresponds to how we have already seen in the previous chapter salvation as the Spirit's work of "killing" the old and "raising" the new life of Christ's life in the Spirit. Now, by seeing Jesus' death in this fashion, we are able to understand violence to be idolatry by how it replaces God's control over one's own life with one's own control for self-preservation. We also see that a more basic condition of violence is the condition of self-preservation that motivates one to be violent. It also shows us the Spirit's presence within Jesus as the reason he did not desire to preserve his own life. Since Jesus' death was the Spirit's presence submitting to the Father's will, non-violence is the way of the Spirit. The Spirit's work of death to one's own will and life to God's will shows the Christian life to be life in the Spirit in which one lives in peace with God by living Jesus' cruciform life on non-violence.

Peace with God: Living in the Spirit of Christ's Politics of Non-violence

Now that we have seen how Jesus lived a life of non-violence as the Son of God in the Spirit, we will see how his followers lived lives of non-violence in Acts and how this theme carries through into Paul's understanding of the Christian life as a son of God in the Spirit. This kind of life is in continuity with Jesus' total trust in the Father to deliver him from his enemies by being non-violent towards them. The boldness of the apostles in Acts to proclaim the gospel was accompanied by a faithful trust in Jesus as Lord to win the victory over their enemies, even if that trust meant their imprisonment, suffering, beatings, or death. This trust in God to deliver means, for Paul, a personal response of non-violence. One cannot carry out vengeance upon one's enemies and trust in God to deliver at the same time, they are mutually exclusive. One either lives in the Spirit trusting the Father or in the flesh's violence by trusting in one's self.

This assurance of the indwelling Spirit gives Christian believers the reason to daily sacrifice their own lives (Rom 12:1) as an expression of gratitude for the great mercy God has shown by pouring out his love in their hearts through the Holy Spirit given to them (Rom 5:5). Sacrificing one's own life was as much a part of Paul's thinking as was faith itself because faith means trusting God with the outcomes of life, even when assaulted for that faith, whether by his own Jewish people or by his own Roman government that took him prisoner, just as Jesus himself did. As we saw in Jesus' life and the lives of his followers in Acts, faith in Jesus is political in that it sacrifices all allegiances to all earthly lords. Being "killed" and "made alive" in repentance and baptism puts an end to all other narratives used to explain one's place in this world and one's allegiances to all other gods used to explain those narratives. For Paul, salvation was identifying with the narrative of Jesus' lordship through his own "cross" and "resurrection." Therefore, sacrificing one's own life was not merely a possible outcome of prophetic speech but was the very meaning of salvation itself, for both Luke and Paul. Neither did Paul think such a sacrificial life of faithfulness to Jesus' own sacrificial life was only for validating his own apostleship (2 Cor 11:1—12:10), but that it was the very mark of the Christian life as a life of peace toward those who would inflict harm. It was this non-violent stance toward harmful and hurtful people that Paul said should be the very identity of the people of God through whom the Spirit gives gifts to the church to be one body of remarkable sacrificial love for one another (Rom 12; 1 Cor 12–14, Phil 2:1–11).

Rightly understanding this discussion in Romans 12, about the love operating in other sons of God (v. 5) as brothers and sisters in Christ (1, 10), is necessary to understand Paul's admonition in Romans 13 for the church to submit to governments. As Paul calls each one in Christ's body to a life of non-violence towards one another by not harming those who curse them (12:14) and to live in peace with each other (12:16), so too does he call them to submit to rulers of governments who have been ordered by God to punish evil doers (13:4). As believers have no reason to fear harm from each other they have no reason to fear harm from governments, if they do not commit the evil the governments are ordered by God to punish. In this context, Paul's discussion of governments in Romans 13 is not concerned about what degree Christians should serve them as much as he was expanding on his previous discussion of submission and non-violence as the marks of Jesus' disciples. There had not yet developed the kind of Constantinian synthesis between the church and culture as to elicit the kind of meaning from this text that Christians were to serve the government with an allegiance greater than their allegiance to Jesus as Lord.[17] Since Jesus is Lord he directs governments according to his own plan and purposes for the world. They are fallen but have been re-enlisted by God back into fulfilling his purposes.[18]

That Romans 13 is actually referring to how Christians are to live in love and non-violence is especially noticeable in how Paul continues his discussion of non-violence following verse 7. Christians are to love one another by owing them only love (13:8), that loving your neighbor as yourself is obeying all the law (13:10), and that each should look out for the interests of others, especially that the strong should care for the weak (ch. 14; 15:1–13). Therefore, the point of Romans 13 is that peace and

17. Ibid., 193–211.

18. Ibid., 141–53.

non-violence is a distinct mark of the church in contrast to the distinct mark of governments to punish the violence of evil doers with a reciprocal form of violence. In this respect, the church is to be an alternative politic to the world's politics, not by way of retreat but by way of engagement with the powers of this world by proclaiming and living out the reign of Christ's lordship over the world in every area of life.[19]

Life in the Spirit Shares with Others: The Cruciform Economics of Contentment

The second trajectory to be investigated is Jesus' contentment with virtually no material possessions in order to see how it runs forward into the lives of the Christians in Acts. We need to see whether this aspect of Jesus' life is also a distinguishing feature of the Spirit's presence. If so, it must also be a distinguishing feature of Christians' lives today for what it means to live a life fully in the Spirit.

The Economics of Contentment and Sharing among the Early Pentecostals

One might think the early Pentecostals were not so much led by the Sprit to share their wealth with the poor as they were the poor who relied on the Spirit to meet their needs and to be content with life's simple necessities. What is most telling about Pentecostalism today is its interpretation of the early Pentecostals that leaves out this aspect of contentment even though their lives were lived with many economic hardships. Most of the early Pentecostals were either from the rural south or urbanites displaced by immigration or urbanization. It was from the "struggling working classes and impoverished unemployed that the Pentecostal movement drew its following in the urban areas of the nation."[20] Here is where it could be asked whether their lives in the Spirit caused them to see economic hardship as how the Spirit works or if their way of seeing how the Spirit works caused them to live lives of economic hardship with joy and contentment? Probably the latter, but since they lacked a clear theological explanation for how they lived as a result of the Spirit, our ability to answer this question is limited. Making this distinction would have been lost on the early Pentecostals simply because they thought anyone filled with the

19. Stassen and Gushee, *Kingdom Ethics*, 168–93.
20. Anderson, *The Vision of the Disinherited*, 122.

Spirit would, like Jesus and the first disciples, be content with what they already possessed even though it was little or nothing. Therefore, not only did they see a theological explanation for their contentment unnecessary, the very idea that an explanation was necessary was itself "unthinkable." Why explain the obvious? Here again, maybe this is the reason why some consider them naïve. They had not yet succumbed to a Constantinian compromise that sees the need to explain away ways of being faithful after the dominant pressure to be unfaithful has won out. Dominant typologies need no explaining, that is how they dominate. Thus, they had no reason to explain their lives as profoundly theological; they just lived their lives that way in the Spirit and thought others would too.

Pentecostalism can no longer afford this lack of theological explanation to be "unthinkable" since the Constantinian compromise within Pentecostalism has caused the earlier economic contentment to be largely lost, at least as a distinguishing feature of life in the Spirit. As a result, Pentecostalism is now paying a high price for its lack of a theological explanation for the economic contentment of their predecessors. For Pentecostals, or any other Christian for that matter, to be people of the Spirit once again, this aspect of Jesus' life and the lives of his followers in Acts must be given priority as a major feature to the shape and direction of the Christian life. Pentecostal leaders and scholars must re-invigorate their fellowships, and especially their own lifestyles, with a rigorous theology of economic contentment if they wish the people they lead to remain people of the Spirit.

Even though many of the early Pentecostals were from the middle to lower income groups, it is especially worth noting that not all of them were from poor, uneducated, or socially marginalized backgrounds. Wacker shows solid evidence that many Pentecostal leaders were at least from the middle-class and a few from upper-middle-class,[21] but one would expect the leaders to be some of the more educated and well-to-do and that the more educated of them would come from more affluent and educated backgrounds than the rank and file. He also points out that several among the more affluent used their resources to establish gospel printing companies, orphanages, and retirement centers but many others "evinced a trajectory of insistent upward mobility and personal achievement."[22] Even if there are some differences of opinion as to the demographic makeup

21. Wacker, *Heaven Below*, 202–3.
22. Ibid., 205.

of the early Pentecostals, there is no disputing the fact that many considered material possessions of this world to be just that, of this world. As such, many considered possessions as God's resources to be used to promote the work of Christ, spreading the full gospel message around the world, and even setting up relief agencies to care for the poor and afflicted as part of that gospel message. This contentment, sacrificial living, and sharing with others less fortunate was simply a way of living for many of them that goes beyond pragmatism. Sacrificing material resources out of contentment is anything but pragmatic.

Just what was it that prompted these people to do such remarkable things with so little? Was it only about being resourceful by making things stretch farther or just doing whatever was necessary to survive? Certainly the American culture was more content with less at the turn of the twentieth century; especially among the rural poor whose daily struggle it was just to survive. Is the fact that many early Pentecostals were from the lower social strata enough reason to explain why they lived the way they did or were they only products of their time? Rather than these sociological accounts that run things backwards into their lives and the lives of his followers in Acts, what if we start with Jesus' life and "run his life forward" into the lives of the early Pentecostals? This will not only allow us to account for their lives theologically but, as a result, will open up an understanding for the shape and direction for the Christian life today. That brings us to the task of explaining the shape and direction of the Christian life as one of communal sharing of resources based on the contentment in which Jesus lived in the Spirit.

Jesus Lived a Life of Contentment in the Spirit

If we consider Jesus' life of no material possessions as a result of the Spirit's presence rather than as merely a circumstance he endured, what would be the result? An honest reader of Luke's narrative cannot deny the fact he spends considerable time explaining the poor economic conditions into which Jesus was born. With this kind of beginning, is Luke not already showing Jesus' life as the Son of the Father in the Spirit to be a mission of living content as the will of his Father; that of trusting his Father? Being born into a family of such low economic status was no mere circumstance he passively endured. It was the will of the Father in the Spirit's presence in order for his life to reverse the structures of human economics. However, our task in this section calls us to investigate this matter with a deeper question than the surface issues that are normally addressed in regards to Jesus and possessions. We must delve deeper by asking, "Was Jesus' mission a calling to simply overturn one form of human oppression of the poor and replace it with another form or was it to reverse a deeper condition within humanity that is masked by other reasons for economic oppression and exploitation?

We see a deeper issue already emerging with Jesus' view of possessions during his temptations and ministry speech in Luke 4. Luke makes it clear that Jesus is filled with the Spirit (4:1) to not give in to Satan's temptation of being king by providing people their basic physical needs (4:3–4). The Spirit also leads Jesus back to Galilee to launch his ministry at the Nazareth synagogue (4:14), a ministry in the Spirit that would proclaim good news to the poor (4:18) and the year of the Lord's favor (4:19). This implies Jesus to be the Year of Jubilee, the setting free and releasing of all debts (4:21).[23] This is already a different sort of economics, not one based on greed for more but one based on contentment with what one has already been given; a radical trust in God as the giver of what one needs for today with no concern for tomorrow. Jesus' contentment in his Father's provisions is a radical trust in God that is unknown to earthly kingdoms and their kings because it does not originate in this world. As the messianic Son of God who bears the Spirit, Jesus claims a kind of sonship with his Father, as his royal Son, which goes beyond any earthly way of understanding kingdoms or being a king. He instructs his disciples to pray and practice the Jubilee Year[24] which, like his refusal of Satan's earlier

23. Yoder, *The Politics of Jesus*, 21–36, 60–71. Yoder gives a good description of this temptation against the backdrop of the widely accepted interpretation that eclipses the economic ramifications of Jesus' messianic mission. "Luke's report of the testing begins with the economic option. The spiritual filter through which we are now used to reading has dealt with the attraction of this temptation as a purely personal and carnal one. Jesus was hungry: would he by miracle abuse his omnipotence selfishly to feed himself? But one does not break a fast of forty days with crusty bread, certainly not with a whole field of boulder-size loaves. The option here, suggested or reinforced by Jesus' own renewed sensitivity to the pangs of hunger, was that his messianity would be expressed by his providing a banquet for his followers. That this is no idle imagination, the later story was to demonstrate. Feed the crowds and you shall be king" (25–26).

24. Ibid., 60–75. "Those numerous versions are in error which translate: 'Forgive us our offenses as we forgive those who have offended us.' Accurately, the *opheilema* of the Greek text signifies precisely a monetary debt, in the most material sense of the term. In the 'Our Father,' then, Jesus is not simply recommending vaguely that we might pardon those who have bothered us or made us trouble, but tells us purely and simply to erase the debts of those who owe us money; that is to say, practice the jubilee" (62).

temptation to provide bread, means a radical trust in God providing one's daily needs for food and survival, like Israel did in the wilderness.

Jesus' contentment in his Father's provisions is a reversal that elicits rejection and scorn from those threatened by it. Of course, those most threatened by Jesus' reversal of the human condition of greed are the ones who, by being in control of their own economics and of others, stand to lose the most from Jesus' reversal. As Jesus lives in the Spirit in submission to his Father's provisions, he reverses the economic conditions upon which their dominance depended.[25] Luke's narrative especially shows Jesus' kingdom reversing the economic conditions by adding nuances not seen in Matthew and Mark. Luke gives these nuances more significance by developing their continuity with the same themes in Acts. A particularly important example is Luke's use of "one's own property" (*ta idia*) in Peter's response of what they had given up to follow Jesus.[26] This comes after Jesus asks the rich man to sell all his possessions and follow him (18:28) and the crowd saying this was impossible for anyone to do. Upon Peter's response, Jesus promises them who had given up "all their own things" to follow him that they would receive much more in this life *and* eternal life in the age to come (18:29–30).

Luke portrays Jesus reversing the condition of economics by how he weaves together in a literary fashion both events and parables. In his actions and teachings, Jesus inaugurates his Father's kingdom economics that operate on a different basis than what the world knows—contentment with little or nothing. Whereas human forms of economics are based on desire for securing one's own possessions, thus securing one's own life, Jesus lives and teaches his Father's economics based on the desire to secure possessions for others, an economics Luke signifies as the Spirit's presence in Jesus' life. The parables of the Pounds (19:11–27), the Vineyard (20:9–19), Jesus cleaning out the Temple of robbers (19:45–48),

---

25. Johnson, *Literary Function of Possessions*, 125–26. This reversal is more than what Johnson has described as a "literary pattern" by which Luke "uses the language of possession symbolically." While Johnson shows how Luke's literary function of possessions contributes to our understanding of Jesus and the church in Acts, he admits this cannot account for all of what Luke meant. "Clearly, the content of the materials on possessions had a significance for the author and his readers not exhausted by their literary function. But what has been lacking till now is a sustained attempt to discover if these materials do make sense at the literary level as integral parts of the story" (129).

26. Ibid., 162. This is an important change for Luke from the synoptic parallels that use "all things" (Matt 19:27; Mark 10:28).

his teaching on paying taxes (20:20–26) and giving (20:45–47), and his teaching on David and the messiah of Ps 110 are all within the context of Jesus' entrance into Jerusalem as Israel's messianic Son. For Luke, these events all coalesce just before Jesus is killed in order to give greater emphasis upon what sort of messiah king Jesus is and over what sort of kingdom he reigns.

Luke demonstrates this kingdom to be the actual reversal of the human condition, a kingdom of radical trust in the Father made possible by the Spirit's presence. The kind of trust Jesus had toward his Father during his life and at his death was the renunciation of using possessions to secure or justify one's own self before God. Jesus performs his Father's kingdom by *not* securing his life with possessions. Rather, Jesus dispossesses his own life not only to be a servant and subvert the economic structures that elicit rejection but, going even further, he trusts God with the rejection he receives as a result of enacting his Father's kingdom. Once again, these two themes reciprocate most profoundly in Jesus' death on a cross, the most graphic reversal of using possessions for self-preservation. Jesus is stripped of his robe and the soldiers gamble for it. On the cross Jesus gives away his last piece of clothing to suffer the shame of nakedness, unable to hide from either his Father or from the mocking people. As Jesus had told them not to worry about getting possessions but to give them away (12:22–34), not to worry about worldly things (21:34–36), but to be a servant (22:24–27), he enacts his own teaching by literally taking on the form of a servant—having nothing and controlling nothing of his own.

By dying on a cross, Jesus demonstrates his own teachings most radically by not securing his own right to earthly possessions but rather denying a right to self-security. Going against all human desire to secure possessions for one's own self, thus attempting to justify one's self, he justifies God by accepting his Father's curse of having his last piece of clothing stripped away and gambled for by the Roman soldiers who were killing him.[27] The public shame Jesus endures in this act of self dispossession is largely lost on those in the west where the near-eastern concepts of honor and shame are not recognized. Thus, in both life and death, Jesus demonstrates the securing of one's own possessions to be idolatry because it replaces God's control over one's life with *one's own control*. It does not allow God to be God. Thus, Jesus' life in the Spirit justified God through

---

27. Ibid., 153–54.

contentment in being God's Son and, as a result, shows contentment in God's provisions to be how one lives in the Spirit.

Peace with Others: Living in the Spirit of Christ's Economics of Contentment

Probably the most vandalized verse in Scripture is Philippians 4:13, "I can do all things through him who strengthens me." It is generally robbed of it meaning by Christians needing a warrant for their continual striving for more of whatever their cravings desire. Understanding this verse in its entire Pauline context reveals just the opposite meaning than personal consumption, achievement, or greed. Paul means he is content and thus "can do" with whatever situation God puts him through in order for the gospel of Jesus Christ to be preached to the Gentiles. Paul begins his letter by describing his disregard for all earthly situations and motives for the greater purpose of Christ being preached (Phil 1:12–30), even disregarding those who preach from wrong motives of personal gain (1:15) even though he was in prison himself for preaching the *true* gospel (1:13–14).

> But I rejoiced in the Lord greatly, that now at last you have revived your concern for me; indeed, you were concerned before, but you lacked opportunity. Not that I speak from want, for I have learned to be content in whatever circumstances I am. I know how to get along with humble means, and I also know how to live in prosperity; in any and every circumstance I have learned the secret of being filled and going hungry, both of having abundance and suffering need. I can do all things through Him who strengthens me (Phil 4:10–13).

The central meaning of this text and a key to Paul's understanding of the Christian life is the word "content." Being content with whatever situation God placed him in was so central to Paul's thinking that he felt it necessary to explain his appreciation for the help they had given him without it being seen as wanting anything. Paul wanted for nothing, ironically, in prison.

Even though the Spirit does not have a prominent place in Philippians, the joy that comes from believing in Jesus Christ is the central theme that overcomes all life's obstacles (1:3; 2:29; 3:1; 4:1). This basic quality of joy is found in those who are in Christ and share in the same Spirit (2:1). Paul describes this unity of being in Christ and the comfort of being in the same Spirit as the basis for unity of mind and purpose among

Jesus' followers. The unity they already had in Christ was to be the basis for them thinking the same thing as Christ, having the same love, having one mind, and one purpose (2:2). For Paul, Christians having the "same mind" is based on the actual reality of Jesus' life as the way of thinking for his followers. How Jesus thought and what Jesus did is not only the pattern by which a believer is to live but an *actual present reality* in which his followers are called to participate fully.

Jesus' followers participate in the reality of his life by having the same Spirit that indwelt him. Jesus' life of humility and service to God and others serve for Paul as the way of life for Christians (Phil 2:6–11). This humility in Jesus was the result of him not desiring to be equal with God, even though he was like God in every way (2:6). He gave up equality with God and became "nothing," a man, even a servant (2:7) and was obedient even unto death, even death on a cross (2:8). This progression descends increasingly downward to the lowliest place within humanity and returns the other way, as in a chiastic structure, ascending upward by God raising him from the dead, giving him a name greater than any other name, so that every knee should bow, everyone in heaven, in earth, and under the earth, and that every tongue should confess that Jesus is Lord (2:9–11). This hymn shows the early church's narrative understanding of Jesus' life not only in the world as he lived, died, was buried, and raised, but of Jesus' life with God on an eternal scale as the result of his earthly life, conflating his eternality with his life within humanity. For Paul, Jesus death on a cross at the hands of humanity and his resurrection from the dead by God is the way one sees reality because, through them, God determined reality.

This actual reality of condescension and humility, made possible by Jesus' own life and death, was to be the actual way of thinking and acting for his followers (2:1) based on their understanding of the cross; not only Jesus' literal cross but the "way of the cross" was to be the Christian's mode of living. This way of thinking and acting, the cruciform life, was the "giving up" of one's own life, the "turning lose" of the desire to "be like God" or to "be God." The concept described by Gerhard Forde, of the "up-ward fall" that we saw earlier, is much more consistent with Scripture in that it shows Jesus' life and death as the actual reversal of God's curse upon humanity in Genesis 3 and is in line here with Paul's description of what happens when the Spirit works Jesus' cross and resurrection in one's life.[28] The Spirit puts "us down where we belong" in relation to our creator so that God can "raise us up" for his glory in Christ. Cross and resurrection then, as God's way of being God to us and for us becomes a Christian's very way of thinking and living in the Spirit. This thinking results in loving God with all one's heart and loving others as one's self, just as Jesus lived. We have already seen the shape of loving God with a life of non-violence that trusts God to be God. Here we see how loving others as one's own self creates an actual real-life equality based on the actuality of Jesus' cross breaking down the economic barriers erected by human sin. Economic equality is based on God's own character and actions and was lived out in the Spirit in Jesus' life as the Son of God.

Thinking the way of the cross is acknowledging God the Father as owner and creator of all things, as Jesus' life and death demonstrated. As Jesus lived in the Spirit with complete contentment in having no material possessions, his followers just do the same in the Spirit and think nothing of it. In the Spirit, they are satisfied in having nothing because they know, again by the Spirit, that they are heirs of all things in Christ. While Jesus had nothing, he "inherited the earth" by having everything. His baptism was the entrance into this mission of living in the Spirit that required no material possessions by which to live. His freedom from possessions was due to the Spirit's presence within him being absolutely dependent upon his Father to supply all his material needs. His dependence on his Father freed him from the bondage of independence that leaves one only bound to depending on one's own self for survival. Likewise for his followers, in repentance and baptism one dies to one's own desire for economic independence from God and others and is raised to new life in Christ to love God and others by seeing all of one's possessions as God's. With all of one's possessions as God's, a follower of Jesus views them as resources to be used to further God's care for others as Jesus did.

As Jesus explained God's character of caring for the sparrows and lilies of the fields and for his equal care for the just and unjust by sending his rain on both (Matt 5:45), so did his followers in Acts share equally of their resources with each other (Acts 2:44–46; 4:32–35). Paul follows suit by explaining justification of sinners as God's setting the disorder of humanity right by Jesus' death on a cross, creating a right order within his community by faith in his death on a cross as the establishment of the new order of the Spirit (Rom 3:23–31). Forgiveness of sins and tres-

---

28. Forde, *Theology is for Proclamation*, 48–49.

passes is God's removal of the law from dictating the old order of death in people's lives. It has no power due to the Spirit's work of placing a believer in Jesus Christ's life who is God's new order for humanity. Jesus' life is the Christian's life (Col 3:4). Jesus' life is the Christian's peace (Eph 2:14). Living in Jesus' life of peace, Jesus' followers live a life of contentment that internally motivates one to share, expecting nothing in return. Paul says this is a gift of the Spirit (Rom 12:8), but he also encourages all to love each other like brothers and sisters and to give more honor to others than one wants for themselves, repeating Jesus' second greatest commandment to love others as yourself (Rom 12:10). Paul makes it even more concrete for Christians by saying they are to share with God's people who need help and to even take strangers into their homes (Rom 12:13). Peter instructs Christians to do the same (1 Pet 4:9).

This cruciform life of sharing one's resources especially with other believers is made possible by Jesus' death on a cross which disarmed the fallen structures of humanity that control economic resources for their own purposes. Jesus' death on a cross, inflicted by humanity, was God's victory over the rulers of human economic structures and their human natures that control them. He stripped the spiritual rulers and powers that hold people captive to their authority. He disarmed them by literally dying to their power in submission (Col 2:15). In doing so, he freed his followers from bondage to the ruling spirits of the world (Col 2:20) and the rules they make to ensure their continued existence over earthly things (Col 2:21). This shows the Spirit who puts believers into Christ, making them other sons of God, to be against the ruling spirits of religion who only keep people in bondage to human commands and teachings; rules that keep people proud but do nothing to control the evil desires of their sinful self (Col 2:23). Laws do nothing to free people from bondage, they only punish those bound to keep them (Gal 2:19; 4:1–9; 5:1, 4). In contrast to natural law, the Spirit "kills" one's sinful desires of the flesh and its laws by "nailing them to the cross" (Gal 2:20) giving that person the Spirit to live as Christ lived, but with joy that only comes from the freedom found in Christ (Gal 5:1). This is true freedom from bondage to human structures, made possible only by dying to one's sinful self in order to live in the resurrection Spirit of Christ's life (Gal 5:16–18, 22–25).

Life in the Spirit Unites with Others: The Cruciform Culture of Racial Unity

As with our first two themes, we began seeing the trajectories of our third theme in chapter 3 of Jesus inaugurating the Kingdom of God that broke down the barriers between social classes and race and in chapter 4 of the Spirit's outpouring in Acts establishing the early church as God's ecclesia of *koinonia* fellowship of all races and ethnicities. We will now continue developing this theme into the other New Testament writers, especially Paul, by showing how they explain the church's unity in Christ based on Jesus' life as the Son of God in the Spirit. Justification for Paul does not mean a spiritual or mystical inner subjective experience or an abstract doctrine of forensic declaration. It means, at a more fundamental level, the actual concrete reality of Jesus' death on the cross and his resurrection from the dead that broke down the barriers established by human injustice. Jesus "set humanity straight" (Eph 2:11–22) "by abolishing in his flesh the enmity . . . so that in Himself he might make the two into one new man, thus establishing peace" (Eph 2:15). Those who are in Christ are to live out the actual concrete reality of unity they already have in Christ by their living unified as one with each other in the same Spirit in which Jesus lived in unity with the racially and socially marginalized. This community that is one in Jesus Christ is to be that new community of racial unity established in the Spirit. Those who live in the Spirit will live in racial unity with others simply because that is what Jesus established in his life in the Spirit and that is what the Spirit did in Acts following Christ pouring out his Spirit upon the church. People who live in the Spirit live in the reality of Christ's *koinonia* fellowship of racial and ethnic unity because that is what the Spirit does.

The Culture of Racial Unity among the Early Pentecostals

While racial unity was exhibited by some of the early Pentecostals, it was obvious that great attention to racial unity and equality would not be a lasting product of the Azusa Street revival. However, with the progress in racial equality in the overall culture of the United States during the past century, Pentecostals have been more willing in recent years to admit to this "forgotten" phenomenon of their early founders, especially in the life of William J. Seymour. Frank Bartleman is now often quoted as saying that at Azusa Street, "the 'color line' was washed away in the blood."[29] Wacker rightfully points out the difficulties in painting too rosy a picture of the interracial worship and practices of the early Pentecostals since it bowed to cultural pressure already present in its initial stages.[30] According to his assessment, "on the whole, pentecostal culture failed to provide a sustained theology of racial reconciliation for whites and blacks alike."[31] The early Pentecostals, while experiencing the effects of the Spirit's unity in Christ breaking down racial boundaries, did not explore the theological reasons for what was already happening in their circles. Wacker explains further why this eventually led to Pentecostalism succumbing to the overwhelming cultural pressure going in the other direction.

> What we see in all of this is that for pentecostals, as for most Christians in America, race relations kept getting mixed up. On the one hand ideals of racial mixing, even harmony, constantly renewed their lives. After all, pentecostal whites and blacks shared a common history, a common land, and, above all, a common faith. On the other hand strong pressures toward racial separation, even animosity, intruded. If whites bore the guilt of enslaving fellow Christians, blacks suffered the more onerous burden, imposed by their Christian consciences, of forgiving whites for wrongs inflicted. But on the whole the pentecostal message offered inadequate help to either group. . . . "Though Holy Spirit baptism implied divine enablement to overcome human frailties," James R. Goff observes, "few seemed clear about its implications or able to accept the radical consequences of its message."
>
> No one should be surprised. Pentecostals were, after all, normal American Christians, subject to all the prejudices and confusions that afflicted most normal American Christians. Pragmatic accommodation to the mores of the age was a survival strategy, not a certificate of moral purity.[32]

These assessments provide further warrant for a theological account able to explain why many of the early Pentecostals did live in racial reconciliation and unity during a time when it was not accepted within the

29. Wacker, *Heaven Below*, 228.

30. Ibid., 226–35.

31. Ibid., 227.

32. Ibid., 234–35.

overall culture, even though it did eventually succumb to the pressure of the American church's Constantinian compromise with the norms of American culture. However, there should at least be some space made for a theological account that does accept the radical consequences of its message, as an answer to Goff's insightful analysis. Progress in the area of racial equality in America obviously does not provide either the biblical theology or the sustained reality of what the Spirit does in Christ's *ecclesia*. If anything, it only glosses over a deeper problem of people thinking that such "progress" is equivalent to inner transformation.

An even greater obstacle to providing such a theological account for racial unity for Christians today, in light of the lives of the early Pentecostals, is the seeming progress that has been made in racial equality in America since the 1950s. The very need for such an account might be lost on those who point to this progress as a reason for complacency or accomplishment. No less could be the complacency among the Pentecostal fellowships today who point to recent overtures of racial harmony during the past couple of decades, such as the "Miracle in Memphis" among the leaders of the predominantly white Assemblies of God and the predominantly black Church of God in Christ.[33] A more recent development is the dialogue between the Assemblies of God and the predominately black United Pentecostal Council of the Assemblies of God initiated by its leader Thomas A. Barclay, a division that has existed since 1919.[34]

The danger with these accounts is the heart-warming nature in which they are described, as if the "righting of all wrongs" could happen simply by a symbolic or "spiritual" exercise that clouds the real problems that are deeply embedded within the structures that have been built on a foundation of racism—a "hidden" structural racism that is intertwined within the larger structured economic inequalities that will always persist in America. What is actually needed to overturn this structurally embedded racism is a theological proposal that calls for the end of the hidden structural racism within Christ's own *ecclesia*, one that especially calls for a structural realignment of all parties involved, literally and materially. How can the church proclaim the reality of Christ's unified body to the world if it is not willing to end its own structural racism first? Without a theological foundation that calls for structural realignment, warm-hearted overtures will continue to give a false sense of accomplishment

---

33. Rodgers, "The Assemblies of God and the Long Journey," 50–61.
34. Harrup, "A Larger Family," 6–10.

that takes pride in nostalgic, but otherwise empty, promises. This will only continue as long as churches continue to build edifices to the glory and victory of racial and economic segregation by building multi-million dollar buildings along the freeways in the wealthiest suburbs so they can more easily forget their Christian brothers and sisters who struggle to keep the lights on in their churches in the economically depressed inner-cities that are still "on the other side of the tracks." This alone shows that stories of racial unity are only stories, with little theological substance of what the Spirit's presence meant for Jesus' life or the Christians' lives in Acts. Hopefully, the account spelled out here will further the conversation and help provide a foundation for deep structural change by making the connections between Jesus' life and the lives of his followers; lives of racial unity and equality based on Jesus' life as the Son of God in the Spirit who makes other sons of God who live like he did. As other sons of God, Jesus' followers are made reconcilers and peacemakers between the most estranged, disinherited, and marginalized people by being put into Jesus' life, which was God's very own reconciliation of all people back to himself and to each other.

Jesus Lived in Racial and Ethnic Unity in the Spirit

As the Son of God, Jesus lived in the Spirit content with his Father's providence over all ethnic and racial identities, beginning with his own. By being content in the Spirit with who he was in his Father, caring most about his Father's house even at age 12 (Luke 2:41–50), Jesus cared more about people who were despised than he did his own reputation. In his Israelite setting this meant caring for those whom Israel had cast out in varying degrees, but, nevertheless, a structured prejudice based on the God-given hierarchical structure of their worship, especially prejudice toward those of other partially Jewish or non-Jewish races and ethnicities. In the Spirit, Jesus performed and proclaimed his Father's kingdom by loving the people his own religion and society had cast out and despised, becoming one of the despised by doing so. Even from his birth into a common working-class family in Nazareth, Jesus would live as the Son of God reversing the human condition of racial prejudice by *being* God's reversal, that is, claiming to be God's anointed Son yet living as a Son no one could possibly believe was God's Spirit-anointed.

Yet in the Spirit's anointing, Jesus thought nothing of himself but only of his Father, which was the Spirit's presence of peace and contentment with who he was in his Father. Again, our two themes coalesce in seeing not only Jesus loving the people society despised and shamed but in seeing his acceptance of the ultimate punishment he would receive from the people doing the despising and shaming. In response to this rejection from the religious and cultural despisers toward the ethnic outcasts, Jesus suffers the same despising and shame as an outcast. He becomes one of them to reverse their shame. As with our other two themes of violence and possessions, Luke shows Jesus reversing the human condition of ethnic oppression by not only identifying with the despised, he became the most despised among them since there was no greater shame and despising by which culture inflicted than crucifying a person on a cross.

Jesus, as the Spirit-anointed Son of God, identifies with society's outcasts even from his birth. That God chose a servant girl Mary in which to conceive his Son by the Spirit and that he chose shepherds (of Nazareth in Galilee no less) to receive the angels' birth announcement actually enact the very prophecies surrounding the events. From Zachariah's prophecy of the dawning new day shining on those in darkness (1:79) and Simeon's prophecy of Jesus being a light for the Gentiles to see (2:32), Luke is setting the stage for Jesus being the reconciliation of those outside Israel and even outsiders within Israel back to God and to each other. As noted earlier, Jesus' baptism by John in the Jordan was certainly unorthodox in its acceptance of those cast out of the "pure" worship in Jerusalem; the young, the poor, the sick, women, and especially Gentiles. Likewise, Jesus' ministry announcement already had put him at odds with Israel's religious order by his claim that the Spirit was upon him to reverse their despising of outcasts. Caring for the poor, captives, blind, down-trodden, and giving Jubilee favor put him on a sure path to being one of society's outcasts himself, since the very notion of such practices was, in itself, judgment upon the prejudices they held against the culturally despised.

Not only did Jesus minister to the poor but all those society labeled as "outcasts" for various cultural reasons, such as tax collectors and women of ill repute. He called Galilean fishermen, tax collectors, "commoners," and religious outcasts to be his disciples. That Jesus went into the home of wealthy Zaccheus, a tax collector, shows he cared for anyone cut off from society's mainstream, whether for being poor, immoral, or evil.[35]

---

35. Johnson, *Literary Function of Possessions*, 139. Johnson seems close to eliminating the poor in Luke as a category by enveloping them into the larger category of outcasts, even though he is right by saying the poor suffer doubly as both socially

Whatever the reason people are outcasts from society, Jesus reverses their condition by not only changing the social status of the despised but releasing them from their sins that cause their outcast status. What does this reversal mean, since being considered a "sinner" was the label given by God himself to his own people of Israel to regulate the very definition and enforcement of holiness within its community? Was Jesus changing even God's definitions or showing how Israel had perverted God's calling of being a light to the Gentiles? Obviously he was doing both by declaring those whom society labeled "sinners" as released from their sins and calling the religious leaders the real sinners by their rejection of his forgiveness, the very thing Israel was called to do all along. Going even further, Jesus calls the forgiven and released to love their enemies, a further reversal of societal norms. Since no ethnic society ever survived by loving its enemies, Jesus was establishing a new society, a new way of being ethnic that burst the "wineskins" of Israel's understanding of ethnicity. This new community was one that would love their enemies by having the Spirit's indwelling. Jesus reversed society's very way of being human. He replaced what humans and their cultures naturally do, only loving those who love in return and who are most like them (Luke 6:27–36), with his Father's kingdom of loving people that culture *most despises* and those who are most *un*like them.

Luke develops this theme best by simply narrating events where Jesus actually reverses the social order and changes its definitions. One clear example is Jesus forgiving the sinful woman simply for her believing in him. Out of this belief she washes his feet with her tears, dries them with her hair, kisses them, and anoints them with perfume (Luke 7:38). The Pharisee, in whose house Jesus was eating, thinks about her with scorn (Luke 7:36–50). The irony is in the Pharisee's scorning of Jesus for him not perceiving her to be a "sinner" while Jesus perceives his scornful thoughts towards the believing "sinful" woman. By a literary and literal reversing, now the Pharisee is the sinner and the woman (by knowing she is sinful) is the righteous one free from sin. Obviously, the woman thought of herself as a sinner else she would not believe that Jesus had released her from her sins. Her faith had *already* released her from her sin. The Pharisee is the sinner by thinking he is righteous. This shows

---

ostracized and poor. "The thematic statements designating the poor specify them as outcasts; the narrative shows us that this poverty is not an economic designation, but a designation of spiritual status."

Luke's description of salvation as belief in Jesus releasing sinners from their sin, not in some inner spiritual sense but in actual reality. By narrative description of Jesus bringing outcasts in and casting out the insiders and by proclaiming the release of prisoners, Luke continues this theme of Jesus reversing society's social order. However, it is not only in a present sense, although it is that, but it is a present reality because it is an eternal reality breaking into the present.

These events demonstrate that Jesus identified with those ostracized out to the farthest margins of society and to the degree to which he was counted as one of them by becoming the most ostracized of all as a criminal being executed on a cross. Since these events literally carried out Jesus' birth and platform announcements of being born in and anointed by the Spirit as the Son of God, being ostracized by the political, economic, and cultural leaders of society was not only a result of the Spirit doing the Father's will in him but the non-violent acceptance of society's punishment was the reciprocal result of being the Son of God in the Spirit. In being God's Son in the Spirit, Jesus justified God rather than himself by going all the way to the most radically "other" of humanity to not only take their place but be one of the most unloved, shamed, scorned, ridiculed, and God-forsaken of all outcasts. One of the other criminals who died next to him was able to perceive this when no one else could. By going to the "other" of humanity Jesus went to the "other" of God (at least to a human perspective), so far "other" than God that no person could say he was God's Son as he hung dying on the cross, ostracized and despised by the most righteous of Israel and the most powerful of Rome. All that any person could say was that Jesus *was* God's curse, but, in *being* God's curse, he eliminated humanity's estrangement that resulted from God ostracizing humanity from his presence in Genesis 3. By becoming God's most ostracized, and paying the ultimate penalty for it, Jesus secured reconciliation for anyone who would believe that his death and resurrection secured their own reconciliation to God and to others. This makes true faith the glad acceptance of being cursed by God and with Jesus' death on a cross being the reversal and the remedy for that curse.

Peace with Others: Living in the Spirit of Christ's Cruciform Culture of Racial Unity

For Paul, the most basic result of salvation in Jesus Christ is the unity his death provided for all people, whether Jews or Gentiles, as sons of the

Father in the Spirit (Eph 2:11–3:6). That Jesus' death broke down all the walls of division between people groups (Col 1:19–22; 3:11), by making one community of *koinonia* fellowship as his own body, is the good news of the gospel. The gospel is God's declaration that through his Son Jesus he has made one people for himself out of all estranged people from all nations. Paul makes this clear to the Galatians who had forsaken the gospel of Jesus Christ (Gal 2:6) only to be foolish by being tricked into believing a false gospel (3:1) that relied on their own power (3:3) of doing good works (3:4). A salvation based on people's abilities is divisive by still requiring people to do the law (5:1–4). All law is divisive by its very nature due to it distinguishing those who can do it from those who either refuse to do or cannot do it. Even the law God gave to Israel was divisive since by it God separated Israel as a sanctified people from the nations and even separated people within Israel from the most holy down the least holy. As such, the law only provided the means for God's people to serve him *within the condition of enmity*, which is all that any law can do. Jesus' death on a cross, on the other hand, *abolished the enmity* between those with the law and those without the law because his death showed all people to be condemned by God whether they were the Jews with the law or the Gentiles who have a law unto themselves (Rom 2:14–15).

Jesus' death especially condemns the most "righteous" of all—those who think they are righteous by their ability to keep any part of the law, which divides (Gal 3:10–11, 17–19). The true gospel, Paul says, is the reality that Jesus' death abolished all divisions between people by reconciling them back to God. Faith is one's belief that Jesus' death accomplished this reality (Gal 2:15–21), the believing of which is from hearing the gospel and which results in one receiving the Holy Spirit (Gal 3:2–5, 14) to be children of God by being in Christ (3:26–27). Only by being in Christ, in whom there is no difference between ethnicities, races, social classes, ages, or genders (3:28), will a person inherit all of God's blessings to Abraham (3:29).

As significant as all the New Testament discussions are concerning these barriers of racial estrangement being broken by the death and resurrection of Jesus Christ, one question still remains. Just exactly what is one to do today, whose life is shaped by the indwelling Spirit given by Christ, about racial unity? The first step is the actual realization that one *has already been made* responsible for racial peacemaking by being adopted by God as another son in the Spirit and, as such, called to a life of racial reconciliation based on the reality that Christ has *already* reconciled one's life back to right relationship with God (2 Cor 5:18–25). Christians are racial peacemakers, not racial discriminators, because they *have been made one body* in the Spirit. This means that to live a life in the Spirit one is to purposefully engage in visibly removing racial barriers and prejudices especially within the *ecclesia* of Christ's body, the church, that have been erected as a result of the church's Constantinian unfaithfulness to Jesus as Lord over the nations. As mentioned earlier, this is especially true regarding the literal and physical dismantling of ecclesial structures erected upon the Constantinian idolatry of racial prejudices.

Conclusion

In this examination of the essence of the Christian life as life in the Spirit, we have been able to see Jesus in his Trinitarian life as the Son of God living in the Spirit by trusting God with his life even unto death on a cross. This led us to Acts where we saw the proclamation of the early church as bringing "death" and "resurrection" to unbelievers who were then baptized into Jesus' life with the Father in the Spirit as other sons of God. This receiving of the Spirit's indwelling allowed us to also make the necessary connections to Paul's description of the Christian life as life in the Spirit, showing the Christian life as total trust in God with one's own life just as Jesus lived. These trajectories were seen as trusting God by being non-violent even to one's enemies, being content with God's provisions in order to share with others in need, and being content with how one has been created by God in order to love all people of other races and cultures, especially within the ecclesial fellowship of the church's *koinonia* "sharedness." This shows the Christian life to be a Trinitarian life of sonship with God in the Spirit by being adopted by God to participate in Jesus Christ's life as a son of God, a life that trusts God and is faithful even unto death and so lives abundantly in Jesus' resurrected life in the Spirit.

6

Concluding Summary and Implications

Summary

In this discussion I have given an account of the Christian life as life in the Spirit. Given the New Testament's witness to the Christian life as one lived in the Spirit, this project will seem to some as highly unoriginal, but, given modern theology's propensity to ignore Christ's life in accounts of the Christian life, there turns out to be considerable room for various kinds of contemporary accounts of the Christian life, including life in the Spirit.

As I discussed in chapter 1, without Jesus' life defining the Christian's life, other accounts are given priority over Jesus' life, not only for what it means to live as a Christian but, more specifically, what it means to live in the Spirit. John Howard Yoder identified this neglect of Jesus' life in *The Politics of Jesus*. There he identified a faulty use of natural theology, such as that of H. Richard Niebuhr, for replacing Jesus' life with other sources like reason, nature, reality, and creation. Stanley Hauerwas has added to Yoder's critique by showing how Reinhold Niebuhr, H. Richard's brother, viewed Jesus as nothing more than the best human possible. Hauerwas demonstrates how this faulty use of natural theology, and the liberal Protestant agenda it supports, as providing a "reasonable" Christianity to assure the church a "winning outcome" in a culture living in rebellion to Christ's lordship.

Although Yoder and Hauerwas have offered helpful critiques of the church's Constantinian unfaithfulness, their accounts are based on Logos-Christology that takes for granted Jesus' divine nature. While not denying the Spirit's necessary presence in either Jesus' life or the Christian's, their christological approach cannot fully explain *how* one lives like Jesus lived because they do not first fully explain *how* Jesus lived as a result of the Spirit's presence. Logos-Christology, while no doubt true, is not as helpful in explaining how others live like Jesus because no one else has ever been born with a divine nature. What is helpful is beginning with *how* Jesus lived as a result of the Spirit. Trinitarian Spirit-Christology provides this framework.

In chapter 2 I surveyed a range of Pneumatologies and Spirit-Christologies to test their adequacy to serve as a basis for seeing Jesus' life and death as a result of the Spirit. This led us to Leopoldo Sánchez's account of Spirit-Christology put forth in his published dissertation, *Receiver, Bearer, and Giver of God's Spirit*, in which Jesus is bearer of God's Spirit in a unique and unrepeatable way. This model gives us the proper basis upon which to describe Jesus' life as a result of the Spirit's presence and as defining for how the church proclaims the gospel in such a way that, through it, God adopts sinners as his sons.

With Sánchez's Spirit-Christology as my basis, I explained in chapter 3 how Jesus' life in the Spirit as God's Son was his calling to procure a life of sonship for others. Hans Frei has helped us see that it was Jesus' identity within the narrative itself that shows his very aim through *both* what he does *and* through the events that devolve around him, especially in the events of the last few days of his life. As the Son of God, Jesus is known not only in *what* he was but in *how* he lived and died; a relational Trinitarian identity as the Son of God in the Spirit. This reciprocal relationship between how Jesus lives in the Spirit and what happens to him shows continuity, even if a seemingly incongruous one, between Jesus being God's Spirit-anointed kingly messiah and the rejection that such a life evokes.

Jesus' baptism by John in the Jordan, a public declaration to bypass Jerusalem's religious establishment, and his declaration at his hometown synagogue in Nazareth to be the fulfillment of Isaiah's prophecy, establish the foundation of this reciprocal relationship between the Spirit's anointing and his establishing God's new kingdom by reversing the human condition of sin. God's new kingdom requires a new kind of king. At Jesus' temptations, Jesus refused to be a worldly king, trusting rather in his Father's way of being king. But what kind of a kingdom would Jesus be inaugurating if his Father's way of being a king entailed being rejected by humanity? How could anyone call him king if being God's king *neces-*

sarily entailed being rejected as king? Luke answers neither of these; he only continues his narrative.

Robert Tannehill helps us see that Jesus' mission as the Son of God is fulfilled by humanity rejecting his mission by its inability to see it, the greatest paradox ever but by God's own design. In Jesus' suffering and death *for* humanity, salvation is procured by the very rejection he receives *from* humanity. Through Jesus' suffering and death, God being *against us* is also God being *for us*. Why else would Luke make it so clear that Jesus is declared to be the Son of God, by a Roman soldier helping kill him no less, just when no person could ever believe it?

The upshot to the kind of death Jesus died trusting his Father in the Spirit was that it took his Father resurrecting him to prove to humanity that *how* Jesus lived his life is *how* one lives in the Spirit. Now we see how right Yoder was to suggest that cross and resurrection is "God's grain of the universe." Also understanding this to be how the Spirit works not only helps ensure that Jesus' death and resurrection remain Trinitarian events but that believing it as one's salvation requires no less of the Spirit's presence to reveal it. That it must be revealed means the Spirit works the constitutive events of Jesus' life in others through the proclamation of his life and death that "kills" the old and "raises" the new, whereby others are adopted as sons of God.

This is clearly seen in Luke's portrayal of Jesus' followers in Acts who now, following the Spirit's outpouring at Pentecost, live cruciform lives as Jesus lived. With the Spirit being given, they live and even die trusting God to resurrect them at the Last Day, just as Jesus had in his life. Luke is careful to portray Stephen's speech and submission to God in death the same way Jesus had lived and died. Also, Peter's sermon at Pentecost and at Solomon's portico, Stephen's speech to the Sanhedrin, and Paul's speech in Athens all reflect this same pattern; Jesus was delivered up unto death but God raised him up in vindication, requiring the Spirit to believe.

That the sermons in Acts require a miracle of the Spirit to believe calls for a reimagining of the church and its ministries in order for faith to happen again. William Willimon suggests we preach again with such boldness that if there is no Holy Spirit our message is doomed to fall on deaf ears. The late Pentecostal preacher David Wilkerson preached this way; preaching in such a way as to evoke the Spirit's presence to believe since no one could ever believe his message and repent without the Spirit. Such were the sermons in Acts, where people, upon hearing them, cried out, "What must we do to be saved?" Peter's answer was for all people, "Repent and be baptized, every one of you, for the remission of your sins, and you will receive the Holy Spirit."

In Acts, the Spirit works sonship with God for others through preaching done with the following three characteristics: first, by requiring the Holy Spirit to work a miracle of faith to believe it, second, by "killing" and "making alive" through the authority Christ gave his apostles, and, third, by being tragic to the individual. This manner of preaching the gospel not only ensures the Spirit's work of adopting other sons of God into Christ's new political, economic, and cultural community of *koinonia* fellowship, it also ensures that baptism remains the sign of God's adoption of other sons into Christ's new community. The believer's baptism is likewise the Spirit's work of "drowning" the old self living in rebellion against God and "resurrecting" the new self to live in Christ's life. Just as believers have been baptized into Christ's death, they have been raised to live in Christ's resurrection (Rom 6:1–11). As the lives of the early twentieth century Pentecostals demonstrate, the indwelling Spirit is the reason people live like Jesus lived; by loving and trusting God by living non-violently, by being content with God's provisions and sharing with those in need, and by being content with how one has been created by God so as to love people of other ethnicities and cultures.

Implications for Further Study

As many Christian faith traditions have lost their footing by their continual allegiance to a Constantinian synthesis that is crumbling out from underneath them, the implications of how Jesus lived out his life of sonship with the Father in the Spirit calls for a reimagining of the church and the Christian life that is faithful to Jesus' life. As these idolatrous footings continue to crumble, Christians in all cultures, especially ones infected with Western ideologies, will be left to forge ahead either by using popular methods to indulge people's quest to find a purpose to their meaningless lives or by allowing, as the church did in Acts, the stone the builders rejected to be the chief cornerstone of the temple God is building with human stones. Just exactly what shape this post-Constantinian ecclesial order will take is yet to be seen. Only one thing is certain; new structures that are just as unfaithful to Jesus' lordship will be offered to take the place of the present unfaithful ones that are crumbling. That the ground underneath is giving way is just another indication that the Constantinian hope of the church "saving the world" is unfounded since only Jesus can save the world. What the church's hope is founded upon is the confession that Jesus is the Christ, the Son of the living God, raised from the dead, and returning to earth to judge the living and the dead. With this confession, God's adopted sons are called to do only one thing, be faithful witnesses to Jesus Christ's lordship.

In light of this proposal for the church to live as the faithful witness to Jesus' lordship before the world, there are many areas of study for theologians and preachers in the church to explore so as to offer faithful accounts of the Christian life in areas that have been previously explained in ways amenable to Constantinianism. I will suggest only three here, one each in the area of church life, the individual's life, and family life. These are ecclesial structure, Christian discipleship, and a Christian view of marriage, respectively.

First, ecclesial structure is an area that not only has great need of a re-examination, it is incumbent upon the church to be found faithful to Jesus' lordship once again by throwing off the idolatrous structural hierarchies patterned after the greed of corporate America. One thing this account of the Christian life should help demonstrate is that the church Jesus established by giving his Sprit is *not* a business. In this post-Constantinian age, there is much more work to be done in developing an ecclesial structure that ferrets out the implications of life in the Spirit in practical ways that advance the church's mission to the world while maintaining its belief in Jesus' lordship over all.

Second, Christian discipleship today is replete with erroneous notions of self-achievement that are influenced by the worldly notion of self-esteem. Faithful ministers of the gospel of Jesus Christ need to not only proclaim the gospel in such a way that requires the Spirit to transform lives into the image of Jesus Christ, but to go further in developing Christian discipleship programs that *begin and end* with the idea of Jesus Christ's identity *replacing* one's need for self-actualization. Such an effort would help bring an end to the self's desire to be "actualized," since, in Christ, the Spirit "kills" the self of flesh and its desires. At a time when many churches bemoan the fact that the majority of their youth leave the church when they go off to college, one thing that might work better than giving them more of what has not worked already is to *make* our youth disciples of Jesus Christ as Jesus commanded us to do. The church might just find this works better in the long run than helping them "feel better" with games, gimmicks, and pop psychology.

Third, a Christian understanding of marriage in light of the Spirit's work of "death" and "resurrection" as God's "grain of the universe" is also desperately needed, especially when many Christian marriage seminars are only an attempt to help people "try harder" at being a "good spouse" and many Christian discussions on gender issues are only a hybrid of American individualism with a little bit of God's "created order of nature" thrown in to appease a Christian's trust in the law of nature and their own abilities in the flesh to achieve such laws. One helpful thing this post-Constantinian era has taught the church is that it can no longer rely on "human nature" to prop up one's belief that God's order of heterosexual and monogamous marriage is "natural." It was certainly not any more "natural" for Paul in Corinth than is it today in Las Vegas. What seems more biblically consistent for the church is to describe marriage and gender in light of faith in Jesus' death and resurrection as overturning and reversing what only seems natural to the human condition of sin that strives to fulfill what is missing with more sin.

In all of these areas, future scholarship is needed based upon an understanding that Jesus Christ's identity supplants one's personal identity in this world. This will yield an understanding in the areas of church structure, discipleship, and marriage that begins with the identity of Jesus Christ as the Son of God in the Spirit as *establishing the identity* of God's adopted sons in the Spirit. This would help Christian ministers and all Christians alike to not only have a better understanding of their place of vocation in the world as witnesses to the lordship of Jesus Christ, but it would also promote unity in the body of Christ based on the actual unity that all his adopted sons *already have* by *having already been put into* Jesus Christ's life in the Spirit by the Spirit.

Bibliography

Ädna, Jostein. "Jesus Symbolic Act in the Temple (Mark 11:15–17): The Replacement of the Sacrificial Cult by His Atoning Death." In *Gemeinde ohne Temple/Community without Temple: Zur Substituierung und Transformation des Jerusalemer Tempels und seines Kults im Alten Testament, anitken Judentum und frühen Cristentum*, edited by Beate Ego, Armin Lange, and Peter Pilhofer, 461–75. Wissenshaftliche Untersuchungen zum Neuen Testament 118. Tübingen: Mohr/Siebeck, 1999.

Alexander, Paul. *Peace to War: Shifting Allegiances in the Assemblies of God*. Telford, PA: Cascadia, 2009.

Alfaro, Sammy. *Divino Compañero: Toward a Hispanic Pentecostal Christology*. Eugene, OR: Pickwick, 2010.

Anderson, Robert Mapes. *The Vision of the Disinherited: The Making of American Pentecostalism*. Peabody, MA: Hendrickson, 1979.

Arendt, Hannah. *On Violence*. New York: Harcourt, Brace, 1970.

Barrett, C. K. *Jesus and the Gospel Tradition*. London: SPCK, 1967.

Bartleman, Frank. *Azusa Street: an Eyewitness Account*. 1980. Reprint, Gainesville, FL: Bridge-Logos, 2006.

Beaman, Jay. *Pentecostal Pacifism: The Origin, Development, and Rejection of Pacific Belief among the Pentecostals*. Hillsboro, KS: Center for Mennonite Brethren Studies, 1989.

Bellah, Robert N., et al. *Habits of the Heart: Individualism and Commitment in America*. Updated ed. Berkeley: University of California Press, 1996.

Bellinger, Charles K. *The Trinitarian Self: The Key to the Puzzle of Violence*. Eugene, OR: Pickwick, 2008.

Bercot, David. *The Kingdom that Turned the World Upside Down*. Amberson, PA: Scroll, 2003.

Berger, Peter L. *The Heretical Imperative: Contemporary Possibilities of Religious Affirmation*. Garden City, NY: Anchor, 1979.

Boersma, Hans. *Violence, Hospitality, and the Cross: Reappropriating the Atonement Tradition*. Grand Rapids: Baker Academic, 2004.

Boff, Leonardo. *Trinity and Society*. Translated by Paul Burns. Maryknoll, NY: Orbis, 1988.

Boyd, Gregory A. *The Myth of a Christian Nation: How the Quest for Political Power Is Destroying the Church*. Grand Rapids: Zondervan, 2005.

Bruner, Frederick Dale. *A Theology of the Holy Spirit: The Pentecostal Experience and the New Testament Witness*. Grand Rapids: Eerdmans, 1970.

Carter, Craig A. *The Politics of the Cross: The Theology and Social Ethics of John Howard Yoder*. Grand Rapids: Brazos, 2001.

———. *Rethinking Christ and Culture: A Post-Christendom Perspective*. Grand Rapids: Brazos, 2006.

Cary, Phillip. *Augustine's Invention of the Inner Self: The Legacy of a Christian Platonist*. Oxford: Oxford University Press, 2000.

Clapp, Rodney. *A Peculiar People: The Church as Culture in a Post-Christian Society*. Downers Grove, IL: InterVarsity, 1996.

Classen, Elaine. "To You Is the Promise: A Rhetorical-Exegetical Study of Acts 2." PhD diss., Pontificia Universitas Gregoriana, 1994.

Coffey, David. *Deus Trinitas: The Doctrine of the Triune God*. New York: Oxford University Press, 1999.

———. "The 'Incarnation' of the Holy Spirit in Christ." *Theological Studies* 45 (1984) 466–80.

Colson, Charles, with Harold Fickett. *The Good Life: Seeking Purpose, Meaning, and Truth in Your Life*. Wheaton, IL: Tyndale House, 2005.

Cox, Harvey. *Fire From Heaven: The Rise of Pentecostal Spirituality and the Reshaping of Religion in the Twenty-first Century*. Reading, MA: Addison-Wesley, 1995.

Craddock, Fred B. *As One without Authority*. Nashville: Abingdon, 1979.

Dayton, Donald W. *Theological Roots of Pentecostalism*. Grand Rapids: Asbury, 1987.

Del Colle, Ralph. *Christ and the Spirit: Spirit-Christology in Trinitarian Perspective*. New York: Oxford University Press, 1994.

Dunn, James D. G. *Baptism in the Holy Spirit*. London: SCM, 1970.

———. *The Christ and the Spirit*. Vol. 1, *Christology*. Grand Rapids: Eerdmans, 1998.

———. *Jesus and the Spirit: A Study of the Religious and Charismatic Experience of Jesus and the First Christians as Reflected in the New Testament*. Grand Rapids: Eerdmans, 1997.

Elshtain, Jean Bethke. *Sovereignty: God, State, and Self*. Gifford Lectures. New York: Basic Books, 2008.

Esler, Philip Francis. *Community and Gospel in Luke-Acts: The Social and Political Motivations of Lucan Theology*. Cambridge: Cambridge University Press, 1987.

Forde, Gerhard O. *The Captivation of the Will: Luther versus Erasmus on Freedom and Bondage*. Edited by Steven Paulson. Grand Rapids: Eerdmans, 2005.

———. *On Being a Theologian of the Cross: Reflections on Luther's Heidelberg Disputation, 1518*. Grand Rapids: Eerdmans, 1997.

———. *The Preached God: Proclamation in Word and Sacrament*. Edited by Mark C. Mattes and Steven D. Paulson. Grand Rapids: Eerdmans, 2007.

———. *Theology Is for Proclamation*. Minneapolis: Fortress, 1990.

Frei, Hans W. *The Eclipse of the Biblical Narrative: A Study in Eighteenth and Nineteenth Century Hermeneutics*. New Haven: Yale University Press, 1974.

———. *The Identity of Jesus Christ: The Hermeneutical Bases for Dogmatic Theology*. Philadelphia: Fortress, 1975.

———. *Theology and Narrative: Selected Essays*. Edited by George Hunsinger and William C. Placher. New York: Oxford University Press, 1993.

Gay, Craig M. *The Way of the (Modern) World, or, Why It's Tempting to Live as if God Doesn't Exist*. Grand Rapids: Eerdmans, 1998.

Grenz, Stanley J. *The Social God and the Relational Self: A Trinitarian Theology of the Imago Dei*. Louisville: Westminster John Knox, 2001.

Habets, Myk. *The Anointed Son: A Trinitarian Spirit Christology*. Eugene, OR: Pickwick, 2010.

Harris, Harriet A. "Should We Say that Personhood is Relational?" *Scottish Journal of Theology* 51 (1998) 214–34.

Harrisville, Roy. *Fracture: The Cross as Irreconcilable in the Language and Thought of the Biblical Writers.* Grand Rapids: Eerdmans, 2006.

Harrup, Scott. "A Larger Family." *The Pentecostal Evangel* (16 January 2011) 6–10.

Hauerwas, Stanley. *Against the Nations: War and Survival in a Liberal Society.* Notre Dame: University of Notre Dame Press, 1992.

———. *A Better Hope: Resources for a Church Confronting Capitalism, Democracy, and Postmodernity.* Grand Rapids: Brazos, 2000.

———. *Dispatches from the Front: Theological Engagements with the Secular.* Durham: Duke University Press, 1994.

———. *In Good Company: The Church as Polis.* Notre Dame: University of Notre Dame Press, 1995.

———. *Sanctify Them in the Truth: Holiness Exemplified.* Nashville: Abingdon, 1998.

———. *Unleashing the Scripture: Freeing the Bible from Captivity to America.* Nashville: Abingdon, 1993.

———. "When the Politics of Jesus Makes a Difference." *Christian Century* (October 13, 1993) 982–87.

———. *Wilderness Wanderings: Probing Twentieth Century Theology and Philosophy.* Boulder, CO: Westview, 1997.

———. *With the Grain of the Universe: The Church's Witness and Natural Theology.* Grand Rapids: Brazos, 2001.

———. *Working With Words: On Learning to Speak Christian.* Eugene, OR: Cascade, 2011.

Hauerwas, Stanley and L. Gregory Jones, eds. *Why Narrative? Readings in Narrative Theology.* Grand Rapids: Eerdmans, 1989.

Hauerwas, Stanley, and Alex Sider. Introduction to *Preface to Theology: Christology and Theological Method*, by John Howard Yoder. Grand Rapids: Brazos, 2002.

Hauerwas, Stanley, and William H. Willimon. *Resident Aliens: Life in the Christian Colony.* Nashville: Abingdon, 1989.

Hauerwas, Stanley, Nancey Murphy, and Mark Nation, eds. *Theology without Foundations: Religious Practice and the Future of Theological Truth.* Nashville: Abingdon, 1994.

Hauerwas, Stanley, et al., eds. *The Wisdom of the Cross: Essays in Honor of John Howard Yoder.* Eugene, OR: Wipf & Stock, 2005.

Hjalmeby, Erik J. *A Rhetorical History of Race Relations in the Early Pentecostal Movement: 1906–1916.* Waco, TX: Baylor University Press, 2007.

Hollerich, Michael J. "Retrieving a Neglected Critique of Church, Theology and Secularization in Weimar Germany." *Pro Ecclesia* 2 (1993) 305–32.

Hunter, Harold D., and Cecil M. Robeck Jr., eds. *The Azusa Street Revival and Its Legacy.* Cleveland: Pathway, 2006.

Johnson, Luke Timothy. *The Literary Function of Possessions in Luke-Acts.* SBL Dissertation 39. Missoula, MT: Scholars, 1977.

Kärkkäinen, Veli-Matti. *Pneumatology: The Holy Spirit in Ecumenical, International, and Contextual Perspective.* Grand Rapids: Baker Academic, 2002.

———. *Toward a Pneumatological Theology: Pentecostal and Ecumenical Perspectives on Ecclesiology, Soteriology, and Theology of Mission.* Edited by Amos Yong. Lanham, MD: University Press of America, 2002.

Keener, Craig S. *Introduction and 1:1—2:47.* Vol. 1 of *Acts: An Exegetical Commentary.* Grand Rapids: Baker Academic, 2012.

Köberle, Adolph. *The Quest for Holiness: A Biblical, Historical, and Systematic Investigation.* Minneapolis: Augsburg, 1938.

Kolb, Robert, and Timothy J. Wengert, eds. *The Book of Concord: The Confessions of the Evangelical Lutheran Church.* Minneapolis: Augsburg Fortress, 2000.

LaCugna, Catherine Mowry. *God for Us: The Trinity and Christian Life.* San Francisco: HarperCollins, 1993.

Lampe, Geoffrey W. H. *God as Spirit.* Bampton Lectures, 1976. Oxford: Oxford University Press, 1977.

———. "The Holy Spirit and the Person of Christ." In *Christ, Faith and History: Cambridge Studies in Christology,* edited by S. W. Sykes and J. P. Clayton, 111–30. Cambridge: Cambridge University Press, 1972.

Lasch, Christopher. *The Culture of Narcissism: American Life in an Age of Diminishing Expectations.* New York: Norton, 1979.

———. *The Minimal Self: Psychic Survival in Troubled Times.* New York: Norton, 1984.

———. *The True and Only Heaven: Progress and Its Critics.* New York: Norton, 1991.

Letham, Robert. *The Holy Trinity: In Scripture, History, Theology, and Worship.* Phillipsburg, NJ: P. & R., 2004.

Liardon, Roberts. *The Azusa Street Revival: When the Fire Fell.* Shippensburg, PA: Destiny Image, 2006.

Lindbeck, George A. *The Nature of Doctrine: Religion and Theology in a Postliberal Age.* Philadelphia: Westminster, 1984.

Long, Michael G., ed. *Christian Peace and Nonviolence: A Documentary History.* Maryknoll, NY: Orbis, 2011.

Macchia, Frank D. *Baptized in the Spirit: A Global Pentecostal Theology.* Grand Rapids: Zondervan, 2006.

Macmurray, John. *Persons in Relation.* Vol. 2 of *The Form of the Personal: being the Gifford Lectures delivered in the University of Glasgow in 1954.* New York: Harper, 1961.

———. *The Self as Agent.* Vol. 1 of *The Form of the Personal: being the Gifford Lectures delivered in the University of Glasgow in 1954.* New York: Harper, 1961.

Mattes, Mark C., and Steven D. Paulson. Introduction to *The Preached God: Proclamation in Word and Sacrament,* by Gerhard O. Forde. Grand Rapids: Eerdmans, 2007.

McClendon, James Wm., Jr. *Doctrine.* Vol. 2 of *Systematic Theology.* Nashville: Abingdon, 1994.

———. *Ethics.* Vol. 1 of *Systematic Theology.* Nashville: Abingdon, 1986.

McDonnell, Kilian. *The Other Hand of God: The Holy Spirit as the Universal Touch and Goal.* Collegeville, MN: Liturgical, 2003.

Menzies, Robert P. *The Development of Early Christian Pneumatology: With Special Reference to Luke-Acts.* Journal for the Study of the New Testament 54. Sheffield: Sheffield Academic, 1991.

———. *Empowered for Witness: The Spirit in Luke-Acts.* Journal of Pentecostal Theology Supplement 6. Sheffield: Sheffield Academic, 1994.

Mittelstadt, Martin William. *Reading Luke-Acts in the Pentecostal Tradition.* Cleveland: CPT, 2010.

———. *The Spirit and Suffering in Luke-Acts: Implications for a Pentecostal Pneumatology.* Journal of Pentecostal Theology Supplement 26. London: T. & T. Clark, 2004.

Mittelstadt, Martin William, and Matthew Paugh. "The Social Conscience of Stanley Horton." *Assemblies of God Heritage* 29 (2009) 15–19.

Nave, Guy D., Jr., *The Role and Function of Repentance in Luke-Acts*. Academia Biblica 4. Atlanta: SBL, 2002.

Neufeld, Thomas R. Yoder. *Recovering Jesus: The Witness of the New Testament*. Grand Rapids: Brazos, 2007.

Neville, Robert C. *God the Creator: On the Transcendence and Presence of God*. Albany: State University of New York Press, 1992.

Niebuhr, H. Richard. *Christ and Culture*. New York: Harper, 1951.

———. "The Doctrine of the Trinity and the Unity of the Church." *Theology Today* 3 (October, 1946) 371–84.

Olena, Lois E. *Stanley M. Horton: Shaper of Pentecostal Theology*. Springfield, MO: Gospel, 2009.

Pannenberg, Wolfhart. *Jesus—God and Man*. Translated by Lewis L. Wilkins and Duane A. Priebe. London: SCM, 1968.

Penney, John Michael. *The Missionary Emphasis of Lukan Pneumatology*. Journal of Pentecostal Theology Supplement 12. Sheffield: Sheffield Academic, 1997.

Placher, William C. *The Domestication of Transcendence: How Modern Thinking about God Went Wrong*. Louisville: Westminster John Knox, 1996.

Prenter, Regin. *Spiritus Creator*. Translated by John M. Jensen. Eugene, OR: Wipf & Stock, 2001.

Rahner, Karl. *More Recent Writings*. Vol. 4 of *Theological Investigations*. Translated by Kevin Smyth. London: Darton, Longman & Todd, 1974.

Rieff, Phillip. *Charisma: The Gift of Grace, and How It Has Been Taken Away From Us*. New York: Vintage, 2007.

———. *The Feeling Intellect: Selected Writings*. Edited by Jonathan B. Imber. Chicago: University of Chicago Press, 1990.

———. *The Triumph of the Therapeutic: Uses of Faith after Freud*. Chicago: University of Chicago Press, 1987.

Robeck, Cecil M., Jr. *The Azusa Street Mission and Revival*. Nashville: Nelson, 2006.

Robertson, Pat, with Bob Slosser. *The Secret Kingdom*. Nashville: Nelson, 1982.

Rodgers, Darrin J. "The Assemblies of God and the Long Journey Toward Racial Reconciliation." *Assemblies of God Heritage* (2008) 50–61.

Rowe, C. Kavin. *Early Narrative Christology: The Lord in the Gospel of Luke*. Grand Rapids: Baker Academic, 2006.

Sánchez M, Leopoldo A. "God against Us and for Us: Preaching Jesus in the Spirit." *Word and World* 24 (2003) 134–45.

———. "A Missionary Theology of the Holy Spirit: the Father's Anointing of Christ and Its Implications for the Church in Mission." *Missio Apostolica* 14 (2006) 28–40.

———. "Praying to God the Father in the Spirit: Reclaiming the Church's Participation in the Son's Prayer Life." *Concordia Journal* (2006) 274–95.

———. *Receiver, Bearer, and Giver of God's Spirit: Jesus' Life in the Spirit as a Lens for Theology and Life*. Eugene, OR: Pickwick, 2015.

Schmemann, Alexander. *Of Water and the Spirit: A Liturgical Study of Baptism*. Crestwood, NY: St. Vladimir's Seminary Press, 1974.

Soards, Marion L. *Speeches in Acts: Their Content, Context, and Concerns*. Louisville: Westminster John Knox, 1994.

Sobrino, Jon. *Jesus the Liberator: A Historical-Theological Reading of Jesus of Nazareth*. Translated by Paul Burns and Francis McDonagh. Maryknoll, NY: Orbis, 1993.

Solivan, Samuel. *The Spirit, Pathos and Liberation: Toward an Hispanic Pentecostal Theology*. Journal of Pentecostal Theology Supplement 14. Sheffield: Sheffield Academic, 1998.

Stassen, Glen H., and David Gushee. *Kingdom Ethics: Following Jesus in Contemporary Context*. Downers Grove, IL: InterVarsity, 2003.

Stassen, Glen H., D. M. Yeager, and John Howard Yoder. *Authentic Transformation: A New Vision of Christ and Culture*. Nashville: Abingdon, 1996.

Stronstad, Roger. *The Charismatic Theology of St. Luke*. Peabody, MA: Hendrickson, 1984.

Swartley, Willard D. *Covenant of Peace: The Missing Peace in New Testament Theology and Ethics*. Grand Rapids: Eerdmans, 2006.

Tannehill, Robert C. *The Acts of the Apostles*. Vol. 2 of *The Narrative Unity of Luke-Acts: A Literary Interpretation*. Philadelphia: Fortress, 1990.

———. *The Gospel according to Luke*. Vol. 1 of *The Narrative Unity of Luke-Acts: A Literary Interpretation*. Philadelphia: Fortress, 1986.

Tanner, Kathryn. *Jesus, Humanity and the Trinity: A Brief Systematic Theology*. Minneapolis: Fortress, 2001.

Taylor, Charles. *Sources of the Self: The Making of the Modern Identity*. Cambridge, MA: Harvard University Press, 1989.

Thielicke, Helmut. *Prologomena: The Relation of Theology to Modern Thought Forms*. Vol. 1 of *The Evangelical Faith*. Translated and edited by Geoffrey W. Bromiley. Grand Rapids: Eerdmans, 1974.

Toulmin, Stephen. *Cosmopolis: The Hidden Agenda of Modernity*. Chicago: University of Chicago Press, 1990.

Turner, Max. *Power from on High: The Spirit in Israel's Restoration and Witness in Luke-Acts*. Sheffield: Sheffield Academic, 1996.

Villafañe, Eldin. *The Liberating Spirit: Toward an Hispanic American Pentecostal Social Ethic*. Lanham, MD: University Press of America, 1992.

Wacker, Grant. *Heaven Below: Early Pentecostals and American Culture*. Cambridge, MA: Harvard University Press, 2001.

Warren, Rick. *The Power to Change Your Life: Exchanging Personal Mediocrity for Spiritual Significance*. Wheaton, IL: Victor, 1990.

———. *The Purpose Driven Life: What on Earth Am I Here For?* Grand Rapids: Zondervan, 2002.

Weaver, J. Denny. "A Footnote on Jesus." *Cross Currents* 56 (2007) 22–35.

———. "The John Howard Yoder Legacy: Whither the Second Generation?" *Mennonite Quarterly Review* 77 (2003) 451–71.

Webster, John. "The Identity of the Holy Spirit: A Problem in Trinitarian Theology." *Themelios* 9 (1983) 4–7.

Wenk, Matthias. *Community-Forming Power: The Socio-Ethical Role of the Spirit in Luke-Acts*. Sheffield: Sheffield Academic, 2000.

Wilkerson, David. *The Cross and the Switchblade*. New York: Geis, 1963.

———. *Hungry for More of Jesus: Experiencing His Presence in these Troubled Times*. Grand Rapids: Chosen, 1992.

———. *The New Covenant Unveiled*. Lindale, TX: Wilkerson Trust, 2000.

———. *Racing toward Judgment*. Old Tappan, NJ: Revell, 1976.

———. *Set the Trumpet to Thy Mouth: Hosea 8:1*. Lindale, TX: World Challenge, 1985.

———. *The Vision*. New York: Pillar, 1975.

Willimon, William H. *The Intrusive Word: Preaching to the Unbaptized*. Grand Rapids: Eerdmans, 1994.

———. *Peculiar Speech: Preaching to the Baptized*. Grand Rapids: Eerdmans, 1992.

———. *Remember Who You Are: Baptism, a Model for Christian Life*. Nashville: Upper Room, 1980.

Willimon, William H., and Stanley Hauerwas. *Preaching to Strangers: Evangelism in Today's World.* Louisville: Westminster John Knox, 1992.

Woods, Edward J. *The "Finger of God" and Pneumatology in Luke-Acts.* Journal for the Study of the New Testament Supplement 205. Sheffield: Sheffield Academic, 2001.

Wright, John W. *Telling God's Story: Narrative Preaching for Christian Formation.* Downers Grove: IL, InterVarsity, 2007.

Wright, N. T. *Jesus and the Victory of God.* Vol. 2 of *Christian Origins and the Question of God.* Minneapolis: Fortress, 1996.

————. *The New Testament and the People of God.* Vol. 1 of *Christian Origins and the Question of God.* Minneapolis: Fortress, 1992.

Yoder, John Howard. "Armaments and Eschatology." *Studies in Christian Ethics* 1 (1988) 43–61.

————. *Body Politics: Five Practices of the Christian Community before the Watching World.* Scottdale, PA: Herald, 2001.

————. "How H. Richard Niebuhr Reasoned: A Critique of Christ and Culture." In *Authentic Transformation: A New Vision of Christ and Culture,* by Glen H. Stassen, D. M. Yeager, and John Howard Yoder, 31–89. Nashville: Abingdon, 1996.

————. *Nevertheless: The Varieties and Shortcomings of Religious Pacifism.* Rev. ed. Scottdale: PA: Herald, 1992.

————. *The Original Revolution: Essays on Christian Pacifism.* Scottdale, PA: Herald, 1972.

————. *The Politics of Jesus: Vicit Agnus Noster.* 2nd ed. Grand Rapids: Eerdmans, 1994.

————. *Preface to Theology: Christology and Theological Method.* Grand Rapids: Brazos, 2002.

————. *The Priestly Kingdom: Social Ethics as Gospel.* Notre Dame: University of Notre Dame Press, 1984.

————. *The Royal Priesthood: Essays Ecclesiological and Ecumenical.* Edited by Michael G. Cartwright. Scottdale, PA: Herald, 1998.

————. "'Spirit' and the Varieties of Reformation Radicalism." In *De Geest in het geding: Opstellen Aangeboden aan J A Oosterbaan ter Gelegenheid van zijn Afsheid als Hoogleraar,* edited by Irvin B. Horst, A. F. de Jong, and D. Visser, 301–6. Alphen aan den Rijn: H. D. Tjeenk Willink, 1978.

————. "The Spirit of God and the Politics of Men." *Journal of Theology for Southern Africa* 29 (1979) 62–71.

————. *To Hear the Word.* Eugene, OR: Wipf and Stock, 2001.

————. *The War of the Lamb: The Ethics of Nonviolence and Peacemaking.* Edited by Glen Stassen, Mark Thiessen Nation, and Matt Hamsher. Grand Rapids: Brazos, 2009.

Yong, Amos. *Beyond the Impasse: Toward a Pneumatological Theology of Religions.* Grand Rapids: Baker, 2003.

————. *Discerning the Spirit(s): A Pentecostal-Charismatic Contribution to Christian Theology of Religions.* Journal of Pentecostal Theology Supplement 20. Sheffield: Sheffield Academic, 2000.

————. Introduction to *Toward a Pneumatological Theology: Pentecostal and Ecumenical Perspectives on Ecclesiology, Soteriology, and Theology of Mission,* by Veli-Matti Kärkkäinen, edited by Amos Yong, xiii–xx. Lanham, MD: University Press of America, 2002.

————. *Spirit-Word-Community: Theological Hermeneutics in Trinitarian Perspective.* Aldershot, UK: Ashgate, 2002.

York, John O. *The Last Shall Be First: The Rhetoric of Reversal in Luke*. Journal for the Study of the New Testament Supplement 46. Sheffield: Sheffield Academic, 1991.

Zizioulas, John D. *Being as Communion: Studies in Personhood and the Church*. Crestwood, NY: St. Vladimir's Seminary Press, 1985.

———. *Communion and Otherness: Further Studies in Personhood and the Church*. Edited by Paul McPartlan. London: T. & T. Clark, 2006.

Name Index

Subject Index

Adoptionism. *See* Christology
"American Dream," 17, 26, 155

Baptism (Christian), 61, 67, 74, 78,
  88n30, 98, 99, 101, 110, 113,
  114–16, 118, 119, 121, 123, 125,
  140–52, 154, 155, 169, 193
  Pentecostal (Spirit), 119, 182

Christian life
  as adopted by God, 3, 5, 27, 28, 30,
    58–61, 3, 64, 71, 78, 92–94, 102,
    106, 108, 113, 117, 123, 143–46,
    150, 154, 155, 162, 164, 189,
    191–95
  as a son of God, 3, 28, 62, 63, 102,
    123, 124, 127, 128, 132, 143, 144,
    169, 189
  as "death" and "resurrection," xi, 57,
    58, 78, 92–94, 98, 99, 100, 102,
    110, 124, 129n58, 130n61, 132,
    133, 143, 145, 146, 150–52, 154,
    155, 169, 178–80, 189, 195
  resurrection (future), 64, 146, 147,
    149, Western (accounts), 99
Christology
  adoptionist, 39, 42, 43
  Chalcedonian, xi, 2, 45, 67
  Incarnational, 29, 47, 52, 54–56
  Logos-Christology, 28, 29, 34, 37,
    39n30, 43–46, 53, 54,59, 60, 62,
    63n95, 65, 190
  Nicene, xi, 2, 39n30, pre-Nicene, 34
  Spirit-Christology, 3–5, 28–31, 35,
    37, 43–47, 50nn65,66, 51–54,

56–68, 70–73, 75, 78, 90, 93, 94,
  132, 158, 166, 191
  western, 56
Church(es), x, xii, xiii, 2n2, 4, 8, 12–16,
  19–23, 25, 31, 32, 41, 42, 45, 47,
  57, 59, 60, 62, 65, 66, 73, 75, 97,
  108–10, 113–26, 129, 132–34,
  136, 139–41, 143, 150–53, 156,
  164, 165, 170, 171, 175n25, 178,
  181, 183, 184, 189–95
  American, 108, 183
  Evangelical, 22n58
  Pentecostal, 156
  New Testament (early), 12, 13, 97,
    102, 104, 113–18, 125, 165, 175,
    178, 181, 189
Constantinian(ism), 8, 12, 16n37, 17,
  19, 20–23, 26, 47, 60, 139, 155–57,
  164, 165, 170, 172, 183, 189, 190,
  193–95
Culture (cultural), 7, 8, 10, 13–20, 30,
  113, 155–57, 164, 167, 170, 181,
  183, 185, 186, 188–90, 193
  American, 17, 19n49, 26, 110, 118,
    134, 138–41, 157, 173, 183
  Greek, 62
  Pentecostal, 182
  post-Constantinian, 59
  western, 136, 138

eccelsia(l), 36, 64, 65, 95, 104, 108, 113–
  18, 121, 123, 124, 143, 149–51,
  153, 181, 183, 189, 193, 194
Ecclesiology, 22, 126
extrinsic(ism), 53n77, 75, 127